Sea-Wolves of the Mediterranean

KHEYR-ED-DIN BARBAROSSA—CORSAIR, ADMIRAL AND KING

Sea-Wolves of the Mediterranean
Moslem Corsairs of the
Sixteenth Century
1492-1580

E. Hamilton Currey

Sea-Wolves of the Mediterranean: Moslem Corsairs of the Sixteenth Century
1492-1580
by E. Hamilton Currey

Published by Leonaur Ltd

Material original to this edition and this editorial selection
copyright © 2011 Leonaur Ltd

ISBN: 978-0-85706-469-1 (hardcover)
ISBN: 978-0-85706-470-7 (softcover)

http://www.leonaur.com

Publisher's Notes

The views expressed in this book are not necessarily
those of the publisher.

Contents

Preface	9
Introductory	11
The Crescent and the Cross	19
The Coming of the Corsairs	29
Uruj Barbarossa	38
The Death of Uruj Barbarossa	49
Kheyr-Ed-Din Barbarossa	59
The Taking of the Peñon D'Alger	69
The Apotheosis of the Corsair King	80
The Raid on the Coast of Italy	91
Barcelona, May 1535	101
The Flight of Barbarossa	112
Roxalana and the Murder of Ibrahim	123
The Prevesa Campaign	133
The Battle of Prevesa	144
The Galley, the Galeasse and the Nef	154
Dragut-Reis	167
The Town of "Africa"	177
Dragut-Reis and the Knights of Malta	186
The Knights of St. John	197
A Great Armada	211
The Siege of Malta	222
Ali Basha	236
Lepanto	248

Ships be but boards, sailors but men:
There be land rats and water rats, land thieves
    and water thieves,
I mean pirates.
Merchant of Venice

Preface

When the ship is ready for launching there comes a moment of tense excitement before the dogshores are knocked away and she slides down the ways. In the case of a ship this excitement is shared by many thousands, who have assembled to acclaim the birth of a perfected product of the industry of man; the emotion is shared by all those who are present. It is very different when a book has been completed. The launching has been arranged for and completed by expert hands; she like the ship gathers way and slides forth into an ocean: but, unlike the ship which is certain to float, the waters may close over and engulf her, or perchance she may be towed back to that haven of obscurity from which she emerged, to rust there in silence and neglect. There is excitement in the breast of one man alone—to wit, the author. If his book possesses one supreme qualification she will escape the fate mentioned, and this qualification is—interest. As the weeks lengthened into months, and these multiplied themselves to the tale of something like twenty-four, the conviction was strengthened that that which had so profoundly interested the writer, would not be altogether indifferent to others. For some inscrutable reason the deeds of sea-robbers have always possessed a fascination denied to those of their more numerous brethren of the land; and in the case of the sea-wolves of the sixteenth century we are dealing with the very aristocrats of the profession. Circumstances over which they had no control flung the Moslem population of Southern Spain on to the shores of Northern Africa: to revenge themselves upon the Christian foe by whom this expropriation had been accomplished was natural to a warrior race; and those who heretofore had been land-folk pure and simple took to piracy as a means of livelihood. It is of the deeds of these men that this book treats; of their marvellous triumphs, of their apparently hopeless defeats, of the manner in which they audaciously maintained themselves against the principalities and the powers of Christendom always hungering for their destruction.

The quality which Napoleon is said to have ascribed to the British Infantry, "of never knowing when they were beaten," seems to have also characterised the sea-wolves; as witness the marvellous recuperation of Kheyr-ed-Din Barbarossa when expelled from Tunis by Charles V.; and the escape of Dragut from the island of Jerba when apparently hopelessly trapped by the Genoese admiral, Andrea Doria. All through their history the leaders of the sea-wolves show the resourcefulness of the real seamen that they had become by force of circumstances, and it was they who in the age in which they dwelt showed what sea power really meant. Sailing through the Mediterranean on my way to Malta in the spring of this year, as the good ship fared onwards I passed in succession all those lurking-places from which the Moslem Corsairs were wont to burst out upon their prey. Truly it seemed as if

"*The spirits of their fathers might start from every wave,*"

and in imagination one pictured the rush of the pirate galley, with its naked slaves straining at the oar of their taskmasters, its fierce, reckless, beturbaned crew clustered on the "*rambades*" at the bow and stern. It might be that they would capture some hapless "round-ship," a merchantman lumbering slowly along the coast; or again they might meet with a galley of the terrible Knights of St. John or of the everredoubtable Doria. In either case the sea-wolves were equal to their fortune, to plunder or to fight in the name of Allah and his prophet.

That which differentiated the sea-wolves from other pirates was the combination which they effected among themselves; the manner in which these lawless men could subordinate themselves to the will of one whom they recognised as a great leader. To obtain such recognition was no easy matter, and the manner in which this was done, by those who rose by sheer force of character to the summit of this remarkable hierarchy, has here been set forth.

E. Hamilton Currey

I wish to record my cordial recognition of the kindness shown to me at Malta by Mr. Salvino Sant Manduca. The picture of the carrack was a gift from him. The galley of the Knights of Malta is a reproduction of a picture hanging in his house. I should also like to thank him for the time and trouble which he took on my behalf during my stay at Malta, and the keen interest he displayed in my subject.

E. Hamilton Currey

Introductory

In all the ages of which we have any record there have been men who gained a living by that practice of robbery on the high seas which we know by the name of Piracy. Perhaps the pirates best known to the English-speaking world are the buccaneers of the Spanish Main, who flourished exceedingly in the seventeenth century, and of whom many chronicles exist: principally owing to the labours of that John Esquemelin, a pirate of a literary turn of mind, who added the crime of authorship to the ill deeds of a sea-rover. The Sea-Wolves of the Mediterranean in the preceding century did not raise up a chronicler from among themselves: for not much tincture of learning seems to have distinguished these desperate fighters and accomplished seamen, descendants of those Spanish Moslems who had, during the Middle Ages, lived in a land in which learning and culture had been held in the highest estimation. Driven from their homes, their civilisation crushed, their religion banned in that portion of Southern Spain in which they had dwelt for over seven centuries, cast upon the shores of Northern Africa, these men took to the sea and became the scourge of the Mediterranean. That which they did, the deeds which they accomplished, the terror which they inspired, the ruin and havoc which they wrought, have been set forth in the pages of this book.

It was the age of the galley, the oar-propelled vessel which moved independently of the wind in the fine-weather months of the great inland sea. Therefore to the dwellers on the coast the sea-wolves were a perpetual menace; as, when booty was unobtainable at sea, they raided the towns and villages of their Christian foes. During all the period here dealt with no man's life, no woman's honour, was safe from these pirates within the area of their nefarious activities. They held the Mediterranean in fee, they levied toll on all who came within reach of their galleys and their scimitars. Places unknown to the geography of the sixteenth century became notorious in their day, and Christian wives and mothers learned to tremble at the very names of Algiers and Tunis. From these places the rovers issued to capture, to destroy, and to enslave: in Oran and Tlemcen, in Tenes, Shershell, Bougie, Jigelli, Bizerta, Sfax, Susa, Monastir, Jerbah, and Tripoli they lurked ready for the raid and the foray. At one time all Northern Africa would thrill to the triumph of the Moslem arms, at another there would go up the wail of the utterly defeated; but in spite of alternations of fortune the sea-wolves abode in the localities of their choice, and ended in establishing those pirate States which troubled the peace of the Mediterranean practically until the introduction of steam.

The whole record of the sixteenth century is one of blood and fire, of torture and massacre, of "Punic faith" and shameless treason; the deeds of the sea-rovers, appalling as they were, frequently found a counterpart in the battles, the sieges, and the sacking of towns which took place perpetually on the continent of Europe.

There was so much history made at this period, the stage of world politics was occupied by so many great, striking, and dazzling personalities, that the sea-wolves and all they accomplished were to a great extent overshadowed by happenings which the chroniclers of the time considered to be of greater importance. In this no doubt they were right in the main; but, in spite of this opinion which they held, we find that time and again the main stream of events is ruffled by the prows of the pirate galleys. Such men as the Barbarossas, as Dragut, and Ali Basha could only have been suppressed and exterminated had the whole might of Christendom been turned against them, for they held in their hands two weapons, the keenest and most powerful with which to attain the objects which they had in view.

The first and more powerful of these was the appeal in a rough and warlike age to the cupidity of mankind. "Those who are content to follow us," they said in effect, "are certain to enrich themselves if they are men stout of heart and strong of hand. All around us lie rich and prosperous lands; we have but to organise ourselves, and to take anything that we wish for; we can, if we like, gather a rich harvest at comparatively small trouble." Such counsels as these did not fall on deaf ears. Driven from the land of plenty—from glorious Andalusia with its fruitful soil, its magnificent cities, its vines and olives, its fruit and grain, its noble rivers and wide-spreading *vegas*—the Spanish Moslem of the day of the sea-wolves was an outcast and a beggar, ripe for adventure and burning for revenge on those by whom he had been expropriated.

Great historians like William Hickling Prescott tell us that, in the course of the seven centuries of the Moslem domination in Spain, the Moors had become soft and effeminate, that "the canker of peace" had sapped, if it had not destroyed, the virile qualities of the race, that luxury and learning had dried up at their source those primitive virtues of courage and hardihood which had been the leading characteristics of those stark fighters who had borne the banner of the Prophet from Mecca even to Cadiz. Torn by faction, by strife among themselves, they had succumbed to the arms of the Northern chivalry; by its warriors they had been driven out, never to return.

When this was accomplished, when the curtain fell on the final scene of the tragedy, and the Moors, after the fall of Granada, were driven across the sea into Africa, there came to pass a most remarkable change in those who had been expropriated. The learning, the culture, the civilisation, by which they had been so long distinguished, seemed to drop away from them, cast away like a worn-out garment for which men have no further use. In place of all these things there came a complete and desperate valour, a bitter and headstrong fanaticism.

It was one of the attributes of the Moslem civilisation in Spain, and one of the most enlightened thereof, that religious toleration flourished in its midst. Jew and Christian were allowed to worship at the altars of their fathers, no man hindering or saying them nay; one rule, and one alone, had to be preserved: none must blaspheme against Mahomet, the Prophet of God, as he was considered to be by the Moslems. The penalty for infraction of this rule was death; otherwise, complete liberty of conscience was accorded.

We have spoken of the two weapons held by the leaders of the sea-wolves. The first, as we have, said, was cupidity; the second was fanaticism, the deadly religious hatred engendered, not only by the wholesale expropriation of the Moslem population, but also by the persecution to which the Moriscoes—as those Moslems were known who remained in Spain—were subjected by their Christian masters. It requires little imagination to see how these two weapons of avarice and intolerance could be made to serve the purpose of those dominant spirits who rose to the summit of the piratical hierarchy. Not only did they dazzle the imaginations of those who followed in their train by promises of wealth uncounted, but they added to this the specious argument that, in slaying and robbing the Christian wheresoever he was to be found, the faithful Moslem was performing the service of God and the act most grateful to his holy Prophet.

Could any rule of life be at the same time more simple and more attractive to the beggared Mohammedan cast on the sterile shores of Northern Africa to starve?

With the main stream of history, to which we have before referred, we have no concern in this book. He who would embark thereon must sail a powerful vessel which must carry many guns. Also for the conduct of this vessel many qualities are necessary: a commanding intellect, acute perceptions, indefatigable industry, complete leisure, are among those things necessary to the pilot. These must be supplemented by a genius for research, a knowledge of ancient and modern languages, and an unerring faculty for separating the few precious grains of wheat from those mountains of chaff which he will have to sift with the utmost care. There are, however, subsidiary rivulets which feed the onward flow of events, and of such is the story of the sea-wolves of the Mediterranean. On these the adventurous mariner can sail his little cockboat, discreetly retiring before he becomes involved and engulfed in the main stream. That he cannot altogether avoid it is shown by the fact that the men who are here chronicled took part in events of first-class importance in the age in which they lived. Kheyr-ed-Din Barbarossa fought the battle of Prevesa against his lifelong antagonist, Andrea Doria. Dragut was killed at the siege of Malta, at the moment almost of the fall of the castle of St. Elmo; had he lived it is more than probable that Jean Parisot de la Valette and his heroic garrison would have been defeated instead of being victorious. Ali Basha was the one Moslem commander who increased his reputation at the battle of Lepanto, because, as was usual in all maritime conflicts of the time, the corsairs, who had the habit of the sea, were more than a match for soldiers embarked to fight on an unfamiliar element.

We shall speak, later on, of the autocratic rule of these leaders who possessed so absolute a domination over the men by whom they were followed. The fact of this absolute supremacy on the part of the chiefs is very curious, as theoretically in the confederacy of the sea-wolves all were equal; we are, in fact, confronted with pure democracy, where every man was at liberty to do what seemed best in his own eyes. He was a free agent, none coercing him or desiring him to place himself under discipline or command. This, be it observed, was the theory. As a matter of fact the corsairs, who were extraordinarily successful in their abominable trade, abode beneath an iron and rigid discipline. This was enforced by the lash, as we shall see later on when it is related how Kheyr-ed-Din Barbarossa flogged one Hassan, a captain who, he considered, had failed in his duty: or by the actual penalty of death, which Uruj Barbarossa inflicted on one who had dared to act independently of his authority.

The theory of equality obtained among the Mediterranean pirates; but the Barbarossas, Dragut, and Ali believed that, in practice, the less interference there was with their designs by those, whom Cardinal Granvelle denominated in a letter to Philip II. as "that mischievous animal the people," the better it would be for all concerned. The conception held of rights and duties of "the mischievous animal" by these militant persons was, that it should behave as did those others recorded of the Roman centurion in Holy Writ: if it did not, and difficulties arose, the leaders were not troubled with an undue tenderness either towards the individual or the theory. Of this we shall see examples as we go on.

This period has been called "The Grand Period of the Moslem Corsairs" because it was in something less than a century, from the year of the expulsion of the Moors from Granada in 1492 to the death of Ali Basha in 1580, that the sea-wolves were at the height of their power, that the piratical States of the Mediterranean were in the making. That subsequently they gave great cause of trouble to Christendom is written in characters of blood and fire throughout the history of the succeeding centuries; but the real interest in the careers of these men resides in the fact that they established, by their extraordinary aptitude for sea-adventure, the permanent place which was held by their descendants. Time and again in the sixteenth century the effort was made to destroy them root and branch: they were defeated, driven out of their strongholds on shore, crushed apparently for ever. But nothing short of actual extermination could have been successful in this; as, no matter how severe had been the set-back, there was always left a nucleus of the pirates which in a short time grew again into a formidable force. The Ottoman Turk, magnificent fighter as he was on land, seemed to lose his great qualities when the venue was changed from the land to the sea. The Janissaries, that picked corps trained as few soldiers were trained even in that age of iron, who never recoiled before the foe but who fought only to conquer or die, seem to have failed when embarked for sea-service. That which the hard teaching of experience alone could show—that the man who fights best upon the sea is he who has the habit of the sea—was at this time not generally recognised, and this it was that rendered the corsairs so supreme on the element which they had made their own. Some among the great ones of the earth there were who appreciated this fact, who, like that great statesman Ibrahim, Grand Vizier to Soliman the Magnificent, recognised what it was to lay their hands upon "a veritable man of the sea"; but the rule was to embark men from the shore and to entrust to them the duty of fighting naval actions.

When "the Grand Period" came to an end, as it did about the date already indicated, the corsairs had become a permanent institution; they remained established at Algiers, Tunis, and other ports on the littoral of Northern Africa as a recognised evil. Pirates they remained to the end of the chapter, the scourge of the tideless sea; but no longer did they array themselves in line of battle against the mightiest potentates of the earth allied for their complete destruction. It was the men of the sea who set up this empire; it was they who defied Charles V., a whole succession of Popes, Andrea Doria and his descendants, the might of Spain, Venice, Genoa, Catalonia, and France. It was they who taught the so-called civilised world of the age in which they lived that sea-power can only be met and checked by those who dispose of navies manned by seamen; that against it the master of the mightiest legions of the land is powerless.

This contention is by no means invalidated by the fact that frequently the corsairs were defeated by land forces embarked on board ship. Thus when Dragut was defending Tripoli against an expedition sent against him in 1559 by the combined forces of Spain, Tuscany, Rome, Naples, Sicily, and Genoa, of one hundred sail which embarked fourteen thousand troops, he was relieved by Piali, the Admiral of Soliman the Magnificent, who came to his assistance with eighty-six galleys, each of which had on board one hundred Janissaries, and who gained so striking a victory over the Christians that the Turkish Admiral returned to Constantinople with no less than four thousand prisoners. But in this case, as in so many others, the actual hostilities took place on shore, where the troops had the opportunity of displaying their sterling qualities.

There is very little doubt that critics will point out that the corsairs were by no means universally successful; that, as in the case of the attack by Hassem, the ruler of Algiers in 1563, on Oran and Marzaquivir (a small port in the immediate vicinity of Oran), in the end the Moslems were badly beaten. This undoubtedly was the case, and there is no desire to magnify the deeds of the sea-wolves or to minimise the heroic defence of Marzaquivir by the Count of Alcaudete, or that of Oran by his brother, Don Martin de Còrdoba, At the last moment of their wonderful defence they were relieved by a fleet sent by the King of Spain, and Hassem had to abandon his artillery, ammunition, and stores and beat a hasty retreat to the place from whence he had come.

There was nothing remarkable in the fact that the corsairs were frequently defeated; what is really strange is that they should have achieved so great a success—success vouched for by the concrete instance that they established those sinister dynasties on the coast of Northern Africa which were the outcome of their piratical activities.

In speaking of them, historians of later date than that at which they flourished are apt to hold them somewhat cheaply, to dismiss them as mere barbarians of no particular importance in the scheme of mundane affairs; as men who caused a certain amount of trouble to civilisation by their inroads and their plunderings. That which is certain is that they were for centuries a standing shame and disgrace to the whole of Christendom.

To those who may perhaps be called the pioneers—that is to say, the men treated of in this book—a certain amount of sympathy and understanding may be conceded; for they had been driven from the land which had been theirs, it was their countrymen and their co-religionists who were being ground to powder beneath the fanatical cruelty of the Spanish Inquisition. That which they did was doubtless abominable, but it cannot be contended that they had not received the strongest provocation both from the material and the religious points of view.

Once the "Grand Period" was passed, that period in which such men as the Barbarossas, Dragut, and Ali flourished, the chronicle of the Moslem States founded by them sinks to the degraded level of sheer robbery and murder; of a history of a tyranny established within one hundred miles of the shores of Europe, and of great kings and princes bargaining with piratical ruffians who held in thrall thousands upon thousands of their subjects. How it came about that the Christian States tolerated such an abuse is one of those mysteries which can never be explained; and if subsequent centuries displayed a greater refinement of manners, a more apt appreciation of all that is softer and kindlier in the human relationships of nation towards nation and of people towards people, they have not perhaps so much to plume themselves upon as had their rude forefathers of the sixteenth century, who, seeing the evil and feeling the effects thereof, did their best to extirpate those by whom this evil was caused.

The question may be asked, how can it be that the lives and actions of such men as these are worth chronicling? It is because, not only that they modified profoundly the course of history in the age in which they lived, but also because that, hidden deep down, somewhere, in these men stained by a thousand crimes, ruthless, lustful, bloodthirsty, cruel as the grave, was the germ of true greatness, some dim spark of the divine fire of genius. Contending against principalities and powers, they held their own; in the welter of anarchy in which they lived they proved that there existed no finer fighting men, which alone give them some claim to consideration; but that which is most interesting to watch is the absolute domination obtained by the leaders over their followers. There is no other record of pirates who commanded on so large a scale; there is none which shows men such as these bargaining on equal terms with the great ones of the earth.

CHAPTER 1

The Crescent and the Cross

There is, in the deeds of men of action, an interest which is never aroused by those persons of brains and capacity by whom the world is really ruled. The statesman in his cabinet is the god within the machine; it is he who directs the acts of nations, it is he who moves the fleets and armies as if they were pieces on the chess-board; to him, as a rule, is the man of action subordinate, obeying his behests. Rule and governance are his, power both in the abstract and the concrete. Seldom in the history of the world do we come across the men who are at one and the same time statesmen and soldiers, who, taking their destiny in their own hands, work it out to the appointed end thereof. But, as we stray in the by-paths of history, we meet with some who, in their day, have influenced not only the age in which they lived themselves, but also the destinies of generations yet unborn. It would seem incredible that mere pirates, such as the Moslem corsairs of the Mediterranean, could be included in this category, and yet, as their story is unfolded, we shall see how the sea-wolves rose from the humblest beginnings to trouble the peace of Europe, to found for themselves dynasties which endured.

Uruj Barbarossa, Kheyr-ed-Din Barbarossa, Dragut Reis, and Occhiali, or All Basha, were men who, in the sixteenth century, did much to change the conditions of the times in which they lived: it was the time of the Renaissance in Europe, a period of splendour in all the arts and sciences. These men added nothing to the knowledge of the civilised world as it then existed, save and except in one particular, which was, as Kheyr-ed-Din explained to Soliman the Magnificent on a certain memorable occasion, that he who rules on the sea will rule on the land also. In the early twentieth century, when all the nations and languages sit at the feet of Captain (now Rear-Admiral) Mahan, and acclaim his "Sea Power" series of books, it is interesting to find that he was anticipated in the most practical fashion possible by a corsair of the sixteenth century.

This period was one in which great men abounded. The Emperor Charles V., Francis I. of France, and Henry VIII. of England, were on the thrones of their respective countries; in Hungary was John Hunyadi, at Constantinople Soliman the Magnificent held rule, while in Rome the "fatal house of Medici" were the successors of Saint Peter. War was a commonplace state of the times, but until the Crescent began to sweep the seas it had its manifestation in the perpetual quarrels of the nations of Christendom, which represented, as a rule, the insatiable ambitions of its rulers. But now new men forced themselves to the front, a new power arose which was very imperfectly understood, and which practically held the sea at its mercy. Gone were the halcyon days of peaceful trade which had been pursued for generations by Venetian and Genoese, by Spaniard and Frenchman; gone also, apparently never to return, was all sense of security for the wretched dwellers on the littoral of the Mediterranean, who lived in daily, and particularly in nightly, dread of the falcon swoop of the pirate galleys.

It is amusing to read the old chroniclers, sticklers as they were for "the dignity of history," continually having to turn aside from the main stream of their narrative of emperors, popes, and kings to descend to the level of the sea-wolves, and to be constrained to set down the nefarious doings of these rovers of the sea. Bell, book, and candle were invoked against them in vain, and mighty monarchs had to meet them in the stricken field not merely once or twice—to their utter undoing and discomfiture—but many times, while victory inclined first to one side and then to the other.

The Osmanli had ever been warriors since the times of the Prophet, of Abu-Bekr, of Othman, and of Ali; but so far their warlike achievements had been always on land, their only sea experience being confined to the crossing of the Straits of Gibraltar, when in the eighth century, under Tarik, they had swarmed into Andalusia, conquered Roderick the Goth, and set up that Moslem domination in Southern Spain which lasted until 1492, just before the events set forth in this book took place. Piracy in all ages is a thing in which a curious shuddering interest has been taken, and the deeds of the outlaws of the sea have never lacked chroniclers. There is for this a reason apart from the record of robbery and murder, which is the commonplace of piratical deeds: it resides in the perennial interest which men take in individual achievement, in the spectacle of absolute and complete domination by one man over the lives and the fortunes of others. This intense form of individualism is nowhere so well exhibited as in the story of piratical enterprise, where a band of men, outside of the law and divorced from all human kind by the atrocity of their deeds, has had to be welded into one homogeneous mass for the purpose of preying upon the world at large. Therefore he who would hold rule among such outlaws must himself be a man of no common description, for in him must be that quality which calls for instantaneous obedience among those with whom he is associated; behind him is no constituted authority, discipline is personal, enforced by the leader, and by him alone. Beneath him are men of the rudest and roughest description, slaves to their lusts and their passions, prone to mutiny, suspicious, and—worst of all—stupid.

It is with these constituent elements that the piratical leader had to deal, trusting to the strength of his own arm, the subtlety of his own unassisted brain. Some among these leaders have risen to eminence in their evil lives, most of them have been the captains of single ships preying on commerce in an indiscriminate manner; but this was not the case with the sea-wolves of the Mediterranean. Primarily sea-robbers they were of course, but as time and opportunity developed their characters they rose to meet occasion, to take fortune at the flood, in a manner that, had they been pursuing any other career, would most certainly have caused them to rise to eminence. Into the fierce and blood-stained turmoil of their lives there entered something unknown to any other pirates: this was religious fanaticism—a fanaticism so engrained in character, a belief held to with such passionate tenacity, that men stained with every conceivable crime held that their passage to Paradise was absolutely secure because of the faith which they professed. Tradition, sentiment, discipline, were summed up in one trite formula; but though we, at this distance of time, may hold it somewhat in derision, it was a vital force in the days of Soliman the Magnificent; and there was an added zest to robbery and murder in the fact that the pirates, as good Mohammedans, were obeying the behests of the Prophet every time that they cut a Christian throat, plundered a Christian argosy, or carried off shrieking women into a captivity far worse than death.

That a pirate should be a warrior goes without saying, that a pirate should be a statesman is a thing almost incredible; but those who will read the story of the life of Kheyr-ed-Din Barbarossa will be forced to admit that here, at least, was a pirate who achieved the apparently impossible. Admiral Jurien de la Gravière has remarked that the Moslem corsairs of the sixteenth century were great men, even when measured by the standard of Henry VIII., of Charles V., of Soliman the Magnificent, of Ibrahim, his Grand Vizier, or of Andrea Doria, greatest among contemporary Christian mariners. To the seaman, of course, there is much that is fascinating in the deeds of his forerunners, and the ships of the corsairs had in them something distinctive in that they were propelled by oars, and were in consequence, to a certain extent, independent of the weather. Like the sailors of all ages, to the sea-wolves gales and storms of all sorts and descriptions were abhorrent; and in consequence they had a well-marked piracy season, which, as we shall see, covered the spring and summer, while they carefully avoided the inclement months of autumn and winter.

In a later chapter an attempt has been made to place before the reader pictures of the galley, the *galeasse*, and the *nef*, which were the names attached to the ships then in use; the name brigantine, far from having the significance attached to it by the sailor of the present day, seems to have been a generic term to denote any craft not included in the names already given.

Although the sixteenth century had outgrown the principle of the general massacre of the enemy by the victors, still chivalry to the fallen foe was far to seek, as all persons captured at sea were, no matter what their rank and status, immediately stripped and chained to the rowers' bench, where they remained until ransom, good fortune, or a kindly death, for which these unfortunates were wont to pray, should come to their release. To a large extent this savagery may be traced to the religious rancour which animated the combatants on both sides, as the fanaticism of the Moslem, of which we have already spoken, was fully matched on the side of the Christians by the bigotry of the Knights of Saint John of Jerusalem, otherwise known as the Knights of Malta, who were vowed to the extermination of what they, on their side, called "the *infidel*." It was an age of iron, when men neither gave nor expected grace for the misfortunes which might befall them in the warrior life which they led. It was distinguished by many gallant feats of arms on both sides, but pity formed no part of the equipment of the fighting man bent on the death or capture of his enemy. Honestly and sincerely each side believed that they were doing the service of the Almighty in destroying the other party root and branch. The amount of human misery and suffering caused by the rise and progress of the Moslem corsairs was absolutely incalculable; the slavery of the rower in the galley in the time of which we speak was an agony so dreadful that in these days it is a thing which seems altogether incredible, a nightmare of horror almost impossible even to imagine.

The life of the *"gallerian"* was so hard that his sufferings in many cases were mercifully ended in death in a very short time, as none save those of iron constitution could stand the strain imposed by the desperate toil and wretched food. Yet there are cases on record of men who had worked at the oar for actual decades, so unconquerable in their strength that even such a life as this had not the power to break them down.

To the peaceful mariner who wished merely to trade, to the individual whose business called him overseas, this epoch must have been one of terror unspeakable. The ordinary perils of the deep were quite enough to keep timid folk at home in those days of clumsy, ill-found sailing ships, which could by no means work to windward, and did not sail remarkably well even with the most favouring breezes; when to this we add that every ship which started on a voyage in the Mediterranean had before her the chance of being captured by the corsairs, it was no wonder that he whose business led him overseas should make his last will and testament and bid a fond farewell to all his relatives.

There is a record in the *Memoires of the Rev. Frère Pierre d'An, Bachelier en Théologie de la Faculté de Paris*, etc., who wrote in a most heartfelt manner concerning the danger of the sea and the perils to be expected from the Barbary corsairs. He says, date 1637:

> An ancient writer, considering how little assurance can ordinarily be placed in the sea, and how hazardous it is to expose oneself and one's goods to its mercy, has remarked, with much reason, that it is infinitely preferable to be poor on shore than to be rich at sea. In which saying he mocks indeed at those ambitious, avaricious, and mercenary men who, in order to gain false glory and the things of this world, expose themselves rashly to the manifest perils which are most of the time the inevitable lot of the seaman. This same consideration causes him also to utter these remarkable words: that he repents himself of but one thing, and that is ever to have travelled by sea when it was possible to have done so by land. And, to say truth, he has good reason to speak as he does, because it is impossible for the most hardy navigators not to tremble with fear when it is represented before their eyes that they must combat with the winds, the waves, and the foam every time that they adventure upon the deep.
>
> Because it is indisputable that this is the very Theatre of the storms, and the place in the world most capable of all sorts of violence and tragic adventure. This, however, does not prevent

those who covet the perishable goods of this world from straying upon the sea, even in unknown and untraversed regions, without ceasing and without rest.

If, however, they abandon the ocean for a time, it is but to return to it again to seek once more war with their ships, in order unjustly to make themselves masters of the bodies and of the riches of others.

Of such it may be remarked to-day are, in all the maritime coasts, the implacable Corsairs of Barbary. For, however great may be the dangers of which we have just spoken, and no matter now many examples they may see of the fury and inconstancy of Neptune, they cease not their irritating performances, kindling warfare in all the coasts of the Christian nations. It is there that they exercise their infamous piracies, and there also that they glory in the most shameful of all commerce—the trade of the brigand.

Which in all towns that are well policed have always met with a swift and just retribution, because the law is ordained against those who maintain such practices.

But such does not happen among these pirates.

On the contrary, it may truthfully be said that, while in towns in which good persons dwell good actions receive the palms and the crown, it is among the Corsairs but to the wicked to whom are given recompense and praise.

In effect the most determined among them—I mean the most unworthy robbers who are best versed in all the infamies of their trade and most accustomed to the practice of violence—are those who are covered with honours, and who pass in the estimation of their fellows for men of heart and courage.

Indeed experience has taught all Christian merchants that the infidels of the coast of Barbary are all brigands.

Among these those of Algiers carry off the prize for riches, for ships, for strength, and for villainy.

The bachelor in theology is somewhat sweeping in his criticisms, and his meaning is, perhaps, somewhat clearer than his grammar. One thing, however, is perfectly plain, that, in the opinion of the reverend brother, those who go to sea are to be divided into two categories, rogues and fools, with a strong preponderance of the worse Element of the two.

Of the corsairs dealt with in this record of their deeds the two

Barbarossas were the sons of a Mohammedan father and a Christian mother. Dragut Reis was a pure Mohammedan, and Ali Basha was a pure-blooded Italian. All these men, as will be seen, raised themselves to eminence in the profession of piracy; in each and every separate case starting at the very bottom rung of the ladder and rising, by sheer stress of valour and character, to the very top. Each in turn became *Admiralissimo* to the Grand Turk at Constantinople. Kheyr-ed-Din Barbarossa commanded the Ottoman fleet at the great battle of Prevesa, at which he met with his life-long competitor at sea, the famous Genoese Admiral, Andrea Doria. Dragut Reis was killed at the siege of Malta in 1565, and Ali Basha was the only Moslem commander who increased his reputation at the battle of Lepanto in 1571, when Don John of Austria shattered the power of the Moslem at sea for the time being.

Although the *"renegado"* was very much in evidence in the vessels of the Moslem corsairs, still of course the bulk of the fighting men, by which the galleys were manned, were Mohammedans, the descendants of the warriors who had swept through Northern Africa like a living flame in the early days of the Mohammedan conquest.

Cut adrift from the homes which had been theirs for over seven centuries—as we shall see in the next chapter—there was nothing left for the erstwhile dwellers in Andalusia but to gain their living by the strong hand. The harvest of the sea was the one which they garnered—a harvest of the goods of their mortal enemies strung out in lines of hapless merchant-vessels throughout the length and breadth of the tideless sea.

It booted not that the great Powers of Europe sent expedition after expedition against them; these they fought to the death with varying fortune, ready, when the storm had passed over their heads, to start once more on the only career which promised them the chance of acquiring riches. Their whole history is a study of warfare, waged as a rule on the petty scale, but rising at times, as in the cases already mentioned, into events of first-class historical importance.

The deeds of the buccaneers of the next century in the Spanish Main sink into comparative insignificance when compared with what was accomplished by such a man as Kheyr-ed-Din Barbarossa, who was known, and rightly known, by his contemporaries, and for many generations of Moslem seamen yet to come, as "the King of the Sea." The capture of Panama by Sir Henry Morgan in January 1671 was possibly as remarkable a feat of arms as was ever accomplished, but it cannot rank in its importance to civilised mankind on the same plane as those memorable battles in the Mediterranean of which mention has been made as having been fought by the Moslem corsairs.

Fighting for their own hand, the booty reaped by these men was incredible in its richness. Sea-power was theirs, and they took the fullest advantage of this fact, fearing none save the great community of the Knights of Saint John of Jerusalem, which, vowed to the destruction of the *infidel*, neither gave nor accepted quarter.

We have said that the real interest in the lives of the corsairs arose from the fact that it was personal ascendancy, and that alone, which counted in the piratical hierarchy. Against Kheyr-ed-Din Barbarossa plots arose again and again, only to be defeated by the address of the man against whom they were directed.

It was one of the cruellest of ages, and rough cruelty was the principal means adopted to ensure success; sheer terror was the weapon of the leader. Thus when one Hassan, a subordinate of Kheyr-ed-Din, failed to take a Spanish ship because she made too stout a resistance, his chief caused him to be soundly flogged and then thrown into prison. Such methods naturally raised up hosts of enemies in the wake of the piratical commanders, ready at any time to do them a mortal injury, and it is little short of miraculous that they should throughout a long period of years have been able not only to maintain, but to increase, their supremacy over the wild spirits of which their following was composed. It was, however, the golden age of autocracy, when men surrendered their judgment to some great leader, content to follow where he led, to endorse his policy at the cost of their lives.

It is the autocrat who is made by the circumstances of his life who ultimately becomes supreme. The leaders among the corsairs were tried by every test of prosperity and of adverse fortune; they emerged from the ruck in the first instance because it was in them to display a more desperate valour than did their contemporaries, and it was only when they emerged triumphant from this, the first test, that they could begin to impose their will upon others. It was then that their real trials began, as the undisciplined are ever prone to suspicion, much given to murmuring against a leader who is not perpetually successful.

As a rule, however, there were but few to criticise, as the office of critic was one fraught with far too much danger to be alluring. In maintaining their authority the leaders stopped at nothing, and the heads of the recalcitrant were apt to part with amazing suddenness from their bodies if they repined overmuch. The Moslem leader was, it is true, merely *primus inter pares*, and was distinguished by no outward symbol of the power which he possessed; but life and death lay in his hands, and life was cheap indeed.

We have spoken hitherto of the leaders, but what of the men of which their following was composed? Rough, rude, and reckless, these latter lived but to fight and to plunder; to them any other life would have seemed impossible, and indeed this was practically the fact. In the communities in which they lived the adult male had no other means of gaining a livelihood. Since their expulsion from their ancient homes no ordered and peaceful method of existence had been possible for them. In the surroundings in which their forefathers had lived the arts of peace had been carried on in a civilisation to which there had been none comparable in the world as it then existed; on all this the Moslem had now to turn his back, and to earn a precarious living by the strong hand. War, sanguinary and incessant, was henceforward to be his lot, and it must be said that he turned to this ancient avocation with a zest which left but little to be desired from the point of view of those by whom he was led. In the new life of bloodshed and adventure he seemed to delight. Like the free-lance in all ages, he seems to have squandered his booty as soon as it was acquired, and then to sea once more, to face the desperate hazard of an encounter with the knights, to raid defenceless villages, to lie *perdu* behind some convenient cape, dashing out from thence to plunder the argosy of the merchantman. Intolerable conditions of heat and cold he endured, he suffered from wounds, from fever, from hunger and thirst, from hope deferred, from voyages when no plunder came his way.

His reward was the joy of the fight, the delight of the ambush skilfully laid, to see the decks of the enemy a dreadful shambles, with the Crescent of the Prophet above the detested emblem of the Cross. Then the return to Algiers laden with spoil: to tow behind him some luckless Christian ship, while aboard his own war-worn galley the drums beat and the trumpets sounded, and the banners floated free to the stainless Mediterranean sky. Then the procession of the captives through the crowded streets laden with what a short time before had been their own property—a mournful cortege of men doomed to an everlasting slavery and of women destined for the harems of the Bashas.

Thus was his life lived, and when death came it came as a rule from the slash of a sabre or the ball from an *arquebus* or a bombard; and then what matter, for had not Hassan Ali or Selim fallen in strife against the enemies of his faith, and did not the portals of heaven open wide to receive the man who had lost his life testifying to the fact that there was but one God, and that Mahomet was the Prophet of God?

True in substance and in fact is that which was said by the Frère Pierre d'An that "it is indisputable that the sea is the Theatre of the storms and the place in the world most capable of all sorts of violence and tragic adventure." Those who "coveted the goods of others straying on the sea," called by the reverend brother "the implacable, corsairs of Barbary," were to make life intolerable on that element for centuries to come, and if the Crescent did not supersede the banner of the Cross in the blue waters of the Mediterranean Sea, it remained as a portent and a dread symbol of human misery and unutterable suffering.

CHAPTER 2

The Coming of the Corsairs

The rise and progress of the Moslem corsairs of the Mediterranean is a most curious and interesting historical fact. The causes which led to results so deplorable to commerce, civilisation, and Christianity are set forth in this chapter in order that some idea may be formed of the state of affairs in that region at the end of the fifteenth and the beginning of the sixteenth centuries, and also that the reflex action of the great triumph of the Christian armies in Spain may be more fully understood.

The maritime Christian States of the Mediterranean at this epoch were at the height of their power and prosperity, but were faced by the might of the Ottoman Empire, against which they waged perpetual warfare. Bitter and unceasing was the strife prosecuted by the Cross against the Crescent, and by the Crescent against the Cross; and riding, like eagles on the storm came the corsairs in their swift galleys ready to strike down the luckless argosy of the merchantman wheresoever she was to be met. But this was not all, as the shore as well as the sea yielded up to them its tribute in the shape of slaves and booty, and Christian mothers trembling in the insecurity of their homes would hush their wailing children with the terror of the names of Barbarossa, of Dragut, or of Ali Basha.

Popes and emperors, kings and princes, found themselves compelled to form leagues against these sea-wolves who devoured the substance of their subjects, and great expeditions were fitted out to fight with and destroy the corsairs. Had Christendom been united no doubt the object would have been attained; but, as will be seen at the end of this chapter, an "Alliance of Christian Princes against the Turks"—which generic term included the corsairs—was not always used in the manner best calculated to injure those common enemies.

When in 1492 Granada was yielded up to "Los Reyes Catolicos,"

Ferdinand of Aragon, and Isabella of Castile, by that luckless monarch known as Boabdil el Chico (or "the little"), the last remnant of the power of the Moors in Spain had gone never to return. On that small hill on the way to the coast still known as *"el ultimo suspiro del Moro"* (the last sigh of the Moor), Boabdil, as he looked for the last time on his lost capital of Granada, is said to have burst into tears. His fierce mother Ayesha had, however, no sympathy for her fallen son: "Thou doest well to weep like a woman for that which thou daredst not defend as a man," was her biting—and totally unjust—comment, and the cavalcade pursued its miserable journey to the coast, from whence it embarked for the kingdom of Fez.

Great was the jubilation in Christendom; for more than seven centuries the followers of the Prophet had dwelt in the land from which Tarik had expelled Roderick the Goth in the eighth century. There they had dwelt and held up a lamp of learning and comparative civilisation which shone brightly through the miasmatic mists of cruelty and bloodshed in the Middle Ages, and none can question that, under Moorish rule in Spain in those centuries, the arts of peace had flourished, and that science, agriculture, art, and learning had found generous and discriminating patronage in the courts of Còrdoba and Granada.

And now all was over the iron chivalry of the North had broken in pieces the Paynim hosts. They were expelled for ever from Christian soil, or else were forced to live in a state of degrading servitude, sore oppressed by an alien rule, in the land which their forbears had won and kept by the sword.

There was jubilation, as has been said, in Christendom, but the knights and nobles who flocked from all parts of Europe to join the standard of the Catholic monarchs had no prevision of the consequences, no idea of the legacy that they were leaving to their descendants.

It is of this legacy that we have to speak, and there has been none more terrible, none fraught with more awful suffering for the human race. The broken hosts of the Moslem chivalry became the corsairs of the Mediterranean: ruthless pirates freed from all restraint of human pity, living only to inflict the maximum of suffering upon their Christian foes, who, having sown the wind at the taking of Granada, reaped in the coming centuries a whirlwind of blood and agony which continued down to the bombardment of Algiers by Lord Exmouth in 1816, and even later than that date.

Warriors to a man, the hosts of Boabdil crossed the Straits of Gibraltar into Africa; warriors but now broken men, from whom had been reft not only their lands and houses but even the chance of remaining in their native country. Religious toleration had been the rule of the Moslem States in Spain. In the name of religion they had been expropriated; therefore toleration was slain, and to exalt the Crescent above the Cross became the duty of every fighting Mohammedan. Into all the ports and harbours of the North African littoral the Moslems intruded themselves, their one preoccupation to revenge themselves upon the Christians, of no matter what race or nationality. There was at this date but small opposition from the rulers of the Pagan States who held in their weak and inefficient hands such strong places of arms as Algiers and Tunis.

Very soon the Moslems acquired the habit of the sea, and very soon the Christian States discovered how different was the Mohammedan dwelling at peace in Andalusia, or at worst fighting with his co-religionists, to the desperate corsairs created by their own act who now ravaged the shores of the tideless sea.

In the years succeeding to the conquest of Granada the corsairs became the scourge of the Mediterranean. France, Spain, Genoa, Venice, were all at odds with them; as the trading vessels, which had hitherto passed to and fro unmolested, were now captured, haled into North African ports, their cargoes sold, and their hapless crews forced to labour, naked and chained to the benches of the pirate galleys, until death came and mercifully put an end to their sufferings.

From Reggio to Genoa, from Venice to Taranto, the cry of rage and fear went up; it was re-echoed from the coasts of France and of the Balearic Islands, while Southern Spain seethed with disaffection, and the Moriscoes, as those Moors who remained in the country were known, were ever on the lookout to assist their bold brethren, the rovers of the sea. Christendom was completely bewildered: hitherto the relations between the nations and the Kings of Tunis, Tlemcen, Fez, and others of the North African potentates, had been of the most agreeable description. Both parties had denounced piracy, and had as far as in them lay done all in their power to discourage this form of robbery. But now all was changed, and, as has been said in the previous chapter, a situation arose analogous to that of the Spaniards in the West Indies a century and a half later when Morgan and the buccaneers were at the height of their maleficent prowess. The situation was analogous, but whereas Morgan, Scott, L'Ollonais, and others terrorised only such forces as Spain possessed in far-distant colonies, the corsairs were a terror to all the great nations of the world.

Granada fell, as has been said, in 1492 amid the rejoicings of the Christian States; but it had been well for Christendom as a whole if the Caliphs of Còrdova and Granada had never been defeated, and they and their subjects driven from their homes: to form the nucleus of those piratical States which existed from this date until well into the nineteenth century, as the scourge and the terror of all those who, during those ages, desired to "pass upon the seas on their lawful occasions." The capture of Granada was separated from the fall of the Byzantine Empire by a period of thirty-nine years, as it was in the year 1453 that Constantinople was captured by the Caliph Mahomet II. Byzantium fell, and perhaps nothing in the records of that Empire became it so well as that last tremendous struggle; and when on May 29th, 1453, the Ottoman legions were victorious, the body of the last Emperor of Byzantium was found beneath a mountain of the slain only recognisable by his purple mantle sewn with golden bees. The Cross which Constantine the Great had planted on the walls 1125 years before was replaced by the Crescent, and the Christian Cathedral became that Mosque of St. Sophia which still endures.

From the earliest days of the Moslem corsairs of the Mediterranean they were in close communication with their co-religionists of the Ottoman Empire; and this for a very good reason, which was that the Turk had not the habit of the sea, but was essentially a land warrior, and, as the story of the sea-wolves progresses, we shall see how in a sense the Grand Turk and the pirates became interdependent in the ceaseless wars which were waged in the epoch of which we treat.

The fall of Constantinople resounded throughout Christendom as though it had been the crack of doom, and all men held their breath wondering what next might portend. So stunned were the maritime States that they took no action, letting "I dare not wait upon I would." Their indecision was fatal. Had the Venetians, the Genoese, and the Catalans at this juncture formed an alliance, they might have chased the Turks from off the face of the waters; but to mutual jealousy and indecision was added fear—fear of this new and mighty power which had arisen and had swept away one of the landmarks of Europe. So it fell out that Genoa entered into an arrangement with the Grand Turk, and Venice concluded a treaty of commerce on April 18th, 1454. It was the Caliph Mahomet who first fortified the Dardanelles, where he mounted thirty heavy guns before which Jacques Loredano, the Venetian admiral, recoiled, reporting to the Republic that henceforward none could pass the Straits. We have, however, nothing to do with the Grand Turk in these pages, save, and except in so far, as he had an effect on the lives of the corsairs. This effect will develop itself as we proceed.

There is one body of men, however, concerning whom it may be as well to treat of briefly in this place, as the lives which they led and the deeds which they performed were inextricably entangled with those of the corsairs. These men were the members of that association first known as the Knights of Saint John of Jerusalem, later as the Knights of Malta. Between them and the corsairs it was war to the death; and not only with these robbers, but also with any ship which sailed beneath the insignia of the Crescent.

In 1291 the Soldan of Egypt chased the Knights Hospitallers, as they were also known, from the soil of the Holy Land; Philip IV. of France welcomed them in the island of Cyprus, and gave them the town of Limasol as an asylum. This for the time the knights were bound to accept, but they were impatient of charity, resentful of tutelage, proud and independent. Considering their own order as the greatest and most stable bulwark of the Christian faith, they bowed before neither King nor Kaiser; and the only boon they asked of great potentates, when allied temporarily with them in their eternal warfare, was that on all occasions theirs should be the post of the greatest danger.

This, indeed, they did not ask as a favour, but claimed as a right. It is easily understood that such desperate warriors, who fought only to conquer or die, were allies sought for eagerly by all professing the same faith.

Fulke de Villaret, grand master of the order in 1310, seized upon Rhodes, which, though nominally belonging to Greece, was at this time a refuge for bad characters of all nationalities. This island was in the most advantageous position, as it commanded the sea-route from Constantinople to Egypt and the ports of Asia Minor, and was also in close proximity to the coast of Caramania, from whence the order could draw the necessary timber for the building of their galleys and incidentally their motive power—in the shape of slaves—for the oars by which they were propelled.

The knights fortified the island until it was practically unassailable in that age. In the meanwhile their navy grew so rapidly that, in 1436, they were actually in a position to fight the Turks in line of battle. To Rhodes came the younger sons of noble families from every nation in Europe, all aflame with ardour to fight for "the religion"; and the great nobles themselves did not disdain to take service in so chivalrous an order.

Their former enemy, the Soldan of Egypt, made a descent on the island in 1440, and in 1444 besieged the place in form; but he was beaten off, after forty-two days' ceaseless fighting, with great slaughter.

"Soldier and sailor too" were the bold Knights of Saint John; for them no toil was too arduous, no danger too great. In heat and cold, in storm and tempest, they plied their trade of war, their holy crusade to extirpate the *infidel* from off the face of the waters. They looked for no material reward, and riches and honours they contemptuously rejected. Strong in their marvellous faith that on their shoulders rested the propagation of Christianity in these latter days, they swept the seas with a calm assumption of victory which caused it to be half assured before the fight began. And when the battle was joined, where could be found such paladins as these men who claimed it as an inalienable right to head the hurricane rush of the boarders from the decks of their galleys, to be ever the leaders when the forlorn hope should mount the breach? Life for the knights of this order was looked at literally with a single purpose—the advancement of Christianity and the downfall of that pestilent heresy which proclaimed that Mahomet was the prophet of God. Against all who bowed the knee in the mosques of the false prophet their lives were vowed, and it is but the barest justice to them to record that on the altar of this their faith these were ungrudgingly poured forth.

Naturally reprisals were the order of the day. Equally fanatical was he who held to the Moslem faith; in consequence many were the attempts to stamp out, once and for all, the prime enemies of the Ottoman Empire. In 1480 a Turkish fleet of one hundred and forty ships issued from the Dardanelles, an army awaited it on the coast of Caramania which was rapidly embarked, and on May 23rd the fleet anchored a few miles from the town of Rhodes. Here, then, was a trial of strength in which the Hospitallers delighted. After repeated attacks in detail, on July 28th a grand assault was made which the Turks considered would be absolutely decisive: it was decisive, but not in the fashion which they anticipated.

The standard of the Janissaries already floated on the first curtain of the rampart when Pierre D'Aubusson rallied the knights for one last desperate effort. "Shall it be said in days to come that 'the Religion' recoiled before a horde of Moslem savages; that the banner of Saint John was soiled by their infamous touch? But this is no time for talk. Ye have swords, Messires; use them!"

Thus the grand master; and then the knights, in their battered armour and with their hacked and dinted swords, flung themselves once more upon the foe. The Janissaries closed in around them; but these fine troops were not what they had been two months before, and the close contact with the Hospitallers, which had endured sixty-five days, had been to them a lesson fraught with disaster: they had already lost six thousand men, and their adversaries were still absolutely undismayed. His helmet gone, his banner held aloft over his head, Pierre D'Aubusson was ever in the thickest of the fray unconquered, unconquerable; and pressing close behind him came the knights, each jealous for the glory of his "Auberge." French, Venetian, Catalan, Genoese German, none can tell who fought best that day; but the Janissaries were beaten, and three thousand of their corpses cumbered the ditch into which they were hurled by their foes; there were besides fifteen thousand wounded in the Turkish camp.

The heart was out of that great army which had embarked to the sound of trumpets and the blessings of the Mullahs but ten weeks before, and they sailed away a beaten force. Mahomet II. swore to avenge his defeat, but his days were numbered, and he died at Scutari on May 3rd, 1481, at the age of fifty-two, and in the thirteenth year of his reign.

In the year 1499 Daoud Pasha, *Admiralissimo* to Bajazet, the successor to Mahomet II., defeated Antonio Grimani the Venetian admiral in that combat known to the Republic as *"La deplorabile battaglia del Zonchio."* The populace of Venice demanded that Grimani should be instantly beheaded, but he not only escaped their vengeance but lived to be nominated as Doge on June 6th, 1521, at the age of eighty-seven: certainly a curious record for an unsuccessful admiral of that date.

In 1500 was formed the "Alliance of Christian Princes" at the initiative of the Borgia Pope Alexander VII. Louis XII., King of France, and Ferdinand V. of Spain announced their adherence to this effort against the Turk, and Pierre D'Aubusson, the veteran grand master of the Knights of Saint John, was nominated as Captain-General of the Christian armies. For the purposes of this war the admiral of the Papal galleys in the Mediterranean, Lodovico del Mosca, purchased from Ferdinand, King of Naples, all his artillery, of which a description is given by the Padre Alberto Guglielmotti, a Dominican friar, author of a work entitled, *La Guerra dei Pirati e la Marina Pontifica dal 1500 al 1560 A.D.*

> There were thirty-six great bombards, with eighty carts pertaining to them; some drawn by horses, some drawn by buffaloes harnessed singly, or two, four, or even six together; two

wagons laden with *arquebuses* for ships' boats; nine with about forty smaller bombards (*bombardelles*) placed three, four, or even six on each wagon; twelve with ordinary pieces of artillery; as many more for the service of twelve big guns; thirty-seven carts of iron balls; three with gunpowder; and finally five laden with nitre, darts, and bullets. Splendid artillery of most excellent workmanship and great power escorted by two thousand men under arms, without mentioning the companies who marched before and after each wagon.

The French king had prepared a fleet and army under Count Philip of Ravenstein; the Spaniards were under the command of Gonsalvo de Còrdoba, the "Great Captain." The history of the "Alliance of Christian Princes" is illustrative of the methods of those potentates at that time. After one or two unimportant skirmishes with the Turks, in which no great harm was done on either side, the French and Spaniards joined together, and seized the Kingdom of Naples: the prudent king of this territory, having sold his artillery to Lodovico del Mosca, did not await the coming of his Christian brethren.

In the territory known to the Romans as Byzacena, which stretched from Algiers to the confines of Tripoli, there was reigning at this period one Abu-Abd-Allah-Mahomed, a Berber Moslem of the dynasty of Hafsit. Between this dignitary and Genoa a treaty of commerce had been arranged and signed. But treaties on the shores of the Mediterranean were capable of very elastic interpretation; they never reckoned with the corsairs, and these latter were in the habit of intruding themselves everywhere, and upsetting the most carefully laid plans. Curtogali, a corsair who had collected a great following, was now a power with which to reckon, and high in the favour of the Grand Turk at Constantinople. This robber presented himself at Bizerta—one of the ports of Abd-Allah-Mahomed—with a squadron of thirty ships, and demanded hospitality. As Curtogali disposed of thirty ships and some six thousand fighting men it would probably have been impossible for Abd-Allah to have refused his request in any case; but he was far from wishing to do so, as, by a convenient interpretation of the Koran, the pirate had to deliver up one-fifth part of all the booty which he reft from the Christians to the ruler of the country in whose harbours he sheltered. There was no place so convenient for the purposes of the pirate as Bizerta: from here he could strike at Sicily, at the Balearic Islands, at Rome, Naples, Tuscany, and Liguria, while at the same time he held the trade slowly sailing along the North African littoral at his mercy. Great were the depredations of Curtogali, and even Pope Leo X. trembled on his throne, while Genoa, Venice, and Sicily seethed with impotent fury.

In the meanwhile who so happy as Abu-Abd-Allah-Mahomed? We cannot do better than to take the description of his position from the pages of the good Padre Alberto Guglielmotti. The Franciscan says:

> He (that is, Abd-Allah) desired peace with all and prosperity for his own interests. Friendly to the merchants in their commerce; friendly to the corsairs in their spoils. Let all hold by the law: the former contentedly paying customs dues, the latter cheerfully handing over a fifth part of their robberies, and Abd-Allah—their common friend—would ever continue at peace with them all. Outside his ports the merchants and the pirates might fall by the ears if they would: that was no reason for him to trouble his head. On the contrary, he would joyfully await them on their return either with customs dues or tribute of the fifth as the case might be.

However well this state of affairs may have suited Abd-Allah, the Genoese held that the situation was far from satisfactory. In consequence they sent an army against Curtogali, and on August 4th, 1516, they captured Bizerta, set free a number of Christian captives, and plundered the town. But they did not capture Curtogali, who, only five weeks after, made a daring attempt to carry off the Pope in person from the sea-shore in the neighbourhood of Rome. Curtogali ended his days as the Governor of Rhodes, from which the Knights of Saint John were finally expelled by Soliman the Magnificent on December 22nd, 1522. This was the greatest blow which the fraternity ever received. On December 24th the Turks made a triumphal entry into the town, and it was said that "Sultan Soliman was not insensible to the sorrowful position of his vanquished enemies, and when he saw the Christian Commander, Prince Philippe Villiers L'Isle Adam, he remarked: 'It weighs upon me somewhat that I should be coming hither to chase this aged Christian warrior from his house.'" At the beginning of the following year the knights left the island, never to return. On the day of this desolate embarkation the herald blew upon his trumpet the "Salute and Farewell" and the identical instrument upon which this call was sounded is still preserved in the armoury at Malta, to which barren island the knights were forced to retreat.

CHAPTER 2
Uruj Barbarossa

In the year 1457 an obscure Roumelian or Albanian *renegado* named Mahomedi was banished from Constantinople by the Grand Turk; he established himself in the island of Mitylene and there married a Christian widow named Catalina, by whom he had two sons, Uruj and Khizr. The father had been a sailor and both sons adopted the same profession. It is from the pages of El Maestro Don Fray Prudencio de Sandoval that we glean these bare facts concerning the birth and parentage of these men who, in after-years, became known to all the dwellers on the shores of the Mediterranean as the "Barbarossas," from their red beards. Sandoval, Bishop of Pampluna, published in the year 1614 his monumental history of the Emperor Charles V., and through his splendid volumes the deeds of the Moslem corsairs run like the scarlet thread which is twisted through a Government rope. It is evident that the fact of having to deal with such rascals annoys the good Bishop not a little, as his severe and caustic comments frequently display. There was incident and accident enough in the life of the famous "Carlos Quinto" without the historian having to turn aside to chronicle the deeds of the pirates; but their exploits were so daring, the consequences thereof were so far-reaching, that the ominous crimson thread had to be woven into any narrative of the times in despite of the annoyance of the man by whom the rope was twisted.

Of Mahomedi we possess no record save the remark concerning him to the effect that *"el qual fue gran mariner."* in what way he displayed his gifts as a seaman we are not told. We have remarked before on the curious fact of how the *"renegado,"* or Christian turned Mohammedan, became the most implacable foe of his former co-religionists. We see in the case of the two Barbarossas that they had no drop of Moslem blood in them, as both parents came from Christian stock: and yet no greater scourges ever afflicted the people from

Uruj and Kheyr-Ed-Din Barbarossa

whom both their father and mother originally sprang than did Uruj and Khizr Barbarossa.

The characters of the two brothers were widely different. The elder was no doubt a "first-class fighting man," a fine seaman, a born partisan leader; but here his qualities came to an end. Rough, cruel, imperious, brutal, he imposed himself upon those who became his followers; but in him were to be found none of the statesmanlike qualities which distinguished his far greater younger brother. His was the absolutely finite intellect of the tactician as opposed to the strategist, who, seeing his objective, was capable of dealing with circumstances as they immediately arose; but, partly no doubt from defective education, but principally from the lack of intellectual appreciation of the problems of the time in which he lived, could never rise to the heights which were scaled by Khizr, better known by the title conferred upon him later on by the Grand Turk as "Kheyr-ed-Din," or "The Protector of Religion."

The sons of Mahomed, that "*gran marinero*," naturally took to the sea, and as a young man Uruj became possessed of a ship—how we do not know, and it were better perhaps not to inquire. In this small craft he repaired to the coast of Caramania to make war upon the Christians; or, in other words, to begin an independent piratical career. Uruj in these days was young and inexperienced, or he would not have chosen this locality for his first venture, as this coast was in close proximity to the island of Rhodes, from whence the great galleys of the Knights of Saint John of Jerusalem set forth to exterminate the enemies of their faith.

So it came about that Uruj, sailing out in his little ship from under the shadow of a wooded point, came in full sight of *Our Lady of the Conception*. There was nothing for it but immediate flight, and Uruj put his helm up and scudded before the breeze; but the great galley "goose-winged" her two mighty lateen sails, and turned in pursuit. The ship which carried Uruj and his fortunes was both fast and handy, and for a time she held her own; but it was only for a time, as those on board *Our Lady of the Conception*, finding that they were not gaining on the chase, put forth their oars and soon changed the aspect of affairs. The galley of the knights carried twenty-seven oars a-side, and each of these oars was manned by nine Moslem slaves. The sea was smooth and favourable for rowing, and soon the ravening pursuit closed in on the doomed corsair. As the interval between chaser and chased became less and less, those on board the pirate ship could see for themselves the fate which was awaiting them, as on the central gang-plank, which separated the rowers' benches, the boatswain and his mates were unmercifully flogging the bare backs of the straining oarsmen to urge them to greater exertions. He who was captured at sea in those days was set to row until he died, and the calculating mercy which causes a man to feed and treat his beast well in order that it may do the better work was not to be relied upon here, as life was cheap and slaves were plentiful. Very soon the beak of the galley overhung the stern of the little ship. Escape was impossible, to fight would have meant the massacre of all on board; the choice was instant submission or a watery grave. Uruj lowered his sail, and he and his little company were ironed and flung into the depths of the galley until such time as they should be wanted to take their turn at the oars. In this ignominious fashion ended his first attempt at independent piracy.

But a storm was brewing, and a heavy sea got up. The sails of the galley were lowered, her beak was put head-on to the wind, and she made for the shore. In this noisome confinement Uruj could hear above the crash of the seas and the whistling of the wind the shrieks of the hapless slaves as the whips of their taskmasters bit through skin and flesh: the galley-slave rowed stark naked chained to his bench. This was to be his fate, and he was well aware of the fact. At last, after nightfall, the galley anchored under the Isle of Castel Rosso, at the entrance of the Gulf of Satalie. It still blew hard, but, in the comparative peace of the anchorage, sounds hitherto hidden by the war of the elements now made themselves manifest. There were the snores of the sleepers, the clank of the leg-chains as the wretched slaves shifted their positions in the attempt to gain an easier place on the bench, there was also the sound of men carousing with loud laughter in the stern of the vessel; but above them all rose the hollow groaning as of one in mortal agony. This proceeded from a slave who was quite close to Uruj. There came a spell in the laughter and loud voices in the stern, and presently an imperious voice spoke: "That noise disturbs me; see that it ceases at once."

An obsequious answer came from out of the prevailing darkness: "It shall cease at once, Excellency." Then came men with lanterns, who unshackled the wretch who groaned and—flung him overboard.

The night grew worse, the wind backed, and the galley began to drag her anchors. The slaves were roused, and the oars got ready to shift her from her dangerous position on what had now become a lee-shore. Uruj had managed to slip his shackles, a defective bolt having given him his liberty; for him it was now or never, and he was a bold swimmer. He had seen enough and heard enough of *Our*

Lady of the Conception, and, as the great oars plunged once more into the sea, the corsair, preferring the mercy of the elements to that of the knights, slipped over the side unobserved and swam for the shore. He reached dry land by a miracle, and from Satalie he found his way to Egypt, where he took service as a mariner in a ship of the Soldan of Egypt which was bound for the coast of Caramania, from which province the Egyptians, as well as the knights, drew the timber which they required for shipbuilding. But again this neighbourhood proved disastrous to Uruj, as the ship in which he sailed was attacked by a Christian galley, and he once more had to save himself by swimming on shore. There was no lack of incident in the life of a corsair of the sixteenth century.

This time he presented himself to Khorkud, the Governor of Caramania, brother to Sultan Selim, the Grand Turk. The Governor, recognising him as an intrepid mariner, ordered the Basha of Smyrna to furnish him with a ship fitted for that *guerre de course*, which he desired to pursue against the Christians. The value of the corsair as an auxiliary was beginning to be recognised among the high Turkish officials. For the complaisance of Khorkud there were two reasons: in the first place, he was acting in the interests of his brother in sending to sea any really capable man to make head against his enemies, and the fact that Uruj was a pirate pure and simple did not weigh for a feather in the balance; in the second place, it was a decidedly good mercantile speculation as he ordered his inferior, the Basha of Egypt, to bear the expense of fitting out the necessary ship—which came to some 5,000 ducats—and doubtless received a handsome percentage on all captures from his grateful protégé.

This latter, as may easily be imagined, had had quite enough of the Caramanian coast, which had turned out a veritable nest of hornets; also, he had no desire at present to cultivate the further acquaintance of the knights, and therefore put the whole width of the Ionian Sea between himself and them, and succeeded in taking several rich prizes. He avoided Mitylene and returned to Egypt, wintering at Alexandria. It may here be remarked that the corsairs, as a rule, regarded the winter as a close season, as in those early days the mariner did not, if he could avoid it, risk his ship by sailing her at this period of storm and tempest. In consequence there was nothing to tempt the pirates to range the seas during these months, and if they had had a successful summer and autumn, as they generally did, they could well afford to lay up and await the coming of spring.

But when storm and rain gave way to the smooth waters and balmy breezes, the sea-wolves were certain of their prey, as the whole length and breadth of the tideless sea was sure to be filled with the ships of the detested Christians trafficking in every direction. In the ethics of the Moslem all ships which sailed under the banner of the Cross, no matter to what nation they belonged, were fair game, even supposing that her insignia were the Crescent—well, supposing the spot to be sufficiently remote, dead men tell no tales, and the pirates were to be trusted to see to it that none escaped.

But, however this might have been, it is quite certain that no qualms of conscience troubled Uruj concerning those others: Genoese, Neapolitans, Catalans, Andalusians, French, or the dwellers of the Balearic Islands, were all fish sent by a bountiful Providence to be enclosed in his net, and he seized upon them without distinction. When in the full tide of his success there was but one thing which preoccupied the mind of the corsair, which was to find a ready market for his spoils and a convenient place in which to rid himself of an embarrassing number of captives. This, however, did not present an insuperable difficulty, as we have already seen in the case of Curtogali, and a similar arrangement was carried out by Uruj Barbarossa and his brother.

Uruj now established himself at the island of Jerba, on the east coast of Tunis, which formed an admirable base from which to "work" the Mediterranean from the piratical point of view. Jerba had originally been conquered and occupied by the Spaniards in 1431, but the occupation had been allowed to lapse, and the island was lying derelict when the Barbarossas made it their headquarters. Here Uruj was joined by his younger brother Khizr, destined to become so much the more famous of the two; he had already made himself some reputation in piratical circles, and now brought his cool judgment and wise counsel to the assistance of that fiery fighting man his elder brother. The first question to be decided was that which we have already mentioned, namely, the disposal of spoil from prospective captures, and with this end in view the corsairs approached the Sultan of Tunis. This potentate made a gracious response to their overtures, and wished them all success in their enterprises. He promised them succour and support on the same terms which Curtogali had obtained, namely, one-fifth of all the spoil landed in his dominions.

The price to be paid was a stiff one, and was so regarded by the active partners in this arrangement; they were, however, young and unknown, and had not the least intention of holding to their bargain when more favourable circumstances presented themselves. Now they held fair speech with the puppet princes of North Africa; the day was to come when they should chase them from their insecure thrones. It was at this time, shortly after the treaty with the Sultan of Tunis was concluded, that the younger Barbarossa received from the Grand Turk the glorious name of Kheyr-ed-Din, or "The Protector of Religion." It was a somewhat remarkable title for a pirate, but perhaps its bestower was slightly deficient in a sense of humour.

Sailing from Tunis in the spring of the year 1512, the brothers, with three galleys, fell in with *The Galley of Naples*, an enormous *nef* with a crew of three hundred. They instantly attacked, but were repulsed, night falling without either side having gained an advantage. This audacious proceeding illustrates the hardihood of the Moslem corsairs at this time. They were amply strong enough to range the Mediterranean and to capture, with no risk to themselves, the weak and unprotected argosies plying their trade in this sea; but this was not the method of the Barbarossas. Villains they may have been according to modern standards, pirates they were unquestionably; but they were grim, hard-bitten, fighting men, who shrank from no dangers in the pursuit of their prey, who reckoned that the humiliation and defeat of their Christian antagonists was as sweet a morsel as the booty reft from their hands. All night the three Moslem galleys and the great *nef* lay becalmed awaiting the conflict which was to come with the break of day; and it is easy to imagine that there was not much quiet sleep on board of either the Moslem or the Christian ships, for both on the one side and the other the issues loomed large. The corsairs had, so far, made no such important capture as this, which, could it be accomplished, would add enormously to their prestige, in addition to such spoils as they might acquire; but the combatants were fairly evenly matched in the matter of numbers, and the fight was one to a finish. The advantage on the side of the corsairs lay in the fact of their being three to one, and their being thus enabled to attack in three separate places at the same time. Terrible must have been that night of waiting for the unfortunates on board *The Galley of Naples*; there was no escape, and on board of her among her passengers were many women, whose fate was too terrible to contemplate should the day go against them. The first assault had been beaten off, it is true, but the struggle had been hard and bitter; would they be equally successful when the assault was renewed?

Even such a night as this, however, comes at last to an end, and the prospect of action must have been welcomed by the men on both sides; of the women with so horrible a fate impending one can hardly bear to think. The ghostly fingers of the dawn touched the grey sea with a wan yellow light, outlining the *nef* and the slender, wicked-looking galleys with their banks of oars; over the surface of the deep a slight mist hovered, as though some kindly spirit of the sea would hide, if such a thing were possible, the deeds which were to come. The three galleys lay close together, and Uruj and his brother held a few last words of counsel.

"It is agreed, then," said the elder; "you, my brother, attack the starboard side and I on the port side, while Hassan Ali (indicating the captain of the third galley) will await the time when we are fully engaged, and will then board over the stern."

"It is agreed," answered Kheyr-ed-Din, and Hassan Ali.

As the strong sun of a perfect May morning in the Mediterranean leapt above the horizon, Uruj loosed his hounds upon their prey; the oars of the galleys churned the clear blue waters into foam, and the air was filled with the yells of the corsairs. "Allah! Allah!" and "Barbarossa! Barbarossa!" they cried. It was a war-cry that was destined to re-echo over many a conflict, both by land and sea, in the years that were to come.

In a simultaneous, and as we have seen a concerted attack, the beaks of the galleys crushed into the broadsides of *The Galley of Naples*, and, ever foremost in the fray, Uruj and Kheyr-ed-Din were the first two men to board. Then, when men were hand to hand and foot to foot, when Moslem *scimitar* rang on Christian sabre, and the air was filled with the oaths and shouts of the combatants, the third remaining pirate craft grappled *The Galley of Naples* by the stern, and a tide of fresh, unwounded men burst into the fray. This was the end; the Christians were both outnumbered and outfought, for among them were many who were not by profession warriors, whereas no man found a footing among the sea-wolves, or was taken to sea as a fighting man, unless he had approved himself to the satisfaction of his captain that he was a valiant man of his hands. We have no record or list of the dead and wounded in this battle, but among the latter was Uruj, who was severely hurt. Not so Kheyr-ed-Din, who escaped scatheless and took command now that his brother was incapacitated. The dead were flung overboard with scant ceremony, and the wounded patched up as best might be, and then *The Galley of Naples* was taken in tow, and the corsairs returned in triumph to Tunis. Faithful to their treaty, so far, they laid one-fifth of their spoils at the feet of the Sultan.

A great procession was formed of Christian captives marching two and two. Four young Christian girls were mounted on mules, and two ladies of noble birth followed on Arab horses sumptuously caparisoned. These unfortunates were destined for the harems of their captors. The Sultan was greatly pleased at the spectacle, and as the mournful procession defiled before him cried out, "See how heaven recompenses the brave!" Jurien de la Gravière remarks:

> Such was the fortune of war in the sixteenth century. A man leaving Naples to go to Spain might end his days in a Moorish bagnio and see his wife and daughters fall a prey to miscreants of the worse description.

It was not till the following spring that Uruj was fit once more to pursue his chosen calling, so severe had been his wounds; but once he was whole and sound again he put to sea accompanied by Kheyr-ed-Din, and this time he had conceived a singularly bold and desperate enterprise. Two years before the famous Spanish captain, Pedro de Navarro, had seized upon the coast town of Bougie, and had unfortunately left it in the hands of a totally insufficient garrison. This departure from the sound rules of warfare had already been punished as it deserved, as the garrison was perpetually harassed and annoyed by the surrounding Arab tribes. The idea of Uruj was to seize upon Bougie by a *coup de main*. The corsair, however, was a far finer fighter than he was a strategist, and was possessed of a most impatient temper. All went well to begin with, as he managed to intercept and to capture a convoy of Spanish ships sent to revictual the place, and had he been content to wait he might have counted with certainty on reducing the garrison by starvation, as it depended on this very convoy for its supplies. In vain the wary and cool-headed Kheyr-ed-Din counselled prudence and delay, but these words were not to be found in the vocabulary of his elder brother. "What had to be done," he replied, "had better be done at once," and at the head of only fifty men landed and assaulted the still uncompleted ramparts of Bougie.

But if Uruj were rash and headstrong, so was not the commander of the Spanish garrison, who, massing his men for the repulse of the assault, waited till the last moment, and then received them with a volley of *arquebuses*, which laid many of them low, and so badly wounded their leader that he had to have his arm amputated on the spot: it says much for his constitution that he survived the operation.

For the time being the brothers had had enough of shore enterprises, and confined themselves strictly to their piratical business at sea, which prospered so exceedingly that they became exceedingly rich and their fame and power increased day by day. As time went on and the wealth of the brothers and partners increased, there entered into the calculating brain of Kheyr-ed-Din the idea that the payment of one-fifth share to the Sultan of Tunis was but money thrown away. Twenty per cent, was eating into the profits of the firm in an unwarrantable manner, he considered, and now that the active partners therein had established so good a business connection, they were quite strong enough to dispense with a sleeping partner. Times had changed for the better, and Kheyr-ed-Din was anxious to take full advantage of the fact; if possible he determined to seize upon and hold some port, in which, not only would they be exempt from tribute, but also in which he and his brother Uruj should be the supreme arbiters of the fate of all by whom it might be frequented.

Of Bougie and its stout Spanish garrison the brothers had had quite enough for the present: they sought, in consequence, for some harbour which presented equal advantages of situation, and their choice fell upon Jigelli, then belonging to the Genoese, who occupied a strong castle in this place.

Jigelli lies well outside the confines of the kingdom of Tunis, about equi-distant from Bougie and Cape Bougaroni, some forty miles from each. It would appear that on this occasion it was the younger of the two brothers who took charge of the enterprise, and there were no slap—dash, unconsidered methods employed. By this time the fame of the Barbarossas had gone abroad from Valencia to Constantinople, from Rome to the foot—hills of the Atlas Mountains, and, to circumvent the Genoese garrison of Jigelli, Kheyr-ed-Din called to his aid the savage Berber tribes of the hinterland of this part of Northern Africa.

Turbulent, rash, unstable as water, were these primitive dwellers of the desert; but they were fighters and raiders to a man, and ready for any desperate encounter if only it held out the promise of loot: they were as veritably the pirates of the land as were the Barbarossas pirates of the sea.

Small chance, indeed, had the five hundred Genoese soldiers by which Jigelli was garrisoned when attacked from the sea by the Barbarossas and by land by an innumerable horde of Berbers who were reckoned to be as many as 20,000. Invested by land and sea, the garrison did all that it was possible for men to do. Provisions and water ran short, ammunition was failing, the ring of their enemies was encircling them day by day closer and ever closer. From the land nothing could be expected but an augmentation of their foes, and day by day the commander of the garrison strained his eyes seaward to watch if haply the proud Republic, to which he and his men belonged, would send succour, or the redoubtable Knights of Saint John would come to his aid.

But the days lengthened into weeks, and the soldiers were gradually becoming worn out by the perpetual strain imposed upon them. There was one chance left, and one alone, which was to cut their way out through the besieging lines. Massacre to a man was their fate in any case, and thus it was that the commander, whose name has not come down to us, mustered his men for the last supreme effort. At dead of night the garrison, having destroyed as far as possible all that might be of use to the enemy, sallied out to their doom. They fought as men fight who know that the end has come; but valour could not avail against the numbers arrayed on the side of the enemy, and they were wiped off the face of the earth. The tribes looted the castle of everything portable, and then retired from whence they had come. For this Kheyr-ed-Din cared nothing; they were welcome to the poor possessions of some hundreds of half-starved Italian soldiers—let them take the shell, for him remained the kernel in the shape of a strong place of arms.

Hardly, however, had the brothers succeeded in this enterprise when that tireless fighter Uruj again attempted the capture of Bougie; but his second attempt was even more disastrous than his first, and he lost half his flotilla. Then he asked for succour from Tunis; but the Sultan, much offended at the idea of the brothers setting up in a piratical business in which he was no longer a sleeping partner, angrily refused.

Chapter 4

The Death of Uruj Barbarossa

The events recorded in the last chapter bring us down to the end of the year 1515, and while every endeavour has been made to present affairs in chronological sequence, it must be remembered that the dates of piratical expeditions are often impossible to obtain: the wrath of the chroniclers at the nefarious deeds of the corsairs greatly exceeding their desire for a meticulous accuracy in the matter of the exact time of their occurrence. Uruj, as has been seen, had by his headstrong folly once again placed his brother and himself in a decidedly awkward situation. By the losses which he had incurred in his second ill-advised attempt on Bougie he had so weakened the piratical confederation that the countenance of some potentate had again become necessary for their continued existence, and the Sultan of Tunis had now repudiated all connection with these ingrates.

But, if craft and subtlety were not to be found in Uruj there was one who never failed to exhibit these qualities when they became necessary, and Kheyr-ed-Din once more came to the front. The Russian peasantry have a saying that "God is high and the Czar is far away." In the sixteenth century the Grand Turk was in every sense "far away" from the struggling corsairs on the littoral of Northern Africa, and was a sovereign of such great and mysterious might that any man with a less fine instinct into the psychology of the times in which he lived than Kheyr-ed-Din would have hesitated long and anxiously before addressing him directly; would probably in the end not have done so at all. But desperate diseases require desperate remedies, and the politic corsair well knew that even the moral support of such an one as the Sultan of Constantinople was worth more than even material aid from a Sultan of Tunis.

Consequently, greatly daring, he sent an embassy to the Sublime Porte with one of his most trusted captains at its head to lay the homage of the corsairs at the feet of Selim I. Very naturally these ambassadors did not go empty-handed, but took with them rich presents and numerous slaves. Selim was much pleased at the attention, coming as it did from such a distance—we have to remember that the coast of North Africa was an immense journey from Constantinople in those days—and the insight of Kheyr-ed-Din was triumphantly vindicated. Not only did the Sultan send a gracious reply in return, but—what was far more to the purpose—he sent a reinforcement of fourteen vessels to the corsairs bidding them to go on and prosper in their efforts to spread the true faith among the Christian heretics.

There is nothing more curious in the history of the corsairs than the perpetual ups and downs of their lives. Thus in the present instance the ill-advised attack of Uruj on Bougie had reduced them to terrible straits; immediately afterwards the action of the Grand Turk once more set them upon their feet and enabled them to pursue an unchecked career of devastation. Aided by the reinforcements sent by Selim, their depredations assumed ever larger proportions, and, had they continued to receive this assistance, the course of history itself might have been changed. Ground to powder beneath the iron heel of their ruthless conquerors, the Moriscoes of Southern Spain were ever waiting the chance to rise and shake off the yoke by which they were so sore oppressed; from far and near reports were coming to hand of the continued successes of the corsairs, and all Andalusia seethed with passionate hope that the day of deliverance was at hand.

But, alas for the vanity of human wishes! in the opening months of the year 1516 Selim recalled his ships and the chance was gone, never again to arise.

It may have been that "the sorrowful sighing of the captives" never reached the ears of the successor of Othman in his palace on the shores of the Golden Horn; in any case, the Sultan was preparing for the conquest of Egypt, and in consequence recalled the ships which he had lent to assist the corsairs. The Moriscoes were thus left without hope, but so far as the corsairs were concerned they were enabled to strike another bargain with the Sultan of Tunis. This monarch had now got over his fit of the sulks, and discovered that customs dues from the peaceful trading mariners, although desirable enough, were not by any means so lucrative a form of revenue as was the one-fifth share of the booty of the pirates. Uruj and Kheyr-ed-Din for their part, although they had captured Jigelli, were totally unable to hold it: the capture had indeed been principally due to the assistance which they had received from the Berber tribesmen, but these nomads had disappeared into the deserts from whence they came, once the looting of the town and fortress had been completed.

The corsair had to be armed at all points, in the moral as well as the material sense, as he was the enemy of all men, and all were vowed to his destruction. Every cruise which he took raised up against him fresh hatred and a more bitter animus, and we must remember that it was not only men individually, but Principalities and Powers that were arrayed in line of battle for his destruction. At the present juncture Spain was specially hostile, for not only had her possession of Bougie been twice attacked by the sea-wolves, but a valuable convoy had been captured. An expedition, in consequence, was sent by the Spaniards against the Barbarossas, but this effort did not result in much damage being done to the offenders. The Spaniards destroyed four piratical vessels which had been abandoned by their crews at Bizerta, and pushed a strong reconnaissance into the Bay of Tunis itself. Here shots were exchanged between the Spanish fleet and the forts—under which Kheyr-ed-Din had drawn up his ships—and the Spaniards then abandoned the enterprise and returned from whence they had come.

In the year 1510 the Spaniard, Count Pedro Navarre, had seized upon Algiers, which town was at this time one of the principal refuges of the Moorish fugitives, who had been driven from Granada, from Còrdoba, and from Southern Spain generally by Ferdinand and Isabella eighteen years previously. To say that the condition of these people was desperate is to speak but the bare truth, for what could exceed the misery of the situation in which they were left after the successful incursion of their Christian foes? What we are apt to lose sight of in the light of present-day circumstances is the fact that these Spanish Moors were a most highly civilised people, far more so indeed than their Christian contemporaries; that they had been driven with fire and sword from the land in which they and their forefathers had dwelt for over seven centuries, and that they now had been cast out literally to starve on the inhospitable shores of Northern Africa. So it came about that the common people exchanged the life of the peaceful and prosperous artisan or husbandman for that of the hand-to-mouth pirate, and the case of knight and noble among them was no better—perhaps rather worse—than the meanest among those who had been expropriated.

Those who know the region in which these unhappy folk lived are aware of the material monuments which still exist and testify to the glorious past; and, seeing what they have seen, it is no great stretch of the imagination to picture to themselves the comfort, the elegance, and the luxury with which the inhabitants of Granada and Còrdoba lived surrounded. Over there, away across some few leagues of shining blue water, were the ruined homes of which many of the banished people still possessed the keys, awaiting the day when Allah and the Prophet should vouchsafe to them that return which they so naturally and ardently desired. To this day the key of the great Mosque at Còrdoba is preserved at Rabat as a sacred relic of former dignity and power—a symbol to the Moslem of his perpetual banishment. If Còrdoba with its mosque—still one of the wonders of the world, with its eleven hundred marble columns—were the principal shrine and holy of holies to these people, there were in addition hundreds of other temples of their faith now for ever desecrated in their eyes by the misfortune which had placed them in Christian hands. In Andalusia were the dishonoured graves of their kinsfolk, and, last and worst of all, in this land still dwelt thousands upon thousands of their co-religionists held in a degrading bondage by their implacable enemies.

The capture of Algiers by Count Pedro Navarro was a crowning misfortune for the exiles, and when this commander seized upon the place he extracted from the inhabitants an oath of fidelity to the Spanish crown; he further erected a strong tower to overawe the town, and to keep its turbulent inhabitants in order. But such an oath as this, extracted at the point of the sword, was writ in water; it meant, of course, the suppression of piracy, and it also meant the starvation of most of those persons who dwelt in the vicinity. How the Moslem population existed for the six years after the incursion of Navarro is a mystery; but they probably moved their galleys, of which they possessed some twenty, further along the coast out of the range of the guns from Navarro's Tower, and secure from the observation of those who held it for the Spanish king.

In the year in which Selim descended upon Egypt the King of Spain, Ferdinand V., died, and grave troubles immediately broke out in Spain. This was an opportunity too good to be missed, as no reinforcements could possibly be expected for the garrison in Algiers as long as these disturbances lasted, and the Algerines took counsel together as to the best means of driving out their enemies. It is a commentary on the detestation in which they held the Spaniards that they should have allied themselves for this purpose with the savages of the hinterland. This, however, was what they did. As in the case of Jigelli, these people could always be relied upon to go anywhere in search of booty, and one Selim Eutemi entered the town at the head of his tribe. But sheer, stark, savage valour could make no impression on Navarro's Tower and the ordnance that was mounted on its walls. The result was a stalemate, as the Spaniards could by no manner of means get out, and neither could their enemies, who swarmed innumerable in the town and the surrounding country, get in. In time, of course, they might hope to bring the garrison to surrender by starvation; but time pressed, and no man knew when the troubles in Spain might be adjusted and help come to the beleaguered. In the meanwhile Selim Eutemi and his men, who had been taught some rude lessons in the power of firearms, kept out of range of the cannon, while the Algerines held yet another council of war, the result of which was that they decided to ask help from Uruj and Kheyr-ed-Din Barbarossa, and to them they appealed. By this time their fame was known to all men, and they could supply that which was lacking—namely ships, artillery, a first-class fighting force, and last, and best of all, the moral support which would stiffen and put heart into the motley horde which at present surged around the gates of the fortress of Navarro.

The Algerines did not appeal in vain, and an instant promise of succour was forthcoming. Kheyr-ed-Din was away at sea, but Uruj, that indomitable fighter, started at once. From whence we are not told, but he must have been somewhere in the neighbourhood, as he and his men marched along the shore; while, keeping pace with them, came a fleet of eighteen galleys and three barques laden with stores. But before proceeding to the assistance of the Algerines Uruj had a personal matter to which to attend, and he wished to combine pleasure with serious business. One of his old companions had seceded from his command and had established himself at Shershell, where he lived the life of an independent corsair within easy striking distance of the Balearic Islands and the coast of Spain, his following composed of a horde of those broken men of whom mention has been made. Shershell was an unfortified town, and surrendered unconditionally upon the arrival of Uruj and his army. Kara-Hassan, for such was the name of this independent corsair, came out to greet his old-time chief; he was met with violent reproaches, and the altercation ended by Uruj having him beheaded on the spot. It was ill to quarrel with the Barbarossas.

Freed from this rival, the Mitylene corsair had now uncontested supremacy on the coast, a supremacy none was likely to contest in the future, as he brooked no opposition, and had come to consider that independent piracy in the Mediterranean was in some sort an infringement of the rights of himself and his brother. One of the most salient peculiarities of the corsairs at this time was the apparent recklessness with which they assailed others who were participants in their nefarious business. Self-interest and policy would seem, to the observer in the present day, to have dictated quite a different course of action; but we shall see, when we come to deal with the life-history of Kheyr-ed-Din, that this infinitely wiser and more intellectual man apparently allowed himself to be swayed by gusts of passion, in which he savagely maltreated those with whom he was associated, and from whom dangerous hostility was certainly to be feared if they escaped with their lives. At this distance of time it is impossible to gauge the motives by which men such as these were actuated, more particularly in the case of Kheyr-ed-Din, whose character was a blend of the deepest subtlety and calculated ferocity.

Having settled with Kara-Hassan, Uruj continued his march along the coast. Arrived at Algiers, he opened in form a siege of Navarro's Tower; but, being unable to make any impression on its defences, he abandoned the siege after twenty days' fruitless fighting, during which he lost a number of men in his assaults. Baffled and furious, he turned on the Berber chieftain, the luckless Selim Eutemi, and caused him to be assassinated, regarding him as being responsible for the failure. The Spanish chroniclers relate, with some wealth of detail, how Uruj personally fell upon Selim Eutemi, when that chieftain was in his bath, and strangled him with his own hands. However this may have been, the Spanish records of the deeds of the corsairs cannot well be taken *au pied de la lettre*; there is no doubt that Selim was murdered, and from that time the Berbers recognised that he who had come to help was now remaining to plunder. Uruj now established himself in the town, and set to work making raids into the adjoining country, carrying off sheep, cattle, and slaves. For the Berbers this was a true awakening. He who now oppressed them had come in the guise of a champion to assist them in the sack and plunder of Navarro's Tower; they had exchanged King Log, who dwelt securely locked up, for a King Stork of the most active description. Although we cannot sympathise with such people, it is quite possible to understand their very natural annoyance at the turn which things had taken, and it does not surprise us (in this age of "Punic faith") that a conspiracy was set on foot between the dwellers of the hinterland and the Spaniards of the fortress.

Uruj was informed of all that was going on through his own spies, and, although he kept his finger on the pulse of the conspiracy, he acted as though the tribesmen were still his very faithful friends and allies. The corsair was more patient than his wont. In this affair he wished for ample proof of delinquency, and also for a vengeance adequate to the occasion when he should discover all the guilty parties; and so some weeks went by while the plot was maturing, apparently, from the point of view of the conspirators, to a successful conclusion. But Uruj had bided his time with a subtlety and *finesse* which would have done credit to Kheyr-ed-Din himself,

It was the custom of the corsair and his chief adherents to attend the principal mosque on Fridays; and therefore, when the conspirators were cordially invited to attend on the following Friday, and, after the service was over, to attend Uruj to his dwelling and there confer with him, they went, nothing doubting, to their deaths. As the discourse of the Mullah came to an end a crash resounded throughout the building: six stalwart swordsmen had flung the great gates of the mosque together, and barred all exit. Excepting the conspirators, twenty-two in number, the remainder of the edifice was filled with the galley's crews of the corsair, men who, had he given the order, would have cheerfully set alight to the sacred building itself and roasted the Mullahs themselves in the flames.

To the corsairs, after they were seated in the mosque, the word had been passed that the Berber tribesmen had meditated this treachery against them, which, had it succeeded, would have meant the death or enslavement of them all. It was therefore a trap of a singularly deadly description into which the countrymen of Selim Eutemi walked on this Friday morning.

The doors being closed, the conspirators were one by one dragged before Uruj, who, bitterly reproaching them, gave order for their instant death. They were haled out through rows of jeering pirates, and beheaded in the street immediately in front of the principal entrance of the mosque. When the slaughter of the twenty-two was accomplished Uruj strode from the mosque over the weltering corpses of the traitors amid the plaudits of his own men, ever ready to acclaim deeds of blood and cruelty. After this there were no more plots against the corsair in Algiers. News of all these desperate doings in Algiers had by this time filtered across into Spain, and El Maestro Don Fray Prudencio de Sandoval recounts how, when the tidings came to Fray Francisco Ximenes, the Cardinal Archbishop of Toledo, that that prelate, much scandalised that the might of Imperial Spain should be flouted by a mere pirate, sent Don Diego de Vera with some fifteen thousand men to recapture the town, and relieve the beleaguered garrison in the tower. This was in the month of September 1516.

Don Diego landed *"en el dia de San Hieronymo,"* and threw up entrenchments within gunshot of the town. Great things were expected of this expedition, as Sandoval notes that in 1513 Don Diego de Vera, in the war against the French, had gained the approval of Count Pedro Navarro ("*avia bien aprovado con el Conde Pedro Navarro*"), and it was not expected that a mere pirate rabble would ever make head against the Spanish troops. De Vera opened fire on the walls of the town from his entrenchments, but hardly had he done so when Uruj, leading his corsairs, which formed the spearhead to an innumerable army of Berbers and Arabs, made a sortie.

> Upon them one day did Barbarossa make an onslaught, and when he saw that the Spanish soldiers were ill commanded, he flung his forces upon them with loud cries. And so great was the fear inspired by Barbarossa that they were routed almost without loss to the Moors; and with much ease did these latter slay three thousand men and capture four hundred on the day of San Hieronymo in this year.

This quotation is given in full to set out the amazing fact that in this battle over three thousand were killed while only four hundred were captured, which shows that it must have been in the nature of an indiscriminate massacre; the only captive of any note was the captain, Juan del Rio. Diego de Vera had had enough of the corsairs, and sailed away with the remainder of his force. Of what became of him or of them there is no record, but he must have been a singularly incompetent commander when he could not make head against a rabble of pirates and Moors with the army at his disposition. Sandoval does not attempt to minimise the defeat, which, of course, would have been impossible; he contents himself with the following delightfully quaint reflection:

> But many, many times Homer nods; this disaster must have come upon us for our sins, upon which it is most important that we should always think and meditate.

Who so triumphant now as Uruj Barbarossa? It is true that the fortress of Pedro Navarro still remained in the hands of its splendid and undaunted garrison, and was destined so to remain for some years to come; but they were impotent for harm, and the conqueror of Don Diego now turned his arms in another direction. Kheyr-ed-Din was at Jigelli when he heard of the victory gained by his brother, and sailed at once with six ships to his support. The town of Tenes fell into the hands of the brothers, with an immense booty, and then

Uruj marched on Tlemcen. The Sultan of Tlemcen, the last of the royal race of the Beni-Zian, did not await the coming of the corsair. All through the northern coasts of Africa the name of Barbarossa was a synonym of terror; the sad fate of Selim Eutemi, of Kara-Hassan, of the twenty-two conspirators of the mosque, had been noised abroad, and the superstitious tribesmen firmly believed that these red-bearded corsairs were the accomplices of Shaitan, even if they did not represent him themselves in their own persons. Who were these men, they asked one another tremblingly, who feared neither God nor devil, and who caused even the redoubtable Spaniards to fly before them like the leaves in front of an autumn gale?

When men begin to talk and to think like this there is not much fight left in them, and so it came about that, after the most feeble of resistances, the Sultan of Tlemcen fled to Fez. Thus, almost without striking a blow, Uruj found himself master of a province from which the Spaniards were accustomed to draw the necessary provisions for the upkeep of the garrison of Oran. But Tlemcen is but some seventy miles from Oran, and Oran is so close to Spain as to be easily reinforced; in consequence Uruj was soon blockaded by the Spaniards, and remained so for seven months. But no blockade could keep Uruj Barbarossa for long within stone walls; sortie after sortie did the gallant corsair lead against the foe, and it was in one of these that he characteristically came by his death. Ever rash and impetuous, he allowed himself to be drawn too far away from possible shelter or support; and, as there was something dramatic in the whole life of this man, so also was there in the manner of his death. They had him trapped at last, this grim Sea-wolf, and he stood at bay in a stone corral used for the herding of goats.

> *As the wolves in winter circle round the leaguer on the heath,*
> *So the greedy foe glared upward panting still for blood and death.*

By his side was his faithful lieutenant Venalcadi. In a breathless melee Christian sword and Moslem sabre clashed and rang. His turban gone, his great curved *scimitar* red to the hilt, the undaunted corsair fought his last fight as became the terror of his name. Almost had he succeeded in breaking through the ring of his foes when Garzia de Tineo, *alferez* (or lieutenant) to Captain Diego de Andrade, wounded him severely with a pike. Uruj stumbled, was struck on the head with another weapon; he reeled and fell. The fight was over, and one of the Barbarossas bit the dust. Garzia de Tineo leaped upon the fallen man and cut off his head. It is recorded that Garzia de Tineo was wounded in the finger by Uruj in the course of the combat, and that for the rest of his life he proudly exhibited the scar as a sign that it was none other than he who had killed the famous corsair.

Uruj Barbarossa was undoubtedly a remarkable man. At a time when the Mediterranean swarmed with warriors none was more feared, none was more redoubtable than he. By sheer valour and tenacity he had fought his way to the front, and the son of the obscure *renegado* of Mitylene died a king. It is true that his sovereignty was precarious, that it was maintained at the edge of the sword; none the less, in that welter of anarchy in which he lived he had forced himself to the summit, and, pirate, sea-wolf, and robber as he was, we cannot withhold from him a meed of the most hearty admiration.

CHAPTER 5

Kheyr-Ed-Din Barbarossa

Uruj had arrogated to himself the title of King of Tlemcen, but with his death this shadowy sovereignty came to an end, and the Spaniards seized upon the province. This, however, did not avail them much, as the Sultan of Fez sent against them an innumerable army, and they in their turn were dispossessed. It was in the year 1518 that Uruj fell beneath the pike of Garzia de Tineo, and now the first place in the piratical hierarchy was taken by Kheyr-ed-Din. In this man the genius of the statesman lay hidden beneath the outward semblance of the bold and ruthless pirate; ever foremost in the fight, strong to endure, swift to smite, he had by now long passed his novitiate, had established an empire over the minds of men which was to endure until the end of his unusually prolonged life. With a brain of ice and a heart of fire, he looked out, serene and calm, upon the turbulent times in which he lived, a monstrous egotist desiring nothing but his own advancement, all his faculties bent upon securing more wealth and yet more power.

He played a lone hand, for he brooked even less than did his truculent brother any approach to an equality with himself among the men who followed in his train. Absolute supremacy was his in the life which he lived, but none knew better than he upon what an unstable basis his power rested. He now called himself the King of Algiers, but still that lean, sun-dried garrison held with desperate tenacity to the tower of the redoubtable Navarro, and any moment a fresh Spanish relieving force might be upon him and chase him forth even as Uruj had been chased from Tlemcen. He saw that he must consolidate his power, must for the present, at any rate, have some force at his back which would provide that material and moral backing which was essential to his schemes. Once before he had successfully approached the Grand Turk, the Padishah, the head of the

Mohammedan religion, and from him he had received that which he had asked; on this former occasion, however, he had not been in the same position as he now occupied.

The corsair must have meditated long and anxiously on the best way in which to approach the autocrat of Constantinople; in the end he probably hit upon the best solution of the problem by again sending an ambassador with precise instructions as to the manner in which he was to act. For this important service his choice fell upon one of his captains, Hadj-Hossein by name, and to him he imparted all that he was to say, and—what was almost as important—what he was not to say.

The duty of the ambassador was to magnify the importance of his master, but to do so in such a manner that the Padishah was not to imagine that a rival to his own greatness had arisen at Algiers. Selim was at this time in Egypt, where he had just completed the conquest of the Mamelukes, and thither did Hadj-Hossein repair. He laid at the feet of the conqueror the respectful homage of the King of Algiers, who, he assured Selim, desired nothing better than to become the vassal of the Commander of the Faithful. Also, he informed him, that in the name of Selim public prayer was offered in the mosques on Fridays, that his image and superscription were struck on the coins, that in every manner possible recognition was made of the fact that he, and he alone, was the chosen of God upon earth. This manner of stating the situation was both delicate and politic. A less wise man than Kheyr-ed-Din might have assumed a note of equality from one Moslem potentate to another, but the corsair was perfectly conscious of his limitations—he knew exactly how the Grand Turk could be useful to him, and he was not going to mar his chance by the display of an untimely arrogance.

Hadj-Hossein proved himself to be a tactful and successful ambassador. The Sultan accepted the homage offered, and made many inquiries concerning the war prosecuted by Hossein's master against the enemies of the true faith in the distant region of Algiers. His queries were all answered with deep submission and the most subtle of flattery, much of which latter was no doubt a perfectly honest expression of opinion. As to the average Mohammedan of this period the Padishah was a being set apart by Heaven to fulfil the decrees of the Prophet.

The ambassador, when he rejoined his master, must have been a proud man, as so well had he fulfilled his mission that he carried back with him to Algiers not only a gracious message, but the insignia of the Sanjak, Scimitar Horse and Tambour, conferred upon that loyal Moslem Kheyred-Din Barbarossa, who, in the words of the Padishah, "abandoning a sterile independence, sought in all the bloody hazards of his life nought but the glory of God and His Prophet." To us this hyperbole, addressed to a pirate, seems merely ridiculous, but in those days of fanaticism the beliefs of men, both Christians and Moslems, are something which it is impossible for us to realise. On either side the way of salvation was the path of conquest, and the man who was heretic to the faith which you professed was rightly served if you could cut him and his off from among the congregation.

It was well for the corsair to make as many friends as possible, as among his enemies he counted all the kings of Christendom; and, looking back on his career, it seems but little short of a miracle that he was not crushed out of existence, not once but a hundred times. But, as has been said already, the root of true statesmanship was in Kheyr-ed-Din. He watched with eager eye the quarrels of the great kings on the continent of Europe; he saw his life-long rival at sea, the greatest of all Christian mariners, Andrea Doria, the Genoese admiral, transfer his allegiance from the French King Francis I. to the Emperor Charles V. He noted and took full advantage of the perpetual squabbles between the Genoese and Venetian Republics, and all the time was in touch with the sea-wolves, who swarmed on the coasts of Africa, and lurked in every creek and harbour of the Ionian Sea. "In all the bloody hazards of his life," to quote once again the words of the Grand Turk, "he could, in the end, depend more or less on the corsairs, whether they ostensibly sailed beneath his banner or whether they did not, as when danger threatened what name was so potent as that of Barbarossa, which his followers asserted to be worth ten thousand men, when shouted on the day of battle!"

That which is most extraordinary in the life of Kheyr-ed-Din is the perpetual danger and stress in which it was lived. Time and again the heavy menacing clouds gathered around his head; strenuous and unceasing were the efforts made by his enemies to destroy his power, to capture the person of this militant robber who flung an insolent defiance to the whole of Christendom. The storms gathered and broke with various effects, which sometimes sent the corsair flying for his life a hunted fugitive, as others saw him once more victorious. But no reverses had the power to damp his ardour, or to render him less eager to arise, like some ill-omened phoenix, from the ashes of defeat: to vex the souls of those who held themselves to be the greatest men on earth.

It was shortly after the death of his brother Uruj that the storm arose which bade fair to sweep, not only Kheyr-ed-Din but all the corsairs of the North African coast, clean out of their strongholds, for the Emperor Charles V., at this time young, eager, and enthusiastic, gave orders for their destruction. These robbers troubled the peace of Europe; they did more than this, they insulted the Majesty of the Emperor, and Charles regarded their perpetual incursions in the light of an affront to his personal dignity. The divinity which hedged such a monarch as the grandson of "Los Reyes Cathòlicos," Ferdinand and Isabella, was a very real thing, and, if offended, was likely to find concrete expression in the most vigorous form. Charles, much annoyed at the necessity for chastising a band of robbers, determined that he would make an end of them once and for all. To Don Hugo de Moncada, the Viceroy of Sicily, to Don Perisan de Ribera at Bougie, to the Marquis de Comares at Oran, orders were sent to prepare their forces for an attack on Algiers.

There was no lack of good-will on the part of the Christian princes, nobles, and governors. The Spanish veterans in Sicily were rusting for want of employment, the levies on the African littoral welcomed anything in the way of war as a distraction from the deadly monotony of their lives. The soldier in these days who rested too long upon his arms became in time practically useless for the purpose for which he existed; but such rulers as Charles V. gave their fighting men but small cause of complaint in the matter of want of employment. The Pope sent his blessing and a contingent, and, to show how serious was the purpose of the Emperor, who took the command in person, let us set forth the total of the expedition which was to utterly destroy and root out the corsairs and their leader:

FLEET

Galleys of the Pope	4
Galleys of Malta	4
Galleys of Sicily	4
Galleys of Antony Doria	6
Galleys of Naples	5
Galleys of Monaco	2
Galleys of Marquis of Terra Nova	2
Galleys of Vicome de Cigala	2
Galleys of Fernando de Gonzaga	7
Galleys of Spain	15
Galleys of Andrea Doria	14
Total Galleys	65
Add Transports	451
Total Fleet	**516**

Sailing-Ship Transport

The Frigate of Malta	1
Division of Spezzia	100
Division of Fernando Gonzaga	150
Division of Spain	200
Total Transports	**451**

We now come to the military side of the expedition, which consisted of:

The Household of the Emperor	200
Noblesse	150
Knights of Malta	150
Servants	400
German Corps	6000
Italians	5000
Spanish from Naples and Sicily	6000
Soldiers from Spain	400
Adventurers	3000
Italian Cavalry	1000
Spanish Cavalry from Sicily	400
Light Cavalry	700
Total Army	**23900**

We next come to the Armament of the Fleet:

Soldiers of the Galleys (50 in each)	3250
Galley Slaves (average 70 in each)	4500
Galley Slaves the Frigate of Malta	80
540 sailing ships of all sorts, mostly small (at an average of 10 each)	4500
Total Personnel of the Fleet	12330
Add Army	23900
Total Personnel of the Expedition	**36230**

It was late autumn when the expedition at last set sail, and the imperious temper of Charles was such that he refused to be governed by the advice of the seasoned mariners, such as Andrea and Antony Doria, and others who dreaded the effect of the gales which the armada was likely to encounter on the coast of Africa. The Emperor was not to be gainsaid, and the fleet set sail. They arrived, says Sandoval, "*en el dia de* San Hieronymo," Saint Bartholomew's day; and there then arose such a storm as the Mediterranean seldom sees. Some of the army had landed, some were still afloat, the corsairs accounted for the luckless soldiers ashore, the elements destroyed many left in the ships: 26 ships and 4,000 men were lost.

Bitterly mortified, Charles, who had personally displayed valour and conduct of unusual distinction in this disastrous expedition, returned to Europe to turn his attention to his everlasting quarrels with the King of France. Meanwhile Don Hugo de Moncada had escaped with a remnant of his forces to Iviza, in the Balearics, where he wintered, and where his men mutinied because he was unable to pay them.

As there was depression almost amounting to despair in the camps of Christendom, so was there concurrently the widest rejoicing in the tents and on board of the galleys which flew the Moslem flag. What mattered it that it was the elements which had saved Kheyr-ed-Din from annihilation? was it not a cause the more for jubilation, as had not the Prophet of God himself come to the assistance of those who were upholding his holy standard? Were not his favours made manifest in that he had sent, to lead his votaries to victory, such an one as Kbeyr-ed-Din Barbarossa?

Pope and Emperor, King, Duke, and Viceroy had tried conclusions with the pirates, and their fleet and army had melted away as the mists melt in the hot sunshine on the Mediterranean; truly were the descendants of the dispossessed Moors of Còrdoba and Granada taking a terrible revenge on those by whom they had been expropriated.

Barbarossa was never one to let the grass grow under his feet; he had the Christians on the run, and he intended to take full advantage of this pleasing circumstance. Accordingly he despatched a trusted lieutenant, one Hassan, with instructions to harass the coast of Valentia, to ravage with fire and sword all those unfortunate towns and villages which he could reach. This corsair entered the Rio de Ampasta and destroyed all before him, the inhabitants fleeing as the news was carried by escaped fugitives and by the red glare of the villages flaming to heaven in the night. Satiated with blood, laden with spoil, and burdened with many wretched captives, Hassan put to sea once more in triumph.

It may here be mentioned how terrible was the damage wrought by the piratical fraternity in the Mediterranean, and the manner in which it has been brought to light in somewhat remarkable fashion quite recently. Since the French occupation of Tunis it was charged against them that they had taken away from the natives of the country those fertile lands which lay upon the shores of the sea, and had given them to French subjects. The facts of the case were that for centuries these lands had been entirely out of cultivation, the reason being that, until the complete suppression of piracy in the Mediterranean took place, none dared to dwell within raiding distance of the sea for fear of being carried off into slavery.

But to return to Hassan. That warrior, having cleared the Spanish coast, got separated from three of his consorts during the night. The next day, at dawn, he sighted a Spanish sailing-vessel, which he thought to make an easy prize. The wind was light, and the galleys—that is to say, the one on which Hassan was aboard and his remaining consort—were soon churning up the waters in pursuit as fast as their oars could carry them. Hassan reckoned on an easy capture, as he made certain she was but a peaceful trader with some score or so of throats to cut. He was, however, badly out of his reckoning, as on board of her was a veteran company of Spanish infantry, stark fighters to a man, who feared no odds, and who were skilfully commanded by Captain Robeira, grown grey in the Moorish wars. With bloodcurdling yells the galleys swept alongside with the fighting men massed on the high poops and forecastles of their vessels. Behind the high bulwarks of the "round ship" (as the sailing craft of the day were denominated to distinguish them from the long ships, or galleys) crouched the Spaniards, their muskets in their hands. Captain Robeira had them perfectly in hand, and not a piece was discharged until the beaks of the galleys crashed into her sides.

Robeira then gave the order to fire, and at the short range into packed masses of men the volley did terrible execution. Completely surprised, the corsairs attempted to board, but were repulsed and driven back with more slaughter. His men becoming demoralised, Hassan withdrew amidst the ferocious taunts of the Spaniards, who had escaped almost unscathed. Sore and angry, the corsairs continued their voyage for another three days, at the expiration of which they arrived at Algiers. Hassan, who had acquired quite a considerable booty, expected a warm reception; this he received, but hardly in the way that he expected. He told his tale to Kheyr-ed-Din, which that commander received in frowning silence; when he had finished the storm burst.

"O miserable coward! dost thou dare to stand in my presence and to confess that thou hast been whipped like a dog by those sons of burnt fathers, the Spaniards?"

The miserable Hassan attempted to justify himself by reference to the booty which he had obtained and the number of captives with which he had returned; but this, far from assuaging the wrath of Barbarossa, only made it worse.

"Dastard and slave! thou boastest that, thou hast destroyed defenceless villages and brought back many captives, but that shall avail thee nothing. No profit shalt thou derive from that. Let the captives be brought before me."

This was done, and to the horror even of those hardened men of blood who followed in the train of Barbarossa, they were all executed. Even this wholesale massacre did not assuage the wrath of the corsair. Standing and surveying the weltering shambles which tainted the air, he pulled ferociously at his red beard, and commanded that they should whip Hassan till the blood ran; when this was done thoroughly and to the satisfaction of the despot, he gave orders that he should be chained and thrust into the prison of the fortress.

Terror stalked abroad in Algiers. No man knew when his turn might come after this awful example of what it meant to incur the wrath of Barbarossa. The corsair gave orders for the execution of Venalcadi, who, it will be remembered, was with Uruj when that warrior came by his death; but Venalcadi was popular among the pirates, and they connived at his escape.

For so cool and politic a man as Kheyr-ed-Din this outburst is wholly inexplicable. Judged by our standards, the flogging of Hassan was not only brutal but silly, as raising up to himself enemies of the most bitter description in the midst of his own followers; and yet cruelty was so engrained in this man that he never forewent his revenge. It is a standing miracle that he escaped assassination in the age in which he lived, and the only explanation would appear to be that men were too much afraid of him to make the attempt.

The immediate result of the flogging of Hassan and the attempted murder of Venalcadi was that the latter collected a following and made war upon Kheyr-ed-Din, who, with incredible folly, then released Hassan, and sent him with five hundred men to fight against Venalcadi. The result was what might have been anticipated: Hassan joined forces with Venalcadi, and together they attacked the tyrant and drove him out of his stronghold.

Kheyr-ed-Din had the one supreme merit of never knowing when he was beaten. Driven from the shore, there was for him always the sea to which to retire; so on this occasion he embarked his family and such of his riches as were portable, and took to the sea once more. *"Yendo a buscar nuevos asientos y nuevos amigos"* (seeking a new home and new friends), says Sandoval.

It was well for the corsairs that the Christians had selected the previous year for their attack, as, had they fallen upon them when Barbarossa was no longer in power at Algiers and the pirates were fighting among themselves, the latter would have been wiped out of existence. It was ill fighting with Kheyr-ed-Din, whether you professed the religion of Christ or that of Mahomet, and this the revolting corsairs were very soon to discover. Barbarossa sailed away from Algiers a hunted fugitive, only to return again as a conqueror.

Eastward the dispossessed ruler of Algiers took his course, and very soon discovered that which he sought—allies to assist him against the revolted Venalcadi and the recalcitrant Hassan. Lurking in the neighbourhood of Bizerta, he discovered El Judeo (the Jew), Cachidiablo (Hunt the Devil), Salaerrez, Tabas, and other corsairs, who collectively composed a formidable force. These were all old acquaintances and some old followers of Kheyr-ed-Din, and to them did he relate the piteous tale of the cowardice of Venalcadi, whom he accused of having deserted his brother Uruj in his direst necessity, thereby causing his death; the abominable conduct of Hassan, who had turned and bitten the hand that fed him. With tears in his eyes did this accomplished actor reluctantly reveal the base ingratitude of which he had been the recipient; so much did he contrive to work upon the feelings of his auditors that they one and all vowed to stand by him, and to replace him as ruler of Algiers, from which he had been thrust by men whose shameful treachery was only equalled by their ingratitude.

Forty sail in strength, they set out to avenge the wrongs of the gentle and long-suffering Kheyr-ed-Din, that master of craft in every sense of the word. Reaching Algiers, they disembarked artillery and stores and began an attack in form; but Venalcadi, whose forces were equal, in fact slightly superior, to those of his antagonists, made a sally, and battle was joined in the open. A most sanguinary combat ensued, in which the forces of Kheyr-ed-Din were decidedly worsted. For a considerable period his fate hung in the balance. Then occurred one of those singular and remarkable things only possible in such an age of anarchy and bloodshed. Barbarossa had in his train sixty Spanish soldiers captured by him from the force of Don Hugo de Moncada. Well did the corsair know their value: there were no finer fighting men in all the Christian armies. Hastily summoning them, he promised them their freedom if they would now throw in their lot with him and assist in the downfall of Venalcadi.

The offer was no sooner made than accepted, and the Spanish veterans, fresh and unwearied, threw themselves into the heart of the fray. Shoulder to shoulder and blade to blade in their disciplined valour, they broke through all opposition; they fought for liberty as well as life, to exchange the noisome confinement of the piratical galley for the free air of their homes and their country. Soon the soldiers of Venalcadi turned and fled back to the city; the day was once again with Kheyr-ed-Din. For four days longer did Algiers hold out, and then a traitor betrayed Venalcadi into the hands of his enemies. Instantly his head was struck off, placed on a pole, and paraded in full sight of the garrison, who were promised their lives on condition of surrender.

The city opened its gates once more, and Barbarossa entered in triumph. The corsair was as good as his word to his Spanish captives, and restored to them their liberty. He went even further, and was liberal in his *largesse* to those who had fought so well for him. If he can be credited with such an emotion as gratitude, he must have felt it for Moncada's stout infantrymen, as, had it not been for them, it would have been his head and not that of Venalcadi which would have decorated the pole. The Spaniards departed to their own country—that is to say, such of them as desired to do so; but one Hamet, a Biscayan, declared that life was so intolerable for a common man such as he in his own country that he desired to throw in his lot with Barbarossa. Thirty-nine others followed his example, abjuring the Christian faith and becoming *renegado*es.

Those of the garrison left alive were glad enough to return once more to their allegiance to their former master. The episode of the mutiny of Venalcadi and Hassan was a lesson not only to them: the fame of it spread far and wide throughout the Mediterranean. Who now could be found to combat Barbarossa? and all along the coasts of the tideless sea echo shudderingly answered—Who?

With the new accession to his strength Kheyred-Din had no difficulty in making himself master of Tunis, and he sent Cachidiablo with seventeen galleys to harry once more the coast of Spain.

CHAPTER 6

The Taking of the Peñon D'Alger

Although Kheyr-ed-Din had made himself master of Algiers, there still remained the fortress of Pedro Navarro in the hands of the Spaniards. This strong place of arms had now been in their practically undisputed occupation for twenty years; from out of its loopholed walls and castellated battlements the undaunted garrison had looked forth while the tide of war both by land and sea had swept by. They had been unmolested so far, but now their day was to come.

In command of the Peñon d'Alger, as it was called by the Spaniards, was a valiant and veteran cavalier, by name Martin de Vargas. For twenty years, as we have said, the gold-and-crimson banner of Spain had floated from its crenulated bastions; since the days of Pedro Navarro it had held its own against all comers. It must have been with a sinking heart that Martin de Vargas and his brave garrison beheld the town fall once again into the hands of Kheyr-ed-Din; they knew, as by this time did all the Mediterranean and the dwellers on the coasts thereof, the implacable enmity of the corsair to the Christians, and how short a shrift would be theirs should they fall into his hands.

On his side Kheyr-ed-Din looked with longing eyes on this remnant of the power of Spain in Africa. Could he but dislodge Martin de Vargas, he had the whole of Northern Africa practically at his disposal; Algiers would then be really his, to fortify for all time against the inroads of his foes. He was master by land and sea, the time was propitious; the corsair decided that the hour had come. He had seen the repulse of his brother Uruj, none knew better than did he the temper of the men by whom the Peñon was held, or the valiance and the unswerving fidelity of that caballero of Spain, Martin de Vargas. He tried to induce that officer to surrender to him, offering every inducement to the Spanish commander to come to terms. He was met with a haughty refusal, couched in the most contemptuous language. He tried the most blood-curdling threats, which were no empty menaces, as his adversary well knew: these were received in silence.

One more embassy he tried, and to this he received the following answer:

> I spring from the race of the De Vargas, but my house has never made it a practice to boast of the glory of their long descent: they professed merely to imitate the heroism of their ancestors. Spurred forward by this worthy desire, I await with calmness all your efforts, and will prove to you, with arms in my hands, that I am faithful to my God, my country, and my king.

Barbarossa summoned to his palace his kinsman and trusted adherent Celebi Rabadan, and they mutually decided that there was nothing they could do save take up arms against this most insolent and uncompromising warrior. In the meanwhile they would try what craft would do; and accordingly two young Moors were introduced into the Peñon, under the pretext that they had seen the error of their ways and were anxious to embrace the Christian religion. Martin de Vargas, like all Spanish *caballeros*, was an ardent proselytiser, and he ordered the two young men to be taken into his own house and instructed by the chaplain of the garrison. The next day was Easter Day, and the two young Moors, while the entire garrison were at Mass, signalled to their co-religionists a prearranged sign indicating that now was the time to attack. Unfortunately for them, a woman in the employment of De Vargas saw them, and they were immediately hanged from the battlements in full view of Barbarossa. That potentate was filled with fury at what he considered an insult to the Mohammedan religion, and again consulted with Celebi as to the feasibility of another assault. It was true, he said, that his messengers had been hanged, but they had made the prearranged signal. Still, the walls were hardly sufficiently breached, he thought, and his own men were singularly disheartened by the ill success of their previous efforts. Did Celebi Rabadan think another attempt desirable?

That person was in a quandary, because he could not gather what it was that Barbarossa wished him to say. He knew that if he recommended an assault, and that it proved once again unsuccessful, that the full fury of the tyrant would fall upon his head; at the same time he was almost equally afraid to broach the idea which had been prevalent in Algiers for some time that Martin de Vargas must assuredly be in league with Shaitan, or he could never have held out in

Andrea Doria, Prince of Oneglea, Admiral to Charles V.

the way that he had done. In consequence he temporised and hesitated, while Barbarossa pulled at his famous red beard and regarded him with scowling brows.

The situation was saved for Celebi Rabadan by an accident. There swam off to the ship a traitor from the Spanish garrison, and this man informed them that his whilom comrades were positively at their last gasp, ammunition all but exhausted, and the food-supply barely sufficient to last another two days.

"To such an end come those who deny the Prophet of God," exclaimed Barbarossa, and gave orders that this news be communicated to all his men, who were to prepare for the final assault on the morrow. He further offered a reward for the capture of Martin de Vargas alive.

On May 16th, 1530, the corsairs once again advanced to the assault. By this time the walls had been battered until a practicable breach had been formed, and over this swarmed thirteen hundred of the starkest fighters of the Mediterranean, In the breach, bareheaded, his armour hacked and dinted, stood the undaunted chieftain of the Spaniards: over his head floated that proud banner which had never cast its shadow on a worthier knight of Spain. The garrison, worn to a shadow by their hardships and their hunger, most of them wounded, and all of them sore spent, were in no case to resist this, the most formidable attack to which they had been subjected. It was all over in a very short time, and a dreadful massacre ensued.

Martin de Vargas, though sorely wounded, was taken alive and conducted to the presence of Barbarossa. Wounded, shaken, bruised, his fortress in the hands of his enemy, the dying shrieks of his murdered garrison still ringing in his ears, the amazing spirit of the man was still utterly unsubdued. "It is to the treason of a ruffian that you owe your triumph," he said to his captor, "and not to your valour: had I received the smallest relief I could still have repulsed and kept you at bay. You have my maimed and mutilated body in your possession, and I hope that you are satisfied. But my body is accustomed to pain, and I therefore defy you and your dastardly cruelty."

To do Barbarossa justice he admired the undaunted spirit of his prisoner, and he replied:

"Fear nothing, De Vargas, I will do all in my power to ease your hurts if you will do that which I ask of you."

De Vargas replied:

"As an earnest of your faith, I demand the punishment of the traitor through whose information you were enabled to take the citadel."

Barbarossa ordered the soldier to be brought before them, and, having nearly flogged him to death, had him beheaded. He then presented the head to De Vargas, saying:

"You observe my complaisance. I now ask you to embrace the Mohammedan faith; then I will overwhelm you with benefits and honours, and make you the Captain-General of my guards."

De Vargas looked at him in indignation and replied:

"Dost thou believe that I, who but now demanded the just punishment of a man who had forsworn himself, could stoop to such an act of baseness as this? Keep your ill-gotten riches; confer your dignities on others; insult not thus a caballero of Spain."

There was a breathless pause. None had ever used such language to Kheyr-ed-Din Barbarossa and lived to tell the tale. Nor was it to be so in this case.

"You and yours have caused me too much trouble," he answered indifferently. He made a sign to the executioner who had beheaded the soldier, and the next moment the head of De Vargas was swept from his body.

The gallant Spaniard, it is to be hoped, came by his end in the way just narrated; but the chroniclers disagree among themselves, and "*El Señor Don Diego de Haedo, Arcobispo de Palermo y Capitan General del Reyno de Sicilia por El Rey Felipe nuestro señor*," states that Barbarossa kept De Vargas in confinement for three months and then had him beaten to death. One can only sincerely hope that the first account is the true one; but Haedo was nearer to the time of the occurrence, and, as he wrote in the reign of Philip II., is more likely to have known the facts. But however this may have been, there was an end for all time of Spanish domination on the north coast of Africa, and from this we may date the permanent establishment of those piratical States in that part of the world.

The star of Kheyr-ed-Din was once more in the ascendant. Not only had he crushed out the incipient mutiny of Venalcadi and taken his life, but he had consolidated his power by the taking of the Peñon d'Alger. He celebrated this occasion in the most practical manner possible: a stop was put to the indiscriminate massacre of the garrison, and five hundred of the Spaniards were captured alive; it was their dreary fate to pull down entirely the tower of Pedro Navarro, which they had defended so gallantly and to utilise the material in making a causeway from the Peñon to the shore. Barbarossa was determined that on no future occasion should his enemies have the chance of dominating his town of Algiers. He was now a sovereign in fact and in deed, regarding even so mighty a monarch as Charles V. with comparative equanimity. Terrible was the wrath of the latter when the news of the fall of the Peñon, the massacre of the garrison, and the death of his trusty servant De Vargas, was brought to him. The sea-wolves seemed to exist but to exasperate him, and this latest news came just at one of the most prosperous epochs of his career.

The titles of "Carlos Quinto," as recorded by Sandoval, read like the roll of some mighty drum. Nor were these titles mere vain and empty boastings, as was so often the case at that time among the minor rulers of the earth. On February 22nd, 1580, just before the fall of the Peñon, he had placed on his own head the iron crown of Lombardy; his viceroys ruled in Naples and Sicily, his dukes and feudatories in Florence and Ferrara, in Mantua and in Milan; there was no more Italy. All these recent acquisitions had been rendered possible by the defection of Andrea Doria, the Genoese seaman, from Francis I. of France to the side of the Emperor. From henceforward it was against this modern Caesar that Barbarossa had to contend; the monarch under whose banner swarmed the terrible Schwartz-Reiters of Germany, for whose honour marched the incomparable infantry of Spain, for whom the fleets of the gallant Genoese sailed in battle-array under the orders of the greatest admiral of the day, Andrea Doria. All these disciplined legions of Christendom were arrayed against the corsair king; banded together for the destruction of that daring pirate whose flag floated in insolent triumph above the white walls of Algiers.

As from this time onwards we shall hear much concerning Andrea Doria, it is fitting that some account should here be given of this great patriot, great soldier, and still greater seaman. Andrea Doria, of the family of the Princes of Oneglia, of Genoa, was born at Oneglia on November 30th, 1468, and was the son of Andrea Coeva and Marie Caracosa, both of the family of Doria. At the death of his mother the young Andrea, then nineteen years of age, was sent to Rome, where his kinsman Dominique Doria, of the elder branch of the family, was captain of the Papal Guard of Pope Innocent VIII. Here he rose rapidly: owing to his extraordinary address in all military exercises, he was marked out for preferment, and would probably have succeeded his kinsman as grand officer, had it not been for the death of Innocent VIII. The successor to Innocent, Alexander VI., was not favourable to the claims of the Dorias; so young Andrea, acting on the advice of Dominique, repaired to the court of Duke Urbino, then regarded as the best school for young nobles desirous of following a military career. After some time spent at the court of Urbino, Dominique counselled that Andrea should enter some other service, as there was no glory to be obtained under a prince who was never at war. Accordingly Andrea passed into the service of the King of Aragon, who, having invaded Naples, was giving plenty of employment to all would-be warriors.

In the record of his early days we find that in the year 1495 he made a journey to Jerusalem to visit the holy places, and that he then returned to Italy, where Ferdinand of Aragon was attempting to recover the kingdom of Naples. "The Great Captain," Gonsalvo de Còrdoba, was warring against Doria's kinsman, Juan Roverejo; this commander had rendered a great service to the Dorias by rescuing David Doria from imprisonment at Ancona, and Andrea decided to throw in his lot with him. He accordingly armed twenty-five cavaliers at his own expense, and joined Roverejo, who put him in charge of the fortress of Rocca Guillelma. In this place Andrea was besieged by Gonsalvo de Còrdoba, the first warrior of the age; here he displayed such extraordinary ability in defence that, on the occasion of a truce, Gonsalvo urged upon Andrea to join the Spaniards. Andrea made answer that honour bound him to Roverejo, but, could he be released from his arrangement with him, he might then consider the proposition of "The Great Captain." Roverejo refused, but, as Charles VIII. immediately afterwards evacuated Italy, Andrea was free to follow his own inclinations, and took service with Lodovico Sforza, Duke of Milan.

From this time onward until 1503 Andrea was constantly employed in war, and made for himself such a reputation that in this year the Republic of Genoa requested him to take command of their navy. This offer he refused, as he said that he knew nothing about the sea. They pressed him, saying that to a man of his genius nothing was impossible, and in the end he gave a somewhat reluctant consent. He soon proved his competence in his new sphere of activity, as his first act was to capture the Fort of the Lantern, in the neighbourhood of Genoa, which was then held by the French for Louis XII. The Republic confirmed his appointment as General of the Galleys with many compliments, and he put to sea and captured three of the war-galleys of the corsairs, also two Turkish ships laden with valuable merchandise. He fitted out the galleys for his own service, sold the merchantmen, and made an immense sum of money.

His next act was to defeat the corsair, Cadolin, who had eight galleys to Doria's six; these he added to his own fleet, which now consisted of fourteen vessels, he having begun with three. As Cadolin was one of the most famous corsairs of the day, this capture made an immense sensation, and all men, Moslems as well as Christians, were asking one another, "Who was this Doria?"

They had their answer, as time passed, in the career of this astonishing warrior, who in his time played so many parts, who served under so many flags, and yet who remained consistently a patriot all the time. As this is not a history of Doria, we have no space to trace out his life step by step as it was lived; suffice it to say that, disapproving of the government of his native Republic under the family of the Adorno, Andrea offered his sword and his fleet to the King of France, Francis I. His offer was received with joy, and he was made Captain-General of the Galleys of France. In his new capacity he sailed for the coast of Provence, which was being devastated by the fleet of Charles V. He sank several of the Spanish vessels, captured others, and secured sufficient booty to pay his soldiers and sailors—a fact most welcome to Francis, who was in desperate straits for money.

Eventually, however, a dispute arose between Francis and Doria, which was to have disastrous effects for the King. At this time Charles V. was suzerain of Genoa, which was held for him by the Adorno. Philippin Doria, nephew of the admiral, met at sea with Hugo de Moncada outside the Gulf of Salerno; a battle ensued, in which Philippin was victorious and Moncada was slain. Amongst others who were captured was the Marquis de Guasto and Camille Colonna; these high officers, together with three of the captured galleys, were sent by Philippin to his uncle at Genoa.

In the meantime some malcontents reached the Court of France and complained to the King that Andrea Doria had not captured Sicily, which they averred he could easily have done. These men were backed up by a certain number of the courtiers, who were bitterly jealous of the fame of Doria and the esteem in which he had been held by Francis. The monarch, easily swayed by any determined and persistent attack, decided to levy a fine on the inhabitants of Genoa as a punishment for the supineness of their countryman, who was his Captain-General of the Galleys; his argument being that they must pay him for the plunder Doria had missed by not taking Sicily when he should have done so.

This was worse than a crime—it was blunder of the very first magnitude, and such a blunder as could only have been made by a very stupid as well as a very arrogant man. Doria by this time was a warrior of European celebrity, and one to whom even kings used the language of persuasion; to attempt to browbeat him was to court disaster.

Francis sent the Vicomte de Tours to Genoa to levy the fine, but the Vicomte did not prosper on his mission. Outside of Genoa he was met by the outraged admiral on horseback at the head of some fifty Genoese nobles and a numerous company of foot-soldiers. De Tours reported that the name and authority of the King of France was held in derision by the fierce old admiral, who so alarmed the envoy himself that he thought it prudent to retire to Florence, from whence he wrote a long letter to his master complaining of his reception by Doria.

This attempt to levy a fine on Genoa was not, however, the only deadly blow which the King of France was aiming at her. The children of Francis were at this time in Madrid, as hostages for the good behaviour of their father, and that monarch was in treaty secretly with Charles to restore Italy to the *status quo ante bellum*, which would have had the effect of handing over Genoa to Antony Adorno. He also began the fortification of Savona, in order that from there he might be in a position to strike at the Genoese—from a military point of view, if necessary—but in any event to cripple the trade of that city. Andrea Doria, as soon as he became aware of this latter action on the part of Francis, was thoroughly roused, and wrote him the letter quoted below, which illustrates the fact that he was quite aware of his own great importance in Europe. It was not a time in which men held such language as did Doria on this occasion unless they were very sure of themselves and their followers.

> *Great Prince,*
> It is an ill use of power to reverse order in human affairs. Genoa has always been the capital of Liguria, and posterity will see with astonishment that your Majesty has deprived it of this advantage with no plausible pretext. The Genoese are well aware how inimical to their interests are your projects with regard to Savona. They beg of you that these may be abandoned, and that you will not sacrifice the general good to the views of a few courtiers. I take the liberty to add my prayers to theirs, and to ask of you this grace as the price of the services I have rendered to France. Should your Majesty have been put to expense, I shall join to my request the sum of forty thousand gold crowns.
> With the humble duty of
> *Andrea Doria*
> Captain-General of the Galleys of France.

Theodore Trivulce, who held Savona for the King of France, was roundly told by Doria that "the people of Genoa would never suffer the taking of Savona by the King of France, as it had from time immemorial belonged to them," and added, "for myself I will sacrifice the friendship of the King in the interests of my fatherland."

The last straw came, however, when the Marshal de Lautrec demanded from Andrea the prisoners taken by Philippin Doria at Salerno. To this Doria returned a curt negative, whereupon Francis sent one Barbezieux to supersede Doria and to seize upon the person of the veteran admiral. But that seaman, now sixty years of age, was not to be taken by any king or soldier. He moved his twelve galleys from Genoa to Lerici, on the east coast of the Gulf of Spezzia, and when Barbezieux arrived he sarcastically told him to take the galleys. Barbezieux had no better fortune than his predecessor, the Vicomte de Tours, and retired discomfited and boiling over with rage to report matters to the King.

It has been said that among the prisoners of Philippin Doria was the Marquis de Guasto. This nobleman had been an interested spectator of the quarrel, and now approached Doria suggesting that he should throw in his lot with Charles. The admiral, who all through had been acting in the interests of his native country, seeing its ruin approaching from the ambitions of Francis, consented, and wrote to his nephew Philippin telling him of his decision, and his reasons for that which he proposed to do. Philippin therefore rejoined his uncle at Lerici with his eight galleys. The negotiations were short, sharp, and decisive, and were conducted through the medium of De Guasto. Charles offered the admiral sixty thousand ducats a year; this was accepted. The only other stipulation made by the Emperor was natural enough, which was that all the Spanish galley-slaves in the fleet of Andrea should be released and their places taken by men of other nationalities. This was of course conceded, and the transaction was complete. Henceforward the most formidable force at sea on the Christian side was at the disposal of the Spanish King.

This transference took place in the year 1528, and it was in the same year that the citizens of Genoa, in recognition of the unexampled services of the admiral to the State, elected him perpetual Doge.

This honour Doria declined, declaring that it was more glorious to have deserved than to possess the honour, and that he considered he could be of more use to his fellow citizens by gaining for them the protection of great princes than by remaining as chief judge in his own country.

The Senate of Genoa, astonished by his noble modesty, hailed him as the father and liberator of his country, ordered that a statue of him should be erected in the public square, that in the same place a palace should be built for him at the public expense, and that it should be called Plaza Doria; further, that he and his posterity should be for ever exempted from taxation, and that a device should be engraved on a plate of copper and attached to the walls of the palace, where it could be seen of all men, announcing to posterity the services that this great man had rendered to his fellow citizens, to be for ever a memorial of their gratitude.

The chronicler of these events draws a parallel between Doria and Themistocles, who, when discontented with the Athenians, passed into Persia and offered his services to Xerxes, to the great joy of that monarch, who cried aloud, "I have Themistocles, I have Themistocles."

Chapter 7
The Apotheosis of the Corsair King

If Charles V. made no such outward manifestation of his joy as did the Persian monarch, he possibly was no less pleased than Xerxes; this he showed by his acts, and the value that he attached to the services of Doria was instanced in the directions which he gave. He ordered the Governors of all his possessions in Italy to do nothing without first consulting the admiral; to lend him prompt aid, whether he demanded it in his own name or in that of the Republic of Genoa. He made him *Admiralissimo* of his navy, with power to act as he liked without even consulting him, as his Emperor. It will be seen that Charles had in him sufficient greatness to trust whole-heartedly when he trusted at all; the faith which he reposed in the Genoese seaman was amply justified by events, and no action of his during the whole of his singularly dramatic reign was ever to result so entirely to his profit. When in after-life Charles had received from the Pope the Imperial Crown, and when, on his return, he put into Aigues-Mortes in Doria's galley, he there met with Francis, who, in a burst to confidence, advised the Caesar never to part with his admiral.

On that stage, which was the blue waters of the tideless sea, we shall, from this time forward, watch the fortunes of those two great sea-captains, Andrea Doria and Kheyr-ed-Din Barbarossa. With them the ebb and flow of conquest and defeat alternated. Great as was the one, it cannot be said that he was greater than the other; but when the supreme arbitrament was within the grasp of both, as it was at the naval battle of Prevesa, neither the Christian admiral nor the Moslem corsair would reach out his hand and grasp the nettle of his fate. Hesitation at this moment, when, in the fullness of time, the rivals stood face to face with arms in their hands, was the last thing that would have been expected of such dauntless warriors, such born leaders of men! and the battle of Prevesa presents a psychological problem of the most baffling and perplexing description. We are, however, anticipating events which will fall into their proper sequence as we proceed.

Kheyr-ed-Din, now firmly established in Algiers, devoted his energies to the undoing of his Christian foes by the systematic plunder of their merchant-vessels. At this period he, personally, seems to have remained ashore, and sent his young and aspiring captains to sea to increase his wealth by plunder, his consequence by the hordes of slaves which they swept into the awful bagnios of Algiers; and Sandoval, that quaint and delightful historian, is moved to indignation and complains with much acrimony of *"las malas obras que este corsario hizo a la Christiandad"* (the evil deeds done to Christianity by this corsair). These were on so considerable a scale at this time that he had to devote to them far more space than he considered consonant with the dignity of history.

But if all were going on well on the coast of Africa for the Crescent, such was far from being the case in the northern waters of the Mediterranean; for Andrea Doria, serving His Most Catholic Majesty at sea, had defeated the Turks at Patras and again in the Dardanelles, which unpleasant fact caused no little annoyance to Soliman the Magnificent. On land the Sultan was sweeping all before him; at sea this pestilent Genoese was dragging into servitude all the best mariners who sailed beneath the banner of the Prophet. There was wrath and there was fear at Constantinople, and the captains of the galleys which sailed from the Golden Horn felt that their heads and their bodies might at any moment part company—the Grand Turk was in an ill humour, which might at any moment call for the appeasement of sacrifice; so it was that men trembled.

It was at this time, in 1533, that Soliman bethought himself of Kheyr-ed-Din. There was no better seaman, there was no fiercer fighter, there was no man whose name was so renowned throughout the length and breadth of the Mediterranean, than was that of the corsair king who was vassal to the Sublime Porte. Soliman was confronted with a new, and, to him, an almost mysterious thing, for the onward conquering step of the Moslem hosts was being checked by that sea-power so little understood of the Turk, and the imperious will of the Sultan seemed powerless to prevent the disasters conjured from the deep.

Soliman the Magnificent, who was not inaptly described by this title, for he was successful as both warrior and statesman, meditated both long and anxiously on the new development of affairs before he made up his mind to the step of calling to his assistance the corsair

SOLIMAN THE MAGNIFICENT

king. But he possessed that truest attribute of greatness in a ruler, the faculty of discerning the right man for any particular post. Brave and reckless fighters he possessed in super-abundance, but somehow—somehow—none of these fiery warriors had that habit of the sea which enabled them to make head against such a past-master in the craft of the seaman as Andrea Doria. The Genoese was chasing the Turkish galleys from off the face of the waters. Constantinople itself was a sea-surrounded city; it was necessary that a check should be administered to the arms of the Christians on this element. It is easy to imagine the preoccupations of the Turkish monarch. The despot rules by force, but he also holds his power by the address with which it is wielded, and he can by no means afford to disregard his personal popularity if he is to make the best use of his fighting men in such a turbulent epoch as was the first half of the sixteenth century. Soliman had the wit to know that he had no mariner who was in any way comparable to Doria; he was also aware that Kheyr-ed-Din had risen from nothing to his present position by his sheer ability as a seaman. It would appear, therefore, a very natural thing that he should invite the co-operation of the King of Algiers, but that with which he had to reckon was the furious jealousy that such an appointment must inevitably arouse among his own subjects.

It says much for the steadfast moral courage of the man that he eventually decided to take the risk; it says even more for the absolute correctness of his judgment that he never afterwards repented of the step which he then took.

Once the mind of the Grand Turk was made up he hesitated no longer. The Capitan de Rodas, one of his personal guard, was sent to Barbarossa to request him to come to Constantinople and take command of the Ottoman fleet. There were no conditions attached; the honour was supreme. Barbarossa loaded the messenger with rich gifts, and overwhelmed him with honours. For Kheyr-ed-Din this was in a sense the apotheosis of his career. The Grand Turk, the head of the Mohammedan religion, had not only recognised his kingship, but had conferred on him an honour unprecedented, unlooked for, and one of the highest value to a man of such an insatiable ambition. Into the cool and crafty brain of this prince among schemers instantly sprang the thought that now at last his kingdom was secure, that in future the whole of the Barbary coast would own no other lord than he.

Preparations for the voyage were immediately begun, and, as an earnest of the new importance which he derived from the advances of Soliman, the corsair actually sent presents to the King of France and proffered him his aid against his enemies. To such a pass as this had one of the most powerful monarchs in Christendom been reduced by the defection of Andrea Doria. Algiers he left in the keeping of his son Hassan, and in charge of Hassan his kinsman Celebi Rabadan and a captain of the name of Agi. In the middle of August, 1533, Barbarossa left Algiers, his fleet consisting of seven galleys and eleven *fustas*. Sailing northward, he fell in with a fleet which he at first feared was that of Doria, but which, fortunately for him, was that of a corsair named Delizuff from Los Gelues. Courtesies were interchanged between the two leaders, and Barbarossa succeeded in persuading Delizuff to accompany him to Sicily, where it was possible they might fall in with Doria, and with their combined forces inflict defeat upon the Christian admiral. Delizuff was nothing loath to join forces with so noted a commander as Kheyr-ed-Din, as he had no desire to tackle Doria single-handed, and at the same time wished to extend the sphere of his plunderings, which had been cruelly restricted recently by the wholesome fear instilled into the sea-wolves by the new admiral of Charles V.

Accordingly, reinforced by the fifteen *fustas* and one galley of Delizuff, the Algerian fleet once more proceeded on its voyage. Although bound for Constantinople at the request of Soliman, at a time when it would have been thought that delay was not only dangerous but impolitic, and although the corsair was endeavouring to merge the pirate in the king who dealt on terms of equality with those whom he now regarded as his brother monarchs, still the old instinct of robbery was too strong to be resisted; the lust of gain and the call of adventure were still inherent in the man whose famous beard was now far more white than red. Advancing age had not tamed the spirit nor weakened the frame of this leader among the Moslems.

Sailing through the Straits of Bonifacio, they touched Monte Cristo, a small island where they found a slave who had formerly belonged to Delizuff. This man was base enough to betray his own native island of Biba into the hands of the corsairs, who sacked it thoroughly and carried off its inhabitants; they also captured thirteen large ships going to Sicily for wheat, and burnt them, making slaves of their crews. In the fight with these vessels Delizuff was killed. Shortly after this, some disagreement arising between the crews of the ships of Barbarossa and the men in Delizuff's fleet, the Algerian commander seized a man out of one of Delizuff's galleys and had him summarily shot. The death of Delizuff naturally caused some confusion in his command, and the high-handed proceeding of Kheyr-ed-Din caused great resentment, not unmixed with fear, as the terror inspired by the Barbarossas was a very real sentiment. Under their command no man knew when or at how short notice his life might not be required of him; but the glamour of success was ever around them, and they never, in consequence, lacked for followers. But the taking out and shooting of one of their comrades was too much for the pirates from the islands of Los Gelues, from whence Delizuff was in the habit of "operating." In the words of Sandoval, "they were not used to such tyranny and cruel usage." In consequence they concerted among themselves and one dark night sailed off, leaving Kheyr-ed-Din to continue his voyage with his original following.

That warrior, nothing disconcerted, pursued his way to the island of Zante, where he fell in with a Turkish *flota*, under the command of the Bashas Zay and Himeral. To these officers of the Grand Turk Barbarossa used most injurious language, bitterly reproaching them with not having sought out and destroyed Andrea Doria, which he declared they ought to and should have done. This is yet another instance of the extraordinary character of the man. These persons were the highest officers in the fleet of the Ottoman Empire; it was more than possible that they would be placed under the command of Barbarossa as soon as his new position as *Admiralissimo* was adjusted at Constantinople; and yet, in spite of these facts, the corsair had taken the very first opportunity which presented itself grossly to insult these men. It is true, as we shall see, that his injurious words came home to roost in the future; but arrogant, conquering, contemptuous, Barbarossa seems to have shouldered his way through life, fearing none and feared by all.

The fact of his known cruelty accounts for much of the dread which he inspired, but it was something far more than this which caused the son of the Albanian *renegado* to ride roughshod as he did over all with whom he was brought into contact. Men felt, in dealing with Barbarossa, that here was a rock against which they might dash themselves in vain. In all his enterprises he spared not himself. He asked no man to do that which he was not prepared to do, but if any failed him there was no mercy for that man; and, although in deference to modern susceptibility no mention is made of the tortures he so frequently caused to be inflicted on his victims, they were none the less a daily spectacle to those who lived under his rule. He possessed, it is true, the rough geniality of the fighting man, a certain "Hail fellow, well met!" manner in greeting old comrades, and yet none of these men there were who did not tremble in an agony of fear when the bushy brows were bent, when the famous red beard bristled in one of his uncontrollable furies. The real secret of his success must have been that, no matter how uncontrollable did his passions appear to be, the man was always really master of himself. Further, he possessed a marvellous insight as to where his own interests lay. He used as his tools the bodies and the minds of the men who were subject to him, and he carried his designs to an assured success by the aid of that penetrating, far-seeing mental power with which, above all else, he must have been gifted. He could drive men, he could lead them, he could invariably persuade when all else failed him. In this we have had an instance when he was chased from Algiers by the combined efforts of Venalcadi and Hassan, whom he had flogged; for no sooner did he meet with other corsairs than he persuaded them to take up his quarrel—which, it must be understood, was none of theirs—and to replace him on that precarious throne from which he had been so rudely thrust. We have already said that he was a man who never knew when he was beaten, and in the years which we have yet to chronicle this characteristic appears again and again; for age had no effect apparently, either mentally or physically, on this man of iron who had by this time reached the age of seventy-seven.

Leaving the high officers of his future master, the Grand Turk, smarting under the opprobrium which he had heaped upon their heads, Barbarossa fared onward with his fleet to Salonica, capturing a Venetian galley on the voyage: from thence he made his way to the Dardanelles, where he anchored and remained several days, to make ready his fleet for the spectacular entry which he intended to make into Constantinople.

The city on the Golden Horn was all agog for the arrival of Barbarossa; no matter what private opinions the inhabitants might have had concerning him, of which we shall hear more presently, they were none the less all curious to a degree to catch sight of this man, so famous in his evil supremacy on that distant shore of Northern Africa.

Kheyr-ed-Din, among his other qualities, possessed in the highest degree that of a successful stage-manager; no pageant which he undertook was ever likely to fail from the want of the striking and the dramatic. It was now his business to impress the citizens of Constantinople with an idea of his greatness, and none knew better than he that it is the outward and visible sign which counts among the orientals, more perhaps than the inward and spiritual grace: he may also possibly have felt that he did not possess the latter to any overwhelming extent. Even before he left Algiers this entry to the chief city of the Ottoman Empire had been in the mind of Barbarossa, who had caused to be embarked a quantity of flags and pennons for the decoration of his grim war-galleys when they should stream into the Golden Horn. There were also bands of music, which, it is to be presumed, utilised the delay in the Dardanelles to attain to something like "a concord of sweet sounds," as the incidents of the voyage from Algiers, so far, had hardly been conducive to much time to spare for band-practice. The galleys were scrubbed and gaily painted; round the ship of Kheyr-ed-Din ran a broad streak of gold on the outer planking to denote the presence of a King of Algiers, and at last all was ready. The fleet weighed anchor, and, with banners flying and bands playing, entered the harbour. The shores were black with spectators; even the Sultan himself deigned to look forth on the coming of the man from whom he expected such great things.

Ceremonial was the order of the day. Soliman the Magnificent was too wise a man not to know what was being said in his capital that day; it was his part to accustom the minds of men to the fact that he, Soliman, had chosen Barbarossa to command his fleet, and that there could be no looking back. The decree had been signed, the invitation had been sent, the man had arrived, there could be no possible retreat from the situation. The anchors splashed into the placid waters close to the shore, and the ships were soon so surrounded by boats as to be almost unapproachable; then came official persons from the Sultan with greetings to the famous seaman; also came Bashas and officers ("*con carga de guerra*," says Sandoval), to offer a welcome and to stare in undisguised curiosity at the man chosen by their sovereign to make head against the famous Andrea Doria. This preliminary courtesy completed, there came the next act in the drama, which consisted in the immemorial custom of the East in the offering of gifts from Barbarossa to the Sultan, from the vassal to his suzerain. The Janissaries, splendid in scarlet and gold, tall above the ordinary stature of man, bristling with weapons inlaid in gold and silver, cleared the common vulgar from the streets approaching the palace of the Sultan; they formed the spearhead of the procession clearing a way for the King of Algiers, who, mounted on a splendid bay stallion, the gift of the Sultan on his arrival, headed the captives who bore the gifts. Of these the exact number is not stated, but the procession was headed by two hundred women and girls, each of whom carried in her hand a gift of gold or silver; one hundred camels were loaded with silks and golden ornaments, and other "curious riches" ("*con otras mil cosas de que hizo ostentacion*"), says Sandoval. There were also lions and other animals, brocades and rich garments.

All of this reads no doubt somewhat too like the tales in the "Arabian Nights"; but we have to remember that, if you have led a long and eminently successful life as a robber, you have necessarily accumulated a store of riches. In the case of Barbarossa he had begun in extreme youth, and was now an old man; he had been quite in the wholesale way as a thief, and now desired to pay a good price for that which he coveted, namely, the post of *Admiralissimo* to the Grand Turk. It may be objected that he had already been offered and had already accepted the post; this is quite true, but there were certain conventions to be fulfilled on the side of the recipient of the bounty of the Sultan quite understood on both sides, although no word had passed on the subject. In those days the man who desired the favour of an Eastern potentate never dreamed of approaching him empty-handed, and the more liberal that he was in the matter of gifts the greater was the favour with which he was regarded. Therefore the principle acted upon by Kheyr-ed-Din on this occasion was both wise and politic; that is to say, he placed certain of his riches in a perfectly sound investment, certain to yield him an admirable percentage, not only in added personal prestige, but also in the placing under his command of such a force as he had never before commanded, with unlimited opportunities of preying on the detested Christian on a far larger scale than it had ever been his good fortune to do before.

The Sultan Soliman was not called "the Magnificent" without just cause; his life was splendid in its social prodigality, as it was in war and in statesmanship; yet even he was somewhat astonished at the amazing richness of the gifts which were laid at his feet by a man whom he knew to be, in spite of the kingly title which he had assumed, merely a rover of the sea. Therefore, in spite of himself, he was impressed. To him, it is true, in his splendour and magnificence, the intrinsic value of that which was brought to him by Barbarossa mattered but little; but the fact that the corsair was in a position to do so opened the eyes of the Sultan to the manner of man with whom he had to deal. Hitherto he had but known of him by hearsay, as the one Moslem seaman who was likely to be capable of making a stand against the terrible Doria, who had now become the plague of the Sultan's existence. He now knew that the man who disposed of such incredible riches must be, no matter what his moral character, a man who stood a head and shoulders over any commander in the Ottoman fleet sailing out of the Golden Horn.

Both materially and psychologically this man somewhat bewildered the despot: and his *alter ego*, the Grand Vizier, happening to be away on a mission to Aleppo, Soliman had no one with whom to confer in a strictly confidential manner; for, after the manner of autocrats, he had but few familiars, in fact it may be said none at all save the statesman mentioned. His reception of the corsair lacked, however, nothing in cordiality. He inquired after the incidents of the voyage, interested himself graciously in all that he was told concerning Africa and the conflicting claims of Christian and Moslem in that region, and was generally courteous to his distinguished visitor. He placed at his disposal a palace and attendants on a scale commensurate with the state of a reigning sovereign, and sent his most distinguished generals to confer with Kheyr-ed-Din. The latter, for the first time in his life, was thoroughly out of his element. His had been the life of the seaman and the soldier to begin with, and of later years that of a rude and unquestioned despot on a savage coast, surrounded by myrmidons to whom his voice had been as the voice of a god. Never had it been his lot before to dwell within the limits of such a comparative civilisation as that which obtained in Constantinople at this date; never before had it been necessary for him to restrain that naturally fiery and impetuous temper of his and to speak all men fairly.

The strain must have been great, the effort enormous, and he knew, as he was bound to know, that his coming had unloosed jealousies and heart-searchings innumerable, with which he could not deal in the usual drastic fashion common to him. The winter was coming on, which was, as we have before remarked, very much of a close season both for the pirate and the honest merchant seaman. In consequence there was not very much chance against the foes of Soliman for the present. When that opportunity offered he promised himself that the courtiers and the soldiers of the Grand Turk would very soon discover that the fame of Kheyr-ed-Din Barbarossa was no empty matter, and that there existed no seaman in all the Ottoman dominions with whom they could compare the "African pirate," as he had reason to believe that he was scornfully called behind his back.

A weaker man would have been daunted by his surroundings, by the manifestly unfriendly atmosphere in which he lived, and by the dread that perhaps, after all, Soliman might go back upon his word. There were no lack of counsellors, he knew very well, who would advise the Sultan to his undoing, if that monarch gave them the opportunity; and, as time passed, so his anxiety grew. Soliman also could not have felt particularly comfortable at this juncture, with a sullen spirit possessing his men "con carga de guerra," bitterly resenting the step which he had taken, and the appointment which he had made. For the present, however, he made no sign, treating Kheyr-ed-Din with distinguished courtesy, but making no reference to the future. Soliman was revolving the problem in his acute mind, doubtless weighing the unpopularity of the step which he had taken against the services likely to be rendered to him by his strange guest. And thus several weeks passed at Constantinople, probably amongst the most trying of all those in the unusually prolonged life of Kheyr-ed-Din.

CHAPTER 8

The Raid on the Coast of Italy

The Grand Turk had spoken, the appointment had been made, Barbarossa had arrived; but though autocrats can cause their mandate to be obeyed, they cannot constrain the inward workings of the minds of men. In spite of the awe in which Soliman the Magnificent was held, there were murmurs of discontent in the capital of Islam. The Sultan had been advised to make Barbarossa his *Admiralissimo* by his Grand Vizier Ibrahim, who was, as we have said, his *alter ego*. This great man had risen from the humblest of all positions, that of a slave, to the giddy eminence to which he had now attained by the sheer strength of his intellect and personality. The Grand Vizier it was who had pointed out to his master that which was lacking in the Ottoman navy: brave men and desperate fighters he had in plenty, but the seaman who cleared the Golden Horn and made his way through the archipelago into the open sea beyond had forces with which to contend against which mere valour was but of small avail. Out there, somewhere behind the blue line of the horizon, did Andrea Doria lie in wait; and if the Moslem seaman should escape the clutches of the admiral of the Christian Emperor, were there not those others, the Knights of Malta, who, under the leadership of Villiers de L'Isle Adam, swept the tideless sea in an unceasing and relentless hostility to every *nef, fusta*, and galley which flew the flag of the Prophet?

It had come to a pass when the Ottoman fighting man was by no means anxious to go to sea. He was still as brave as those marvellous fanatics of seven centuries before, who, in the name of God and of His Prophet Mahomet, had swept all opposition aside from the path of Islam, had conquered and proselytised in a manner never paralleled in the world before. At the call of the Padishah, for the honour of the Prophet, the sons of Islam were as ready to march and to fight as had ever been the warriors of the earlier Caliphs. But they had ever been soldiers; the habit of the sea was not theirs, and they found that, time after time, such sea-enterprises as they did undertake were shattered by the genius of Doria, or broken into fragments by the reckless, calculating assaults of the knights. And so it came about that there was but little heart in the navy of the Padishah, and those who served therein had but slight confidence in those by whom they were led. To use a metaphor from the cricket-field, it was time "to stop the rot" by sending in a really strong player. He was not to be found within the confines of orthodox Islam, and must be imported from outside.

The man had been found; could he be forced on an unwilling and discontented populace? Who, it was asked in Constantinople, was this man who had been called in to command the ships of the Ottomans at sea? They answered their own question, and said that he was a lawless man, a corsair: were there not good seamen and valiant men-at-arms like the Bashas Zay and Himeral, who should be preferred before him; this man who had come from the ends of the earth, and of whom nobody knew anything good? Again, could he be trusted? Something of the history of the Barbarossas had penetrated to the capital of Turkey, and it was known that scrupulous adherence to their engagements had not always characterised the brothers: who should say that he might not carry off the galleys of the Grand Turk on some marauding expedition designed for his own aggrandisement? There was yet more to be urged against him: not only was he infamous in character, but he was no true Mussulman, for had not his father been a mere *renegado*, and—worst of all—had not his mother been a Christian woman?

It was thus that the talk ran in that blazing autumn in Constantinople. Naturally there were plenty of persons who carried reports to Kheyr-ed-Din, and that astute individual soon made up his mind as to the most advantageous course for him to pursue. With the full concurrence of the Sultan, he left Constantinople and journeyed to Aleppo to see Ibrahim. The latter was both cunning and tenacious. Removed from the capital, the tide of gossip and discontent only reached him at second-hand; but he was not to be deterred by popular clamour even had he been in the midst of it. None knew better than he who and what was Barbarossa; in fact, it may be confidently asserted that none in Constantinople had anything like the same knowledge of this man and all that concerned him. Ibrahim had not named Barbarossa to his sovereign without weighing all the pros and cons of the matter, and that which was now happening in the capital had been fully anticipated by him. It pleased the Grand Vizier very much that Kheyr-ed-Din should take this long journey to see him; not from any ridiculous idea that this was an act of homage due to the dignity of his position—Ibrahim was far too great a man for such pettiness—but because it enabled him to see for himself what manner of man was this redoubtable pirate on whom he was relying to defeat the enemies of the Sublime Porte at sea. The corsair must have made the most favourable impression possible on the Grand Vizier, as that statesman wrote to Soliman:

> We have put our hands on a veritable man of the sea. Name him without hesitation Basha, Member of the Divan, Captain-General of the Fleet.

The Grand Turk had no intention of going back upon the appointment already made, but he was none the less pleased to receive from his Vizier so strong an endorsement of his policy; and now the time had come to stop the mouths of the murmurers and scandal-mongers of Constantinople. Accordingly he formally recalled Barbarossa from Aleppo, gave him, with his own hand, a sword and a royal banner, and invested him with plenary power over all the ports of his kingdoms, over all the islands owning his jurisdiction, command of all ships, vessels, and galleys, and of all soldiers, sailors, and slaves therein. The die was cast, the erstwhile corsair, the son of the *renegado* of Mitylene and his Christian wife was henceforward the supreme head of the Ottoman fleet.

The following description of the famous corsair may be found interesting at this juncture.

Barbarossa was at this time seventy-seven years of age. Courageous and prudent, he was as far-seeing in war as he was subtle in peace. A tireless worker, he was, above all things, constant in reverse of fortune, for no difficulties dismayed him, no dangers had power to daunt his spirit. His ruddy skin, his bushy eyebrows, his famous red beard, now plentifully streaked with white, his square, powerful frame, somewhat inclined to stoutness, above all, his penetrating and piercing eyes, gave to his aspect a certain terror before which men trembled and women shrank appalled.

All this harmonised well with his reputation as a chief so resolute, so pitiless, that it was the boast of his followers that his very name shouted in battle put to flight the Christian vessels. His smile was fine and malicious, his speech facile, revealing beneath the rude exterior of the corsair the subtle man of affairs, who, from nothing, had made himself King of Algiers, and was now, by the invitation of Soliman the Magnificent, *Admiralissimo* of the Ottoman navy.

Well may Jurien de la Gravière say that "in the sixteenth century even the pirates were great men."

It has been stated that in speech Barbarossa was facile. He was not only so, but he possessed a power of addressing such a man as Soliman in terms which, while delicately flattering that mighty monarch, gave him also a lead which he might follow in the future disposition of such power as he possessed at sea.

On his return from Aleppo Kheyr-ed-Din was received in audience by the Sultan. We must be pardoned if we give the long speech which he addressed to his new master in its entirety; and we have to remember that the man who made it was now an old man who, all his life, had been absolutely free and untrammelled, owing allegiance to no one, following out his own caprices, and sweeping out of his path any whom he found sufficiently daring as to disagree with him. That this ruthless despot should have been able so to change the whole style and manner of his address so late in life is only one proof the more of the marvellous gifts which he possessed.

It was in the following words that the corsair addressed the Sultan:

> Dread Sovereign, fortune itself has made it a law to second you in all your enterprises because that you are always ready to declare war upon the enemies of Mahomet the Prophet of God, on whom be peace. You have extended the limits of your vast possessions, you have vanquished and slain the King of Hungary, you have humiliated Charles V., this Emperor with whom the Christians dare hold you in comparison. These have been the recompenses received by you for the pure flame with which your zeal for the religion of Mahomet has ever burned.
>
> But these successes and these triumphs are not capable of contenting that thirst for glory with which your being is animated, and I am humbly desirous of indicating to you the means of culling fresh laurels. Experience has taught me the way, and I can assert, without fear of being accused of vanity, that in this matter I can be of great assistance to your Majesty.
>
> That which fortune has done for me in the past that will it continue to do for me in the future. Age has not enfeebled me, continual exercise has but rendered me stronger; I can therefore promise to you the most ready service both by land and sea. The desire which has always been mine to persecute the Christians caused me to conceive the idea of serving in your sea-army.

If Heaven is favourable to my vows, the Spaniards will soon be chased from Africa; the Carthaginians, the Moors, will soon be your very submissive subjects; Sardinia, Corsica, Sicily, will obey your will. As for Italy, it will soon be desolated by famine when I attack it in formidable force, without fearing that the Christian Princes will come to its aid.

Mahomet II., your illustrious grandfather, formed the project of conquering this country; he would have succeeded had he not been carried off by death. If I counsel you, dread Sovereign, that you should carry war into Europe and Africa, it is not that I desire your arms should be turned back in Asia from against the Persians, the ancient enemies of the Ottomans. I require but your sea-army, which is no use against the Persians. While you shall be conquering Asia I shall be subduing Africa. The first enterprise which I shall undertake will be against Muley Hassan, the King of Tunis; he has all the vices and possesses not one single virtue. He is a man of sordid avarice, of unexampled cruelty; he has rendered himself odious to the entire human race.

He had twenty-two brothers, all of whom he has caused to be murdered. That which is a common failing among tyrants is his: he dare not place himself at the head of his troops. He prefers to endure the outrages which he suffers at the hands of the Moors to taking up arms and inflicting upon them a salutary vengeance. He had the baseness to enter into an alliance with the Spaniards, and to favour their conquests in Africa. It will be all the easier for me to exterminate this wild beast because I have with me his brother, who prayed me to save him from the cruelty of Muley Hassan.

When I besiege Tunis I shall present him to the inhabitants, who love him as much as they hate Muley Hassan. They will open their gates to me, and I shall gain the town without the loss of a single man: it will be then you who will be master. On my way thither I will do what harm I can to the Christians; I will endeavour to defeat Andrea Doria, who is my personal enemy and my rival in glory: should I succeed in defeating him your Majesty will possess the empire of the sea. Be then persuaded, great Prince, by me, and believe that he who is master of the sea will very shortly become master on land.

It is somewhat difficult to fathom the reasons which induced Barbarossa to treat Soliman to his sanctimonious diatribe concerning the

King of Tunis; coming, as it did, from a pirate, it was merely ludicrous, and could not for one instant have deceived the remarkably shrewd person to whom it was addressed. The corsair stated the facts correctly, but the reasons which led to an Eastern autocrat disposing of his family in this manner were so obvious at the time that, if Soliman felt any emotion at all concerning the event, it was probably one of admiration! Regarded from the practical, apart from the sentimental side, what the proposition amounted to was that Barbarossa should attack a king with whom the Grand Turk had no sort of quarrel, and that, once his territory had been reft from him, that it should be handed over to the ruler of Constantinople for the greater glory of the Sublime Porte. What mental reservations there were on the part of the corsair we are not told, but had Soliman known him better he would have been aware that never had Barbarossa pulled any chestnuts from the fire of life which were not intended for his own eating; and that it was extremely unlikely, at his time of life, that he was now going to alter the habits of his long and strenuous career.

There was one thing, however, that Kheyr-ed-Din was not; he was no bragger or boaster, and, whatever may have been his mental reservations in his interview with the Sultan, that which he stated he would do, that he did. And now the time had come when the grim old Sea-wolf had done with intrigue and the unaccustomed atmosphere of a Court and went back to his native element, the sea.

Soliman, it must be said to his credit, was no man to deal in half-measures, and when once he had given his trust he gave it wholeheartedly, generously. In consequence he gave Barbarossa eighty galleys, eight hundred Janissaries, eight thousand Turkish soldiers, and eight hundred thousand ducats for expenses (some three hundred thousand pounds sterling of our money). All the necessary preparations were carried out under the orders of Barbarossa, who was given a roving commission to do what seemed best to him for the advancement of the glory of his master and the discomfiture of his Christian foes. The commission which he now received was practically that which had been given by Charles V. to Doria, the most flattering with which any man can be entrusted, as in his hands were left issues of peace and war usually only vested in the sovereign.

All through the early summer of 1534 the dockyards and the arsenals of Constantinople hummed with the note of preparation; Ibrahim had returned from Aleppo and threw himself, heart and soul, into these activities, which meant the sailing of the Ottoman fleet under the command of "that veritable man of the sea," Kheyr-ed-Din

Barbarossa. Stilled were the murmurs of the year before; the corsair, invested with plenary powers by the Sultan himself, was now in a position to make his authority felt; added to this, the more sensible of the malcontents had been won round by the Grand Vizier to the view that as, so far, the Ottoman navy had been conspicuously unsuccessful at sea, it was just as well to make use of the most capable Moslem seaman upon whom they could lay their hands. As to his moral character, that they could afford to discount, and as to the question of his faithfulness or the reverse, it was pointed out with irresistible logic by Ibrahim, that never before had the Sea-wolf had such glorious opportunities of plunder as now, when he could count ten ships for every one that had followed in his wake before.

It was in July 1534 that the Ottoman fleet left Constantinople, and Kheyr-ed-Din began operations by a descent upon Reggio, which he sacked. On August 1st he arrived at the Pharos of Messina, where he burnt some Christian ships and captured their crews; then he worked north from Reggio to Naples, ravaging the coast and depopulating the whole littoral, burning villages, destroying ships, enslaving people. In this expedition he is said to have captured eleven thousand Christian slaves. There is perhaps nothing more amazing in the whole history of this epoch than the number of the slaves captured by the corsairs, and the damnable cruelties exercised upon them; these were, of course returned by the Christians with interest whenever possible. As an instance of the treatment to which the slaves were subjected it is only necessary to mention the course taken by Barbarossa when he left Algiers in the previous year. There were at that time seven thousand Christian captives in his power; immediately before starting he had the entire number paraded before him, and, under the pretext of having discovered a plot, which in no circumstances could possibly have existed, owing to the supervision of the slaves, he caused twenty of them to be beheaded on the spot in order to strike terror into the remainder during his absence.

Back to the Golden Horn streamed ship after ship laden with plunder and with slaves. "The veritable man of the sea" was proving the correctness of the choice of the Sultan, the acumen of the Grand Vizier who had recommended his appointment. Barbarossa was determined to leave nothing undone to prove to Soliman that his choice had indeed been a worthy one when he had selected him as admiral of his fleet: also he had in his mind those others who spoke slightingly of him as "the African pirate"; they should know as well as their master of what this pirate was capable. Northward the devastating host of Barbarossa took its way; the fair shores of Italy smoked to heaven as the torches of the corsairs fired the villages. Blood and agony, torture and despair, followed ever on the heels of the sea-wolves of the Mediterranean. And now a fresh pack had been loosed, as it was, of course, in enormously increased strength that Barbarossa returned to the scene of so many of his former triumphs.

Plunder and slaves were all very well in their way, and acceptable enough on the shores of the Golden Horn; but Kheyr-ed-Din had a pet project in view on this particular cruise, which was to capture Julia Gonzaga and to present her to Soliman for his harem. The lady destined by him for this pleasant fate was reported to be the loveliest woman in Europe, a fitting gift for such an one as the Grand Turk. The fame of her surpassing loveliness had reached even the corsairs. She was the widow of Vespasian Colonna, Duchess of Trajetto, and Countess of Fundi; she had now been a widow since 1528, and lived at Fundi, some ninety miles north-east of Naples. Barbarossa laid his plans with his accustomed acuteness, and it was only through an accident that they miscarried.

There was one undeniable advantage in the system which swept off into slavery the whole of the inhabitants of a country-side, and that was, if at any time you required a guide at any particular point on the coast, he was sure to be forthcoming from one of the vessels in the fleet. Now Barbarossa did not exactly know where Julia Gonzaga was to be found, so he set his captains to work to discover the necessary slave. This was soon accomplished, and there was really no occasion for a slave on this occasion, as a *renegado* of Naples knew the castle in which Julia Gonzaga was residing at the time, and readily agreed to act as guide to the expedition sent to accomplish her capture. Kheyr-ed-Din had made a sudden dash along the coast with some of the swiftest of his galleys for the purposes of this capture. In consequence the people in Naples and the neighbourhood were not even aware that the piratical squadron was on the coast before they anchored, as near as it was practicable to do, to the residence of the Duchess of Trajetto. The fleet actually arrived after dark, having kept out to sea and out of sight during the day.

As soon as the anchors were down a party of two thousand picked men were landed and marched silently and with all expedition to the castle of Fundi. The escape of the Duchess was really providential. She had already gone to bed, and the fierce marauders were actually within the grounds of the castle before her distracted people became aware of their presence. But fortunately some among them kept their heads, and it also so happened that her bed-chamber was the opposite side of the castle to that by which the pirates approached. A horse was brought round under the window of the room, and, in her night-dress with nothing but a shawl wrapped around her, was Julia Gonzaga lowered out of her window on to the back of her horse. As she galloped for dear life down the avenue of her home she heard the shrieks of her miserable household murdered in cold blood by the furious pirates who had thus been balked of their prey.

Dire was the vengeance taken by the corsairs. They sacked Fundi and burned the town; they killed every man on whom they could lay their hands, and carried off the women and girls to the fleet.

Kheyr-ed-Din was furious with anger and disappointment. "What is the value of all this trash?" he demanded, with a thundering oath, of the commander of the unsuccessful raiders, surveying as he spoke the miserable, shivering women and girls. "I sent you out to bring back a pearl without price, and you return with these cattle."

Thus balked of his prey, Barbarossa swung his fleet round to the southward and westward and sailed for Sardinia, where, from the Straits of Bonifacio to Cape Spartivento, he left no house standing that would burn, or man alive who was not swept in as a captive. The descent of the corsairs in force, such as Kheyr-ed-Din now had at his disposal, was one of the most awful calamities for a country that it is possible to imagine. When Sardinia had ceased to yield up either booty or slaves the fleet sailed for Tunis, where it arrived before Bizerta on August 15th. The arrival of the corsairs was totally unexpected, and caused the greatest consternation. The story which Barbarossa had told to Sultan Soliman concerning the reigning King Muley Hassan was correct in every detail, and there is no doubt that he was a bloody and cruel tyrant of the worst description.

Therefore when the wily Barbarossa sent on shore and informed the *sheiks* and *ulemas* of the place that he had come in the name of the head of the Mohammedan religion to free them from this monster by whom they were oppressed, and that he intended to place on the throne the brother of Muley Hassan, Raschid, who had miraculously escaped from the fate which had overtaken all the other members of his house, the townspeople were inclined to listen to his advances and to admire the picture which he drew of the peace and prosperity which would accrue to them should Raschid, and not Muley Hassan, be on the throne of their country. That which he inferred in all his dealings with these people was that he had Raschid with him ready to step into the shoes of his unpopular brother as soon as the latter should be deposed by a justly indignant populace. The fact of the matter was that Kheyr-ed-Din had taken the fugitive prince with him to Constantinople, thinking to make use of him, and that, when he was sailing, Soliman had absolutely forbidden him to remove Raschid from his capital.

Completely deceived, the townspeople allowed the landing of eight hundred Janissaries. The tyrant, who was, as Barbarossa had told the Sultan, a craven coward, waited for no further demonstration of force, but incontinently fled into the interior with such valuables as he could carry. As soon as this was reported to Barbarossa he landed in force and entered the town, and then the townspeople noticed that the soldiers were all shouting for Soliman and for Barbarossa. They then demanded that Raschid should be produced according to promise, but naturally he was not forthcoming. Those who had acclaimed the soldiers of Soliman as liberators now began to arm against them, and they very shortly discovered, from some Tunisians who had come in the fleet from Constantinople, that Raschid had been left behind in that city.

CHAPTER 9
Barcelona, May 1535

Some idea of the terror inspired by the actions of the sea-wolves at this date is contained in the following extract from *The Golden Age of the Renaissance*, by Lanciani:

The Bastione del Belvedere, which towers in frowning greatness at the north-east end of the Vatican Garden and commands the approach to the Borgo from the upper-end valley of the Tiber, was begun by Antonio de Sangullo the younger, and finished by Michel Angelo after the death of Antonio, which took place on September 30th, 1546. This great piece of military engineering must not be considered by itself, but as a part of a great scheme of defence conceived by Paul III, to protect the city against a hostile invasion from the sea. The Pope could not forget that, in August 1534, the fleet of infidels commanded by Barbarossa had cast anchor at the mouth of the Tiber to renew its supply of water, and that if its leader had thought fit they could have stormed, sacked, and plundered the city, and carried off the Pope himself into slavery without any possibility of defence on the Christian side. This point has not been taken into due consideration by modern writers; the fortifications of Rome, designed or begun or finished at the time of Paul III., have nothing to do with the sack of 1527, with the Connétable de Bourbon, or with the Emperor Charles V. All the bastions, that of the Belvedere excepted, point towards the sea-coast, which was perpetually harried and terrified by Turkish or Barbary pirates. These would appear with lightning-like rapidity in more than one place at a time, and carry off as many unfortunate men, women, and children as they could collect.... To prevent the recurrence of such disasters the sea-coast was lined with watch-towers, the guns of which could warn the peasants of the approach of suspicious vessels.

That Paul III. had good warrant for the precautions which he designed to take is not only instanced by the fact of Barbarossa anchoring in the mouth of the Tiber on the occasion of the raid with which we are at present concerned, but from what had occurred to his predecessor on the Papal throne in 1516. Pope Leo, son of Lorenzo the Magnificent, was accustomed to leave Rome in the autumn for hunting, and fishing in the sea, of which latter pastime he was particularly fond. One of his favourite resorts was the castle of Magliana, five miles from Rome, on the banks of the Tiber. On September 18th, 1516, he left Rome and proceeded to Civita Lavinia, on the Laurentian coast. Here he was waited for by the corsair Curtogali, who, with fifteen ships off the coast and an ambush on shore, was ready to carry him off. Curtogali is supposed to have derived his information as to the movements of the Pope from some traitor about the Papal Court who desired the downfall of "the fatal House of Medici."

Some one, however, warned the Pope, who fled, accompanied by his retinue, at a headlong gallop to Rome, never drawing bridle until he reached the safe seclusion of the Vatican.

We must now return, however, to that eagle who fluttered so sorely the dovecotes, both Christian and Moslem, and whose loudly proclaimed faith in the Prophet never permitted his religion to stand inconveniently in the way of his material advancement in the world. The soldiers and sailors of the corsair entered Bizerta shouting for Soliman and Barbarossa. There was no mention of Raschid, that Prince of the Hafsit dynasty, whom Kheyr-ed-Din had declared to the townspeople he had come to restore to the throne of his ancestors. Too late the town sprang to arms, under a chief named Abdahar, and in the first instance accomplished a considerable success. Barbarossa's men were unprepared, and a number of them were slain. Driven into a bastion of the walls, a party of the corsairs were desperately defending themselves, when one Baetio, a Spanish *renegado*, discovered that a cannon behind them pointing seawards was loaded. He succeeded, with the assistance of others, in slewing it round and discharged it at close quarters into the packed masses of the enemy. This caused a frightful demoralisation to set in; the corsairs rallied and soon swept all before them. The massacre turned from the one side to the other, and it is said that no less than three thousand of the unfortunate townspeople were slain. Barbarossa only called off his men when they were wearied out by the slaughter.

Kheyr-ed-Din now graciously accepted the submission of the townsfolk; that is to say, such of them as were left, and took charge of the entire kingdom as governor for the Sultan of Turkey. He sent out ambassadors to the neighbouring Arab and Berber chieftains of the hinterland, repaired fortifications, appointed magistrates—all ostensibly in the name of that phantom prince whom the Tunisians were destined never to see, and who never returned to his native country.

King of Algiers, *de facto* King of Tunis, *Admiralissimo* to Soliman the Magnificent, his name a portent in Christendom, his fame reaching from Spartel to Tunis, and from the shores of France to the foothills of the Atlas, Kheyr-ed-Din Barbarossa was at the height of his power. Never before had a corsair risen to such eminence, never again was there destined to be so magnificent a sea-robber. Thus it was that the year 1535 opened gloomily for all those Powers whose coasts were washed by the tideless sea. Italy, torn and bleeding, her strong men slain, her fairest matrons and maids carried off into the most odious captivity, was lamenting the terrible fate to which she had been exposed by the raids of the pirate admiral. In Catalonia, in Genoa, in Venice, along what is now known as the Riviera, men trembled and women wept; for who could say that it might not be upon them that the next thunderbolt might fall? In Venice taxation was raised to the breaking strain to provide galleys wherewith to combat the foe, while the Genoese fortified their coasts and poured out money like water upon arms, armaments, and ammunition. Says Sandoval:

> From the Straits of Messina to those of Gibraltar none living in Europe on the shores of the sea were able to eat in peace or to sleep with any sense of security.

The Emperor Charles V. was roused to action, stung by the intolerable humiliation of the position into which he had been placed by a mere corsair.

King of Sicily, Naples, and Spain, as well as Emperor of Germany, in any direction he might turn he would find a trail of blood and fire over the fair face of his dominions in the Mediterranean. Although it might gall his pride to admit that his enemy was formidable, Charles was too wise a man, too experienced a warrior to underrate his foe. He repaired the fortifications of Naples and Sicily at great cost: he wrote letters to the Pope, to Andrea Doria, to the Viceroys of Naples, Sicily, and Sardinia, to the Marquis de Vasto, and Antonio de Leyva to collect all the arms and munitions necessary for the attack on Barbarossa. He sent orders to Don Luis Hurtado de Mendoza, Marquis de Mondejar, Captain-General of the Kingdom of Granada, to collect money and to have men ready in the ports of Andalusia. He gave orders for eight thousand German soldiers to hold themselves in readiness; these were to be joined by the veterans of Coron and Naples, which body counted four thousand more; in Italy he also raised another eight thousand men. All this was done under the seal of secrecy, which the Emperor most peremptorily ordered was to be observed.

But news travelled in the first half of the sixteenth century, although newspapers, war correspondents, and telegraphs were not; when all the feudatories of the greatest king in Christendom were busy it was impossible for the matter to remain hidden. Even had it been within the range of possibility to conceal what was going on there was one circumstance which would have rendered all effort to this end nugatory. Charles had invited Francis of France to join in this holy war against the scourge of Christendom: not only did Francis refuse to join, but he had the incredible baseness to betray the scheme to Barbarossa. It would be pleasanter to think that some mistake had been made in this matter, but unfortunately it is beyond dispute, as the facts have been placed on record by Sandoval, whose history, it must be remembered, was published in 1614. In this matter he is quite precise, as he states that a "Clerigo Francese," one Monsieur de Floreta, was sent with despatches from Francis to Barbarossa at Tunis, and that this treacherous envoy from Christendom gave the corsair king all the available information that he had been able to collect before starting.

This was typical of that "Golden Age of the Renaissance" in which it took place; when real devotion to all arts, sciences, and amenities of a higher civilisation went hand in hand with crime of the vilest and treachery of the basest description. Well might Barbarossa, and such as he, laugh to scorn the pretension that his Christian enemies were one whit better than were they, when they could point to the fact that, to serve a private revenge, a great Christian king could betray his co-religionists to their Moslem foes. Shamelessly did the sea-wolves seek their prey wherever it was to be found; their methods were villainous and seemingly without excuse, but, after all, there was some colour, some shadow of right in what they did, for their argument was that they were merely getting back from Christendom that which had been reft from them in the near past in the kingdoms of Còrdova and Granada. But who shall find excuse for the Christian kings, governors, and princes at this epoch? They sought their prey no less ravenously than did the pirates, and with just about the same amount of justification: witness the sacking of Rome by Charles V. in 1527, and the unexampled act of treachery just recorded of Francis of France.

Kheyr-ed-Din had lived all his turbulent life among wars and rumours of wars: the head of the tiller, the hilt of the *scimitar*, the butt of the *arquebus*, had been in his hand since early youth; bloodshed and strife were the atmosphere in which he lived and breathed. Desperate adventures by land and sea had been his ever since he could remember; there was no hazard that he had not run, no peril which he had not dared. But now even he, the veteran of far more than one hundred fights, was grave and preoccupied when he considered the greatness, the imminence of his peril. The "Clerigo Francese" had put him in possession of the fact that Carlos Quinto was exerting all his strength for the combat which was to come; and Barbarossa was far too old a fighter, far too wise a warrior, to underrate by one soldier or by one galley the forces that the Emperor could put into line against him; from far and near his foes were gathering for his destruction, and he did not deceive himself in the least as to what the fate of his followers and himself would be should the Christian hosts be victorious.

But, nevertheless, such an emergency as this found the man at his best: ready to take fortune at the flood when she smiled upon him, he was perhaps at his very greatest in adversity; and when all around him trembled and paid one of their infrequent visits to the Mosque to implore the aid of the Prophet, the veteran corsair was coolly reviewing the situation, seeking a way to weather the tempest before which lesser men shrank appalled, declaring that the end had come. The storm was coming in a squall of such violence as even he had never before experienced, but, thanks to his friend the King of France, he had been forewarned. He sent at once to his master, Soliman the Magnificent, at Constantinople, to impart to him the direful intelligence; then the bagnios were thrown open, and, under pitiless lash and scourge, the Christian captives toiled from dawn till dark to repair the fortifications of Tunis. Silent and unapproachable, conferring with none, the grim old Sea-wolf sat in his palace overlooking the bay and considered the question of whether he should give battle by land or sea when the time came. If it were possible, he came to the conclusion that it should be the latter; he had been evicted from his kingdom on land once before, but he knew that in the open ocean few cared to face Barbarossa, and he might fall on Doria first and the Knights of Saint John of Jerusalem second if matters turned out favourably for him. In any case, he must summon all the aid that was possible.

East and west flew the galleys of Kheyr-ed-Din, scudding before the wind if that were favourable, or churning the surface of the sea with straining, strenuous oars should the wind be foul or a calm prevail.

It was an appeal for aid to the Moslem corsairs from Algiers, from Tlemcen, from Oran, from Los Gelues (or Jerbah), and from all the countless islands of the Archipelago, where they lurked to seize their prey—Tunis, which flew the Crescent flag of the Prophet, was in danger—let them rally against the grandson of the man who expelled the Moors from Spain.

Grim and sinister, the corsairs came flocking to the standard of Barbarossa. Well they knew that, should he fall, it was but a matter of time for them all to be chased from off the face of the waters. Of cohesion there was but little among them, and, in spite of the bond of a common religion and a common hatred of the Christian, they were swayed far more by a lust for plunder than by such considerations as these. In times of imminent danger, however, men naturally crave for a leader, and in piratical circles all was now subordinated to the instinct of self-preservation.

Meanwhile, in Christendom their great enemy was maturing his plans. To the Marquis de Cañete, Viceroy and Captain-General of the Kingdom of Navarre, Charles wrote, confiding to his care the charge of the Empress, with instructions that her orders were to be implicitly obeyed during his absence. Having done this he journeyed to Barcelona, at which city he arrived on April 8th, 1535. Here he was immediately joined by the armada of Portugal—twenty *caravelas* raised, armed, and paid for by the King, Don Juan of Portugal. This fleet was commanded by the Infante Don Luis, brother to the Empress, and carried on board the vessels of which it was composed a whole host of nobles and gentlemen of quality, who had come to fight under the approving eyes of the Caesar of the modern world.

On May 1st came Andrea Doria with twenty-two galleys, and those already in the harbour crowded the sides of their vessels to watch the arrival of the famous Genoese seaman.

Four abreast in stately procession the great galleys swept into the harbour. With that love of "spectacle" so inherent in the southern nature, everything was done to ensure the military pomp and circumstance of the coming of the first sea-commander of the Emperor. At first with furious haste, and then slowing down to make the approach more stately, the fleet of Andrea moved on. From mast and yard and jackstaff of the galleys of the admiral floated twenty-four great banners of silk and gold embroidered with the arms of the Emperor, with those of Spain, of Genoa, and of the Dorias, Princes of Oneglia. The principal standard bore upon it a crucifix, broidered at the sides with pictures of Saint John and the Virgin Mary; another represented the Virgin with her Son in her arms. With the sound of trumpets, clarions, *chirimias,* and *atambours* the fleet moved to within a short distance of the Portuguese and saluted them; then, as the thunder of the guns ceased and the light wind blew away the smoke, they circled round and stopped abreast of the royal vessel on which Charles had embarked. Once again the guns barked a royal salute, while knights and nobles, seamen and soldiers hailed their Emperor with frenzied shouts of *"Imperio! Imperio!"*

Then Andrea Doria stepped into his boat and was rowed across the shining water to visit the Emperor, who received him, we are told, "with great honour and many tokens of love."

On May 12th arrived Don Alvaro de Bazan, General of the Galleys of Spain. This magnificent caballero made an entrance in much the same state and circumstance as did Doria, and during the remainder of the stay of the armada in Barcelona there was much banqueting and feasting and drinking of healths to the Emperor and confusion to the Moslem foe. It was once again as it had been in those days in which Ferdinand and Isabella had descended upon the doomed city of Granada, and had built, in full sight of its defenders, the town which they called Santa Fe (or the Holy Faith) as an earnest that they would never leave until that symbol of their faith had triumphed. To witness this victory the best blood of Europe had flocked, and now, forty-three years later, when the audacious Moslem had raised his head once more, the descendant of the warriors who had followed "Los Reyes Catòlicos" rallied to that standard which Carlos Quinto, their grandson, had set up on the shores of Catalonia. Sandoval devotes pages of his work to the names, styles, and titles of the noble *caballeros* who joined the army for the destruction of Barbarossa.

On May 16th Charles embarked in the *Galera Capitana* of Andrea Doria, accompanied by many grandees and *caballeros* of the Court, as well as illustrious foreigners like Prince Luis of Portugal, and held a review of the armada. There was much expenditure of powder in salutes to the Emperor, and all vied with one another in shouting themselves hoarse in honour of the great monarch who deigned to lead in person the hosts of Christendom against the *infidel,* who had defied his might and dared to offer him battle. On May 28th the Emperor travelled some leagues inland, starting before dawn, to visit the Monastery of Nuestra Señor a de Monferrato, in which was kept a singularly holy image of the Virgin. Here he confessed and received the sacrament, and then returned to Barcelona.

On May 30th he embarked in the Royal Galley, the *Galera Bastarda*, which had been prepared for him by Andrea Doria, his Captain-General of the Galleys. This vessel seems to have somewhat resembled the barge of Cleopatra in the magnificence of its appointments, as its interior was gilded, and it was fitted up with all the luxury that could be devised at this period. Silken carpets and golden drinking-vessels, stores of the most delicate food and of the rarest wines, were embarked to mitigate, as far as possible, the inevitable hardships of a sea-passage, and there were not lacking instruments of music wherewith to beguile the Caesar with concord of sweet sounds. Perhaps that which strikes the modern seaman most in this recital of all the useless matters with which the vessels of the great were burdened at this period is the extraordinary number of flags and banners with which they went to sea.

The catalogue of those in the *Galera Bastarda* makes one rather wonder how there was room for anything else of more practical usefulness when it came to fighting. There were in this galley twenty-four yellow damask banners, inscribed with the imperial arms; a pennon at the main of crimson taffeta of immense length and breadth, with a golden crucifix embroidered thereon. Two similar ones bore shields with the arms of the Emperor, and there was a huge flag of white damask sewn with representations of keys, communion chalices, and the cross of Saint Andrew, in crimson, with a Latin inscription. There were yet two others of scarlet damask "of the same grandeur," embroidered round the edge with "Plus Ultra," the device of Spain. Among a further varied assortment was one which bore the inscription: *"Send, O God, thine angel to guard him in all his goings."*

The fleet under the command of Andrea Doria numbered sixty-two galleys and one hundred and fifty *nefs*. There were also a miscellaneous assortment of small craft, known in those days as "brigantines," employed in the carriage of stores and ammunition. We have seen, on a former occasion, what terrible losses attended one of these armadas when really bad weather was encountered, and therefore it is not surprising that, on his second venture, Charles should have selected the finest season of the year for his descent upon the coast of Africa. They were brave men, these Mediterranean seamen, and the risks which they ran in their strangely formed, unseaworthy craft were of course much enhanced when they were loaded to the gunwale with stores, provisions, horses, banners, and last, but by no means least, a mob of seasick soldiery.

The Emperor Charles V.

Into this armada were crowded twenty-five thousand infantry and six hundred lancers with their horses.

Cagliari, in Sardinia, was the last rendezvous of the expedition, and here it arrived in the early part of June, where a week was spent in making the final preparations; and at last, on June 10th, a start was made for the coast of Africa.

Meanwhile in Tunis Kheyr-ed-Din was working double tides. He was kept well informed by his spies of all that was going on, and his preparations for defence were as adequate as they could be made; the corsairs, as we have said, had come flocking in at his call. He had withdrawn as many of his fighting men from Algiers as he deemed prudent. Knowing that the attack was directed against him personally, he had not much fear that it would be diverted at the last moment. It would have been true strategy on the part of Charles to have done this, but the Emperor considered that his honour required that the attack should be an absolutely direct one, and so Algiers was left on one side, to the ultimate upsetting of his plans. We say this because, although in this case he was to take Tunis and to restore to the throne of that country the puppet King Muley Hassan, and although he was to rescue some twenty thousand Christian captives, he did not capture Barbarossa, who was to live for many years to continue and to carry on his unceasing war against the Christians.

There was no artifice left untried by the despot of Tunis. To the African princes, Moors as well as Arabs and Berbers, did Kheyr-ed-Din send embassies. For these he chose cunning men well versed in the means of exciting the furious passions of these primitive and ferocious peoples, and it was their mission to represent Muley Hassan as an infamous apostate who was prompted by ambition and revenge, not only to become the vassal of a Christian king, but to conspire with him to extirpate the Mohammedan faith. The subtle policy inflamed these ignorant and bigoted Mohammedans to the point of madness, and from far and near they threw in their lot with the man who represented himself to be the rallying-point for all those in Africa who desired not only to preserve their holy religion but also their personal liberty. From Tripoli and Jerba, from Bougie and Bona, from the shores of Shott-el-Jerid, through all the dim hinterland that stretches from thence north-westwards to Algiers, the tribesmen came flocking in. The wild riders of the desert had been rounded up, and it is said that no less than twenty thousand horsemen, in addition to an innumerable crowd of infantry, responded to the call of the master schemer who was but using these guileless savages to further his own personal ends. The land-pirates of the desert, those stormy petrels whose lives only differed from those of the followers of Kheyr-ed-Din in that they carried on their depredations on the land instead of on the sea, camped in their thousands in the environs of Tunis and boasted of the deeds which they were about to perform. Kheyr-ed-Din stimulated their enthusiasm with presents of the most costly description. Ever wise and politic, he knew when it was necessary to pay royally, and on this occasion surpassed himself in prodigality. For all this he himself cherished no illusions; he had the measure of the fighting men of his foes at his fingers' ends, and the most that he expected from these wild irregulars was that they might, perchance, stay an onset and worry the imperial army with dashing cavalry raids. But that they should hold their own with the incomparable infantry of Spain, or make head against the stolid valour of the German men-at-arms, was not contemplated by Barbarossa. In his Janissaries, in his hard-bitten fighting men from the galleys, he could expect much; but there were but some few thousands of these, while the disciplined host against which he was called upon to combat was at the least twenty-five thousand—the flower of the imperial forces. The situation was unique, one on which the world had never looked before—all the might of Christendom going up against one who, no matter by what titles he might choose to describe himself, was no more than a vulgar robber. He was, however, a robber on such a scale as had never before been equalled—a force which remained unsubdued during the whole of his extraordinary and unusually protracted career.

CHAPTER 10

The Flight of Barbarossa

Autocracy in the sixteenth century was a very real and concrete fact. The orders of great kings were, as a rule, implicitly obeyed, and, when they were not, there was likely to be trouble of the worst description for those by whom they had been contravened. It is this that causes us to regard as most extraordinary one of the happenings in the armada which sailed from Barcelona for the coast of Africa. A most peremptory order was issued that no women, no boys, no one, in fact, save fighting men of approved worth, should find a place in the ships. Says Sandoval:

> There were not allowed in the armada women, boys, or useless persons, but only those who were capable of fighting.

It appears, however, that the women paid no sort of attention to this ordinance, and the historian gravely relates that:

> .... it was no use turning them out of the ships as, as soon as you sent them down one side they returned and climbed up the other.

It seems almost incredible, but is none the less a fact, that four thousand women accompanied the expedition and landed at Tunis. The autocracy of the Emperor apparently stopped short where women were concerned, or else he was indifferent whether they came or not.

On June 16th the armada arrived before Tunis, and the army disembarked to attack the fortress known as La Goletta. Into this strong place of arms Barbarossa had sent some six thousand of his best men, mostly Turkish soldiers, under the command of Sinan-Reis, a *renegado* Jew, and one of the fiercest and most faithful of his followers. To the camp of the Emperor came the fugitive King, Muley Hassan, in whose cause the armada had nominally been assembled—how nominal this was we shall see later by the light of the treaty concluded between him and the Emperor. Charles had complete command of the sea for the time being, and, in consequence, the ex-Sultan was amazed at the profusion and luxury which reigned in the camp of the Christians; and he concluded that these indeed must be the lords of the earth, as luxury and profusion was hardly the note of such courts as then existed in the northern portion of the African continent.

Although the army was landed, and with it artillery for the bombardment of the Goletta, there remained, of course, "the army of the sea," under the orders of the redoubtable Doria; and while the Marquis del Guasto, who was in supreme command on shore, prepared to batter down the defences of the fortress on the land side, the attack was carried on simultaneously from the sea by the galleys. The actual presence of the Emperor stimulated the various nationalities under his eyes to vie with one another in deeds of daring, and they contended among themselves for the posts of the most honour and danger. The attacks of the African horsemen were brushed on one side by the disciplined valour of the Andalusian cavalry, while the great guns thundered from land and sea against the walls of the doomed Goletta. Sinan and his Ottoman soldiers performed prodigies in the way of repairing breaches in the walls as soon as they were made; but Kheyr-ed-Din from the city watched the progress of the bombardment gloomily, as he saw and knew that the fall of the Goletta was but a matter of days. All this time he was far from idle; sortie after sortie did the dauntless old warrior lead in person against those engaged in the task of bombardment. Time and again he heartened the Arab and Berber levies to attack, but the sallies were repulsed, and the lightly armed Africans were driven like chaff before the wind when they swooped down on the lines of investment.

But the time came at last when Sinan and his gallant Turks could hold the place no longer; the walls were breached in six or seven places, and Spaniards, Germans, and Italians made a simultaneous attack. Sinan fighting to the last, evacuated the fortress, and retired actually through the water across a shallow part of the bay to the city, with the remnant of his once magnificent force; and now Barbarossa knew that the end was come, and that Tunis must pass from his hands to those of the Christian Emperor. It was not only the fall of the Goletta that troubled him, but the equally important fact that by this the fleet of the enemy was enabled to lay hands upon his own fleet, consisting of eighty-seven galleys and *galliots*, together with his arsenal, and no less than three hundred cannon, mostly brass guns of excellent construction, mounted on the walls and planted on the ramparts. The surprising amount of this artillery gives a measure of the strength of the fortress and the efforts it must have cost the besiegers with such a man as Sinan in command.

That the end was near was known to all, and not the least of their embarrassments was the presence within the city walls of some twenty thousand Christian captives. The city was large, the defences were spread out over a great area, it was abundantly evident that it could not be held, and, in consequence, Barbarossa summoned his principal officers and communicated to them his decision.

> We will not remain here to be slain like rats in a trap by the accursed of God by whom we are attacked. No, rather will we perish, sword in hand, as our fathers have done before us; but first there is a danger against which we have to guard. Within these walls are twenty thousand prisoners who will rise against us at the first opportunity; let us, then, first put them to death, and then we will leave this place and show our enemies how the true Moslems can die.

Even those hardened men of blood shrank before the horror which was proposed to them by their chief, and Sinan-Reis took up his parable and spoke the minds of all when he said that follow him to the death they would cheerfully do, but stain themselves with so awful a massacre was to place themselves outside the pale of humanity for ever. It was seldom that they crossed his mood, and Barbarossa listened in frowning silence, accepting as a partial excuse that time pressed, and to put to death twenty thousand persons would occupy longer time than they could spare. On the morrow a battle was fought which, as Kheyr-ed-Din anticipated, ended in the complete rout of the Moslems. Everywhere the Corsair King was in the forefront of the battle, and it is said that he disposed of fifty thousand men on this occasion; but this is probably an exaggeration, and in any case the bulk of his forces consisted of those African levies which, in a pitched battle against European troops, were practically useless owing to their want of discipline and cohesion. Very soon the hosts of the Emperor had prevailed, and the Arabs and Berbers had fled back into the wilderness from whence they had come and whither it was useless to pursue. Barbarossa, at the head of such of his corsairs and Turks as were left—a number estimated at some three to four thousand—burst through all opposition and also escaped, travelling so rapidly that pursuit was abandoned almost at once. And then the event happened which the

Moslem leader had foreseen: some of the Christian captives managed to get free from their shackles within the city and released others; they overpowered those left to guard them, and threw open the gates to the soldiery of the Emperor.

Then occurred one of those awful horrors of which this time was so prolific: before Charles or his generals could prevent them the soldiery had swept into the town and commenced to slay, to plunder, and to ravish, without distinction of age, sex, or nationality. Ostensibly these Christian warriors had come to rescue the inhabitants of Tunis from the oppression of Barbarossa, but while that chieftain was in full flight across the mountains to Bona, those by whom he had been defeated entered the town, which they had come to save, and perpetrated a massacre so awful that it is said that no less than thirty thousand people perished. It is a terrible blot on the escutcheon of the Emperor; as, although he and his generals deprecated the massacre—and indeed to do them justice tried to prevent it—this is no excuse for allowing their men to get out of hand, when they must have been aware of the inevitable result: as the Moslem corsairs at their worst were equalled in their iniquities by the European soldiery, once the strong hand of discipline had relaxed its grip.

It may have been that the Emperor was displeased with this excess of zeal on the part of his army; but, if it were so, the chroniclers are silent concerning the matter, being far too busy singing the praises of the Caesar to think of such a trifle as the massacre of most of the persons whom he had come to deliver. The wretched inhabitants of Tunis must have found it somewhat difficult to distinguish between the corsair, who killed three thousand of their fellow townsmen, and the Christian Emperor, who had massacred ten times that number. Charles, however, reaped great glory from an expedition which had but one good result, which was, that he succeeded in rescuing twenty thousand captives; these men, very naturally, on their return to their homes in every corner of Europe, magnified the wonderful deeds of that prince who had been instrumental in securing their release, and the massacre of the Tunisians was conveniently ignored. Charles had defeated Barbarossa and expelled him from Tunis; he had now displayed his magnanimity and altruism by the terms which he imposed on the miserable Muley Hassan. As far as that individual was concerned, he certainly deserved nothing better; but, as a finale to an expedition blessed by the Pope, and looked upon almost in the light of a modern crusade, it certainly displays a remarkably keen eye for the main chance.

The preamble of the treaty runs as follows:

That the King of Tunis, recognising that he had been expelled from his kingdom by Barbarossa, and that the Emperor in person, with a powerful armada, had come and expelled this tyrant, taking from him the fortress and town of Tunis and restoring them to the King Muley Hassan: that this monarch is most grateful for so magnificent a service, and in recognition thereof contracts to liberate all Christian captives who may be in his realm, to give them a free passage to their homes, and from this time forward binds himself to extend to all Christians kind and generous treatment.

There can be no exception taken to this, which was the least which the Emperor had the right to expect; but this was only, as we have said, the preamble.

Muley Hassan was further made to contract to hold his kingdom in fee to the Spanish Crown, to covenant that no corsair should use his ports for any purpose whatsoever, that the Emperor should not only retain the Goletta but that all other fortified seaports should be put into his hands, that the King of Tunis should in future pay twelve thousand crowns per annum 'for the subsistence of the Spanish garrison of the Goletta, that he should enter into no alliance with the enemies of the Emperor, and should annually present, as an acknowledgment of his vassalage, six Moorish horses and six hawks.

Muley Hassan had exchanged the comparatively dignified position of a prince in exile, who has been expropriated by the strong hand, for that of the puppet of one of the greatest enemies of his religion. Neither he nor his people were one whit the better for the change, and, as far as vassalage was concerned, they would in all probability, in the state of religious feeling at the time, have sooner been subordinate to the Moslem corsair than to the Christian King.

Barbarossa, as we have seen, frankly acknowledged that he sought his own advantage, and, when he possessed himself of Tunis, made no pretence of any altruistic motive. The Emperor, on the other hand, having come in the guise of a Christian reformer, simply stole the kingdom from Barbarossa and kept it for himself. Incidentally he released the captives, which enabled him to pose once more as the great champion of the oppressed. But, however this may have been, there is no doubt that he had performed a notable feat of arms, and even the most mighty monarch then in Europe felt uplifted by the fact that he had defeated the greatest of the corsairs: accordingly, on

Muley Hassan, King of Tunis

July 25th Charles wrote to England, France, Portugal, Milan, Florence, Venice, Genoa, Siena, Mantua, and Naples:

> So it was in a few days the whole of Europe was acquainted with his good fortune.

Martin Nunez, "Caballero de Toledo," was sent on a special embassy to the Pope to acquaint the Pontiff at first hand of all that happened, and the success which had attended the arms of the Emperor, and also to thank his Holiness for the assistance which he had rendered by sending the Papal galleys. Jorge de Melo, a Portuguese caballero, was sent to his own country with despatches, and other nobles and high officials were despatched to the Emperor's Viceroys in the various parts of his dominions. In the long circular letter which Charles addressed to all these potentates—and which is reproduced in its entirety by Sandoval—he says "that the Christian captives found in Tunis amounted to something like eighteen to twenty thousand, that Barbarossa had escaped with some five thousand Turks, corsairs, and *renegadoes*, of which three thousand were on horseback and two thousand afoot; that, as they suffered from great scarcity of provisions, and the almost total lack of water, many were falling by the way, and many others were being murdered by their quondam allies for such goods as they possessed, or for the value of their arms and clothing."

We must now return to Kheyr-ed-Din. What the sufferings of that chieftain and the remnant of his gallant army must have been in their flight to Bona they alone knew. It was the height of summer, and burning tracks of desert and rugged mountain passes had to be surmounted; naturally they could have carried but very little food, and water they had to find on the way. In addition to this, as we have seen in the despatch of Charles, the tribesmen turned against them, cutting off stragglers and murdering and plundering as opportunity offered. Barbarossa himself was an old man, so old that it seems nothing short of a miracle that he should have survived the hardships of this awful march. Not only did he do this, but apparently arrived at Bona in condition to continue his journey by sea at once, had he cared to do so. He had lost his newly acquired kingdom, he had lost nearly his entire fleet, his arsenal and stores were in the hands of his enemies; if ever a man was completely crushed it was he on this memorable occasion. As we have said before, however, it was in times of the greatest stress when the indomitable character of this man rose to meet the occasion, and, while his foes were congratulating one another that at last there was an end of the scourge of the Mediterranean and the bugbear of Christendom, the hunted fugitive was merely preparing himself for fresh acts of aggression.

The real fact of the matter was that he was above all and before all a seaman. The defeat of Kheyr-ed-Din meant merely the transference of his malign activities from one sphere to another—from the sea to the land, or from the land to the sea. King he called himself, and king *de facto* he was both in Algiers and Tunis, reigning with unexampled cruelty, a prototype of those other corsair kings by whom he was succeeded. But the real source of his power lay, not in stone walls and fortifications, nor in ill-trained levies of African tribes, but in his own genius for command at sea, and the manner in which he was able to inspire with his own dauntless and desperate spirit those hardy mariners who followed in his train, the descendants of the "Moriscoes" who hailed from the ancient Moorish kingdoms of Còrdoba and Granada.

Thus it was in the present instance. He had been unable to withstand the might of Caesar and his legions, but Tunis was not the whole of Northern Africa, nor had quite all his eggs been kept in that one basket. He had kept fifteen galleys in reserve at Bona, and, in consequence, on his arrival there, was able to embark at once. This he did, and hardly had he done so when there appeared upon the scene fifteen galleys commanded by Adan Centurion and John Doria. Kheyr-ed-Din had had enough of fighting just for the present; his men and he were wearied out by the hardships of their flight, and accordingly he drew up his galleys under the fort at Bona and awaited an attack, should the enemy care to deliver one. But Adan Centurion's heart failed him; to cut out the old Sea-wolf from under one of his own batteries was more than he had the stomach for, and he accordingly sailed away. *"Fue sin duda la perdida grande"* (this no doubt was a great pity), is the comment of Sandoval, who goes on to say that, had the Genoese been the men that they had been aforetime, this would never have been, and that they would have gone in and burnt or disabled the galleys of the corsair, slain their leader, or driven him ashore. Hot on the tracks of Adan Centurion and his nephew John came the veteran Andrea Doria with forty galleys, but he was too late, and the bird had flown; had it been he who had arrived in the first instance, then it is more than probable that matters would have turned out differently, and Kheyr-ed-Din had then and there terminated his career. It is true that Andrea possessed himself of Bona, and the Corsair King was shorn of yet another of his land-stations, but for the time he had cut himself adrift from the land, and had gone back to that element in which he was particularly at home.

Doria left Bona in the charge of Alvar Gomez and a company of Spanish troops and then sailed away, if possible to find and capture Barbarossa, thus to set the seal of completeness on the victory which had been won by his master the Emperor. Another stronghold of the corsairs was now in most competent hands, as Alvar Gomez Zagal was one of the most renowned *caballeros* of Spain, son of that Pero Lopez de Horusco on whom the Moors themselves had bestowed the title of "Al Zagal," or "The Valiant," on account of his extraordinary bravery.

On August 17th Charles re-embarked his army and evacuated the country, leaving, however, one thousand Spanish veterans, under the command of Bernard de Mendoza, in charge of the Goletta, as a permanent memorial of the expedition, and as a guarantee that the wretched Muley Hassan should fully comply with the treaty obligations which had been imposed upon him. It is true that Barbarossa had not been captured, but his city had been taken, his fleet had been destroyed, and he himself was now a fugitive, unable any further to trouble the peace of Christendom or the dignity of the Emperor by whom he had been so soundly chastised. In consequence the Caesar departed well pleased with himself and with those who had been acting under his orders, to whom he distributed orders and titles, as a memento of the occasion upon which they had finally broken up the power of those by whom his peace had so long been troubled.

One of the difficulties in dealing with the career of Kheyr-ed-Din Barbarossa is that, in times when he was unsuccessful, or when, as on the present occasion, he had received a severe setback, it is next to impossible to find out what he was doing or where exactly he was preparing for his next coup. In this case, in particular, the old-time historians were thanking God that the Emperor had rid the world of a particularly pestilent knave, and ceased to trouble themselves much about him until he forced himself once more upon their notice. Had Charles at this time recognised the greatness of the man whom he had just so signally defeated he might have changed the course of history. Had he, instead of sailing back to Europe, content with that which he had accomplished in Tunis, pushed his attack home on Algiers, he might have made himself master of the whole of Northern Africa, as, in the disorganised state in which the corsairs now found themselves, they could certainly have offered no effective resistance. But to the Emperor these rovers of the sea presented themselves merely in the light of robbers. Robbers, it is true, on a somewhat large scale, but still not persons of sufficient importance to detain him from the infinitely more pressing affairs which awaited him on the opposite shores of the Mediterranean Sea.

In addition to the fifteen galleys which Kheyr-ed-Din picked up at Bona he had in reserve at Algiers some fifty others. Escaping the attention of Adan Centurion and John Doria, and the infinitely more formidable squadron of Andrea, he headed once more for Algiers, and for a time seems to have remained quiet, no doubt recuperating from the fatigues, disappointments, and physical hardships which he had so recently undergone. He was apparently undisturbed during the winter by his Christian enemies, and was in consequence able to think out his future plans of campaign and to collect and put heart into his scattered followers, who, in ones and twos, were gradually, such of them as were left, finding their way back to the headquarters of piracy and its indomitable chieftain. That cool calculator of the chances of life knew that this must be so; the power of the corsairs generally had received the worst blow it had ever encountered since the dispossessed Moriscoes had taken to the sea for a living; those of them who remained alive were without ships—that is to say, without their only means of making a livelihood—and that they should gravitate towards Algiers and its master was as nearly a certainty as anything human could be. And, as was anticipated by the chief, so it came to pass. Into the city straggled broken, starving, sullen men who had lost their all, for whom the future held nothing but misery and despair unless they could get to sea once more.

It was on occasions such as this that the intellectual eminence of Barbarossa was so marked. Rough and cruel as he was, he possessed nevertheless a magnetic power over the minds of men, on which, when it so pleased him, he could play with the most extraordinary effect. And now, when the rank and file of the corsairs were ragged, hungry, and smarting under defeat, he dealt with them tenderly and graciously; and the sum of his teaching was to the effect that they had but to follow him once more and all the evils from which they were suffering would be presently remedied. So it came about that men who, before the defeat, had commanded ships of their own, were glad enough to become units on board the galleys of Kheyr-ed-Din, animated by the pleasing hope that soon again, under the leadership of this man, they might regain all, nay more, than they had lost. It must be remembered that Barbarossa argued from sound premises when he held out such hopes as these to the desperate remnant of the corsairs in Algiers in that sad winter of 1535. He was the greatest of them all, and they, as well as he, knew this to be a fact: if they had lost their all in the past battles, they had been fighting in a common cause to preserve their own lives and their liberty to plunder the Christian at sea. And now there was work and there was bread to eat for those who once again would throw in their lot with their old leader; and, although it may be said that these men had no alternative, still they threw themselves with heartiness into that which the master mind decreed should be their work, and this was none other than the preparation of the galleys for another campaign against the Christian.

"What matter, comrades?" said the veteran on one occasion when he was superintending the fitting out of the galleys. "These dogs have gone back from whence they came, and they have left that creature, Muley Hassan, to do their will in Tunis. It is true that there is Mendoza and his thousand Spaniards in the Goletta, but did not Martin de Vargas hold the Peñon here? And where is De Vargas, and in whose hands is the Peñon now? We know from whence the garrisons of Spain draw their supplies, and believe me that there will be hungry men in the Goletta in this coming year. Once we get to sea again, there will be more than enough for every good man who believes in the Prophet, and who has the sense to follow Barbarossa. For every ducat that you have lost see, in the coming year, if you do not gain ten; the Christians are off their guard now, and they think that they have done with me because they have captured Tunis." He laughed his great, jovial laugh. "By the beard of the Prophet—upon whom be peace!—they have yet to find out the man with whom they have to deal."

It took a master mind to instil heart of grace into men who so recently had had so bad a beating as these; but in the end they began to cheer up, and to recollect how Barbarossa had sooner or later always risen from defeat as strong or stronger than before; also they recalled the fact that he was the chosen of the Padishah, and that that potentate, the representative of the Prophet on earth, would assuredly come to his assistance now that Tunis, which had been taken in his name, had been reft from Barbarossa by the Christians. Gradually hope took the place of despair, and when the corsairs took to the sea in the early part of the following year it was with renewed confidence in both themselves and their leader.

CHAPTER 11
Roxalana and the Murder of Ibrahim

At the coming of spring Barbarossa was at sea again with thirty-two ships ready for any eventuality, his crews aflame with ardour for revenge against those by whom they had been so roughly handled. He chose for the scene of operations a place on the coast of Majorca some fifteen miles from Palma; from here he commanded the route of the Spaniards from their country to the African coast, and it was against this nation that he felt a great bitterness owing to recent events. Eagerly did the corsair and his men watch for the Spanish ships, the heavier vessels lying at anchor, but the light, swift galleys ranging and questing afar so that none might be missed. Very soon the vigilance of the Moslems was rewarded by the capture of a number of vessels, sent by Bernard de Mendoza laden with Turkish and Moorish slaves, destined to be utilised as rowers in the Spanish galleys. These men were hailed as a welcome reinforcement, and joyfully joined the forces of Kheyr-ed-Din when he moved on Minorca, captured the castle by a surprise assault, raided the surrounding country, and captured five thousand seven hundred Christians, amongst whom were eight hundred men who had been wounded in the attack on Tunis—all these unfortunates were sent to refill the bagnio of Algiers.

This private war of revenge was, however, destined soon to come to an end, as Soliman the Magnificent in this year became involved in disputes with the Venetian Republic, and recalled "that veritable man of the sea," as Barbarossa had been described by Ibrahim, to Constantinople.

In this city by the sea there had taken place a tragedy which, although it only involved the death of a single man, was nevertheless far-reaching in its consequences; for the man was none other than that great statesman Ibrahim, Grand Vizier, and the only trusted counsellor of the Padishah. He who had been originally a slave had risen step by step in the favour of his master until he arrived at the giddy eminence which he occupied at the time of his death. It is a somewhat curious commentary on the essentially democratic status of an autocracy that a man could thus rise to a position second only to that of the autocrat himself; and, in all probability, wielding quite as much power.

Ibrahim had for years been treated by Soliman more as a brother than as a dependent, which, in spite of his Grand Viziership, he was in fact. They lived in the very closest communion, taking their meals together, and even sleeping in the same room, Soliman, a man of high intelligence himself, and a ruler who kept in touch with all the happenings which arose in his immense dominions, desiring always to have at hand the man whom he loved; from whom, with his amazing grip of political problems and endless fertility of resource, he was certain of sympathy and sound advice. But in an oriental despotism there are other forces at work besides those of *la haute politique*, and Ibrahim had one deadly enemy who was sworn to compass his destruction. The Sultana Roxalana was the light of the harem of the Grand Turk. This supremely beautiful woman, originally a Russian slave, was the object of the most passionate devotion on the part of Soliman; but she was as ambitious as she was lovely, and brooked no rival in the affections of Soliman, be that person man, woman, or child. In her hands the master of millions, the despot whose nod was death, became a submissive slave; the undisciplined passions of this headstrong woman swept aside from her path all those whom she suspected of sharing her influence, in no matter how remote a fashion. At her dictation had Soliman caused to be murdered his son Mustafa, a youth of the brightest promise, because, in his intelligence and his winning ways he threatened to eclipse Selim, the son of Roxalana herself.

This woman possessed a strong natural intelligence, albeit she was totally uneducated; she saw and knew that Ibrahim was all-powerful with her lover, and this roused her jealousy to fever-heat. She was not possessed of a cool judgment, which would have told her that Ibrahim was a statesman dealing with the external affairs of the Sublime Porte, and that with her and with her affairs he neither desired, nor had he the power, to interfere. What, however, the Sultana did know was that in these same affairs of State her opinion was dust in the balance when weighed against that of the Grand Vizier.

Soliman had that true attribute of supreme greatness, the unerring aptitude for the choice of the right man. He had picked out Ibrahim from among his immense entourage, and never once had he regretted his choice. As time went on and the intellect and power of the man became more and more revealed to his master, that sovereign left in his hands even such matters as despots are apt to guard most jealously. We have seen how, in spite of the murmurings of the whole of his capital, and the almost insubordinate attitude of his navy, he had persevered in the appointment of Kheyr-ed-Din Barbarossa, because the judgment of Ibrahim was in favour of its being carried out. This, to Roxalana, was gall and wormwood; well she knew that, as long as the Grand Vizier lived, her sovereignty was at best but a divided one. There was a point at which her blandishments stopped short; this was when she found that her opinion did not coincide with that of the minister. She was, as we have seen in the instance of her son, not a woman to stick at trifles, and she decided that Ibrahim must die.

There could be no hole-and-corner business about this; he must die, and when his murder had been accomplished she would boldly avow to her lover what she had done and take the consequences, believing in her power over him to come scatheless out of the adventure. In those days, when human life was so cheap, she might have asked for the death of almost any one, and her whim would have been gratified by a lover who had not hesitated to put to death his own son at her dictation. But with Ibrahim it was another matter; he was the familiar of the Sultan, his *alter ego* in fact, It says much for the nerve of the Sultana that she dared so greatly on this memorable and lamentable occasion.

On March 5th, 1536, Ibrahim, went to the royal seraglio, and, following his ancient custom, was admitted to the table of his master, sleeping after the meal at his side. At least so it was supposed, but none knew save those engaged in the murder what passed on that fatal night; the next day his dead body lay in the house of the Sultan.

Across the floor of jasper, in that palace which was a fitting residence for one rightly known as "The Magnificent," the blood of Ibrahim flowed to the feet of Roxalana. The disordered clothing, the terrible expression of the face of the dead man, the gaping wounds which he had received, bore witness that there had taken place a grim struggle before that iron frame and splendid intellect had been levelled with the dust. This much leaked out afterwards, as such things will leak out, and then the Sultana took Soliman into her chamber and gazed up into his eyes. The man was stunned by the immensity of the calamity which had befallen him and his kingdom, but his manhood availed him not against the wiles of this Circe. Ibrahim had been foully done to death in his own palace, and this woman clinging so lovingly around his neck now was the murderess.

The heart's blood of his best friend was coagulating on the threshold of his own apartment when he forgave her by whom his murder had been accomplished. This was the vengeance of Roxalana, and who shall say that it was not complete?

The Ottoman Empire was the poorer by the loss of its greatest man, the jealousy of the Sultana was assuaged, the despot who had permitted this unavenged murder was still on the throne, thrall to the woman who had first murdered his son and then his friend and minister. But the deed carried with it the evil consequences which were only too likely to occur when so capable a head of the State was removed at so critical a time. Renewed strife was in the air, and endless squabbles between Venice and the Porte were taking place. With these we have no concern, but, in addition to other complaints, there were loud and continuous ones concerning the corsairs. Venice, "The Bride of the Sea," had neither rest nor peace; the pirates swarmed in Corfu, in Zante, in Candia, in Cephalonia, and the plunder and murder of the subjects of the Republic was the theme of perpetual representations to the Sultan. The balance of advantage in this guerrilla warfare was with the corsairs until Girolame Canale, a Venetian captain, seized one of the Moslem leaders known as "The Young Moor of Alexandria." The victory of Canale was somewhat an important one as he captured the galley of "The Young Moor" and four others; two more were sunk, and three hundred Janissaries and one thousand slaves fell into the hands of the Venetian commander. There being an absence of nice feeling on the part of the Venetians, the Janissaries were at once beheaded to a man.

The whole story is an illustration of the extraordinary relations existing among the Mediterranean States at this time. Soliman the Magnificent, Sultan of Turkey, had lent three hundred of his Janissaries, his own picked troops, to assist the corsairs in their depredations on Venetian commerce. Having done this, and the Janissaries having been caught and summarily and rightly put to death as pirates, the Sultan, as soon as he heard of what had occurred, sent an ambassador, one Yonis Bey, to Venice to demand satisfaction for the insult passed upon him by the beheading of his own soldiers turned pirates. The conclusion of the affair was that the Venetians released "The Young Moor of Alexandria" as soon as he was cured of the eight wounds which he had received in the conflict, and sent him back to Africa with such of his galleys as were left. There was one rather comical incident in connection with this affair, which was that when Yonis Bey was on his way from Constantinople to Venice he was chased by a Venetian fleet, under the command of the Count Grandenico, and driven ashore. The Count was profuse in his apologies when he discovered that he had been chasing a live ambassador; but the occurrence so exasperated Soliman that he increased his demands in consequence.

Barbarossa, who had spent his time harrying the Spaniards at sea ever since the fall of Tunis, was shortly to appear on the scene again. He received orders from the Sultan, and came as fast as a favouring wind would bring him. Kheyr-ed-Din had been doing well in the matter of slaves and plunder, but he knew that, with the backing of the Grand Turk, he would once again be in command of a fleet in which he might repeat his triumph of past years, and prove himself once more the indispensable "man of the sea."

Soon after his arrival his ambitions were gratified, and he found himself with a fleet of one hundred ships. Since the death of Ibrahim, and the incident which terminated with the despatch of Yonis Bey to Venice, the relations between the Grand Turk and the Venetian Republic had become steadily worse, and at last the Sultan declared war. On May 17th, 1537, Soliman, accompanied by his two sons, Selim and Mohammed, left Constantinople. With the campaign conducted by the Sultan we are not concerned here; it was directed against the Ionian Islands, which had been in the possession of Venice since 1401. On August 18th Soliman laid siege to Corfu, and was disastrously beaten, re-embarking his men on September 7th, after losing thousands in a fruitless attack on the fortress. He returned to Constantinople utterly discomfited. It was the seventh campaign which the Sultan had conducted in person, but the first in which the ever-faithful Ibrahim had not been by his side.

This defeat at the hands of the Venetians was not, however, the only humiliation which he was destined to experience in this disastrous year; for once again Doria, that scourge of the Moslem, was loose upon the seas, and was making his presence felt in the immediate neighbourhood of Corfu, where the Turks had been defeated. On July 17th Andrea had left the port of Messina with twenty-five galleys, had captured ten richly laden Turkish ships, gutted and burned them. Kheyr-ed-Din was at sea at the time, but the great rivals were not destined to meet on this occasion. Instead of Barbarossa, Andrea fell in with Ali-Chabelli, the lieutenant of Sandjak Bey of Gallipoli. On July 22nd the Genoese admiral and the Turkish commander from the Dardanelles met to the southward of Corfu, off the small island of Paxo, and a smart action ensued. It ended in the defeat of Ali-Chabelli, whose galleys were captured and towed by Doria into Paxo. That veteran fighter was himself in the thickest of the fray, and, conspicuous in his crimson doublet, had been an object of attention to the marksmen of Chabelli during the entire action. In spite of the receipt of a severe wound in the knee, the admiral refused to go below until victory was assured. He was surrounded at this time by a devoted band of nobles sworn to defend the person of their admiral or to die in his defence. His portrait has been sketched for us at this time by the Dominican Friar, Padre Alberto Gugliel-motto, author of *La guerra dei Pirati e la marina Pontifica dal 1500 al 1560.* The description runs thus:

> Andrea Doria was of lofty stature, his face oval in shape, forehead broad and commanding, his neck was powerful, his hair short, his beard long and fan-shaped, his lips were thin, his eyes bright and piercing.

Once again had he defeated an officer of the Grand Turk; and it may be remarked that Ibrahim was probably quite right in the estimation, or rather in the lack of estimation, in which he held the sea-officers of his master, as they seem to have been deficient in every quality save that of personal valour, and in their encounters with Doria and the knights were almost invariably worsted. For the sake of Islam, for the prestige of the Moslem arms at sea, it was time that Barbarossa should take matters in hand once more.

The autumn of this year 1537 proved that the old Sea-wolf had lost none of his cunning, that his followers were as terrible as ever. What did it seem to matter that Venetian and Catalan, Genoese and Frenchman, Andalusian and the dwellers in the Archipelago, were all banded together in league against this common foe? Did not the redoubtable Andrea range the seas in vain, and were not all the efforts of the Knights of Saint John futile, when the son of the *renegado* from Mitylene and his Christian wife put forth from the Golden Horn? What was the magic of this man, it was asked despairingly, that none seemed able to prevail against him? Had it not been currently reported that Carlos Quinto, the great Emperor, had driven him forth from Tunis a hunted fugitive, broken and penniless, with never a galley left, without one ducat in his pocket? Was he so different, then, from all the rest of mankind that his followers would stick to him in evil report as well as in the height of his prosperity? Men swore and women crossed themselves at the mention of his name.

"Terrible as an army with banners," indeed, was Kheyr-ed-Din in this eventful summer: things had gone badly with the crescent flag, the Padishah was unapproachable in his palace, brooding perchance on that "might have been" had he not sold his honour and the life of his only friend to gratify the malice of a she-devil; those in attendance on the Sultan trembled, for the humour of the despot was black indeed.

But "the veritable man of the sea" was in some sort to console him for that which he had lost; as never in his own history—and there was none else with which it could be compared—had the Corsair King made so fruitful a raid. He ravaged the coasts of the Adriatic and the islands of the Archipelago, sweeping in slaves by the thousand, and by the end of the year he had collected eighteen thousand in the arsenal at Stamboul. Great was the jubilation in Constantinople when the *Admiralissimo* himself returned from his last expedition against the *infidel*; stilled were the voices which hinted disaffection—who among them all could bring back four hundred thousand pieces of gold? What mariner could offer to the Grand Turk such varied and magnificent presents?

Upon his arrival Barbarossa asked permission to kiss the threshold of the palace of the Sultan, which boon being graciously accorded to him, he made his triumphal entry. Two hundred captives clad in scarlet robes carried cups of gold and flasks of silver behind them came thirty others, each staggering under an enormous purse of sequins; yet another two hundred brought collars of precious stones or bales of the choicest goods; and a further two hundred were laden with sacks of small coin. Certainly if Soliman the Magnificent had lost a Grand Vizier he had succeeded in finding an admiral!

All through the earlier months of 1538 the dockyards of Constantinople hummed with a furious activity, for Soliman had decreed that the maritime campaign of this year was to begin with no less than one hundred and fifty ships. His admiral, however, did not agree with this decision; to the Viziers he raged and stormed.

"Listen," he said, "O men of the land who understand naught of the happenings of the sea. By this time Saleh-Reis must have quitted Alexandria convoying to the Bosphorus twenty sail filled with the richest merchandise; should he fall in with the accursed Genoese, Doria, where then will be Saleh-Reis and his galleys and his convoy? I will tell you: the ships in Genoa, the galleys burned, Saleh-Reis and all his mariners chained to the rowers' bench."

The Viziers trembled, as men did when Barbarossa stormed and turned upon them those terrible eyes which knew neither fear nor pity. "We be but men," they answered, "and our lord the Sultan has so ordained it."

"I have forty galleys," replied the corsair; "you have forty more.

With these I will take the sea; but, mark you," he continued, softening somewhat, "you do right to fear the displeasure of the Sultan, and I also have no wish to encounter it; but vessels raised and equipped in a hurry will be of small use to me. In the name of Allah the compassionate and his holy Prophet give me my eighty galleys and let me go."

In Kheyr-ed-Din Barbarossa sound strategical instinct went hand in hand with the desperate valour of the corsair. To dally in the Golden Horn while so rich a prey was at sea to be picked up by his Christian foes was altogether opposed to his instincts: never to throw away a chance in the game of life had ever been his guiding principle.

Soliman, great man as he undoubtedly was, had not the adamantine hardness of character which enabled his admiral to risk all on the hazards of the moment; or possibly the Grand Turk was deficient in that clearness of strategical instinct which never in any circumstances forgoes a present advantage for something which may turn out well in a problematical future. Soliman, sore, sullen, and unapproachable, dwelt in his palace brooding over the misfortunes which had been his lot since the death of Ibrahim. Barbarossa, who so recently had lost practically all that he possessed, and who had reached an age at which most men have no hopes for the future, was as clear in intellect, as undaunted in spirit, as if he had been half a century younger: to be even once more with those by whom he had been defeated and dispossessed was the only thing now in his mind. The capture of Saleh-Reis and his convoy would be a triumph of which he could not bear to think. Further, it would add to the demoralisation of the sea forces of the Sultan, which were sadly in need of some striking success after the defeats which had so recently been their portion. The Sultan had decided that one hundred and fifty ships were necessary; his admiral thought otherwise. There was too much at stake for him to dally at Constantinople; his fiery energy swept all before it, and in the end he had his way. On June 7th, 1538, he finally triumphed over the hesitations of the Viziers and put to sea with eighty sail.

The Sultan, from his kiosk, the windows of which opened on the Bosphorus, counted the ships.

"Only eighty sail; is that all?" he asked.

The trembling Viziers prostrated themselves before him.

"O our Lord, the Padishah," they cried, "Saleh-Reis comes from Alexandria with a rich convoy; somewhere lurking is Andrea Doria, the accursed; it was necessary, O Magnificent, to send succour."

There was a pause, in which the hearts of men beat as do those who know not but that the next moment may be their last on earth.

The Sultan stared from his window at the retreating ships in a silence like the silence of the grave. At last he turned:

"So be it," he answered briefly; "but see to it that reinforcements do not lag upon the road."

If there had been activity in the dockyards before it was as nothing to the strenuous work that was to be done henceforward.

Before starting on this expedition Kheyr-ed-Din had made an innovation in the manning of some of the most powerful of his galleys, which was of the utmost importance, and which was to add enormously to the success of his future maritime enterprises. The custom had always been that the Ottoman galleys had been rowed by Christians, captured and enslaved; of course the converse was true in the galleys of their foes. There were, for the size of the vessels, an enormous number of men carried in the galleys of the sixteenth century, and an average craft of this description would have on board some four hundred men; of these, however, the proportion would be two hundred and fifty slaves to one hundred and fifty fighting men. That which Kheyr-ed-Din now insisted upon was that a certain proportion of his most powerful units should be rowed by Moslem fighting men, so that on the day of battle the oarsmen could join in the fray instead of remaining chained to their benches, as was the custom with the slaves. It is, however, an extraordinary testimony to the influence which the corsair had attained in Constantinople that he had been able to effect this change in the composition of some of his crews; it must have been done with the active co-operation of the Sultan, as no authority less potent than that of the sovereign himself could have induced free men to undertake the terrible toil of rower in a galley. This was reserved for the unfortunate slave on either side owing to the intolerable hardship of the life, and results, in the pace at which a galley proceeded through the water, were usually obtained by an unsparing use of the lash on the naked bodies of the rowers.

This human material was used up in the most prodigal manner possible, as those in command had not the inducement of treating the rowers well, from that economic standpoint which causes a man to so use his beast of burden as to get the best work from him. In the galley, when a slave could row no more he was flung overboard and another was put in his place.

The admiral, however, even when backed by the Padishah, could not man a large fleet of galleys with Moslem rowers, and, as there was a shortage in the matter of propelling power, his first business was to collect slaves, and for this purpose he visited the islands of the Archipelago. The lot of the unhappy inhabitants of these was indeed a hard one. They were nearer to the seat of the Moslem power than any other Christians; they were in those days totally unable to resist an attack in force, and in consequence were swept off in their thousands.

Seven islands cover the entrance to the Gulf of Volo. The nearest to the coast is Skiathos, which is also the most important; it was defended by a castle built upon a rock. This castle was attacked by Barbarossa, who bombarded it for six days, carried it by assault, and massacred the garrison. He spared the lives of the inhabitants of the island, and by this means secured three thousand four hundred rowers for his galleys. He had to provide motor-power for the reinforcements which he expected. In July he was reinforced from Constantinople by ninety galleys, while from Egypt came Saleh-Reis, who had succeeded in avoiding the terrible Doria, with twenty more; the fleet was thus complete.

Barbarossa ravaged Skios, Andros, and other islands, putting them under contribution, and in this manner raised some eight thousand ducats; from a pen of guinea-fowl to a king's ransom, nothing escaped the maw of this most rapacious of corsairs. Candia and some other islands yielded up some small spoil, but the sufferings of such insignificant folk as the wretched islanders were soon lost to the sight of the Christian world in the magnitude of the events which were now impending.

Kheyr-ed-Din Barbarossa, Corsair, Admiral, and King, the scourge of the Mediterranean, and Andrea Doria, Prince of Oneglia, Admiral of the modern Caesar, Charles V., Emperor and King, were at last to meet face to face.

CHAPTER 12

The Prevesa Campaign

Some thirty-five miles to the south-eastward of Cape Bianco (the southernmost point of the island of Corfu) lies Prevesa, at the entrance of the Gulf of Arta, or, as it was known in classic times, the Ambracian Gulf. In these seas, in the year 31 B.C., was fought one of the most memorable battles of antiquity, for it was here that Octavius, afterward Augustus Caesar, defeated the forces of Antony and Cleopatra. There have been many controversies of late years as to whom the original idea of breaking the line in naval combats is due: anyhow, it can claim a respectable antiquity, as it was practised at the battle of Actium by Octavius, who by a skilful manoeuvre caused Antony to lengthen his line, which he then cut through and attacked the ships of Cleopatra, which were in support: this was too much for the lady, who fled with her sixty ships, followed by Antony, to his eternal disgrace. The remainder of his fleet fought bravely for a time, but was eventually defeated, the land army also surrendering to Octavius. The date of the actual battle of Actium was September 2nd, 31 B.C.: it was in September 1538 that the battle of Prevesa between Andrea Doria and Kheyr-ed-Din Barbarossa took place, and the conditions of the battle were almost exactly similar.

To this very place came, 1569 years later, the Christian and the Moslem, the Crescent and the Cross, each under its most renowned leader, each side burning with an inextinguishable hate. It was one of the peculiarities of this warfare that into it entered so much actual personal feeling, each side hating the other for the love of God in the most poisonous fashion. Save and except the battle of Lepanto in 1571 (with which we shall deal later in the story of Ali Basha, or Occhiali as he was called by his Christian opponents) the contest at Prevesa was far the most important ever fought by those strange oar-propelled vessels known as galleys. It was memorable in many ways, but particularly so for the ages of the men in chief command. Andrea Doria was at this time seventy years of age; in fact, Guglielmotti gives the date of his birth as 1466, thus making him two years older. That amazing veteran Kheyr-ed-Din Barbarossa, who died in his bed at Constantinople on July 4th, 1546, at the age of ninety, must have been eighty-two. Vicenzo Capello was sixty-eight, as the epitaph on his tomb at Venice in the church of Santa Maria Formosa says that he was seventy-two in the year of his death, 1542.

Once again Christendom was nerving itself for a supreme effort against the corsairs, and, during the time that Barbarossa was raiding and ravaging among the islands of the Archipelago, the Christian fleet was gradually assembling. At first it numbered some 150 galleys, 81 Venetian, 36 Pontifical, and 30 Spanish; Charles V. sent, at the last moment, 50 ships on which were embarked 10,000 troops. The force totalled altogether 59,000 to 60,000 men, 195 ships, and 2,594 cannons. This was no doubt a most formidable armada, but the policy of those by whom it was composed was not all directed to the same end. While Charles desired, above all things, to exterminate the corsairs for good and all, which was, in the circumstances, the only sound view of the matter, the Venetians were for fighting defensive actions to maintain their supremacy in the Ionian Islands, and were disposed to let the future take care of itself. There was not, in consequence, that absolute unanimity among the various commanders of the expedition as was necessary for its complete success.

The concentration of the Christian fleet took place at Corfu. The Venetians arrived first, with Vincenzo Capello in command; Marco Grimani brought thither the Papal contingent; they anchored and waited, but Andrea Doria did not appear. Days lengthened into weeks, and Grimani and Capelli chafed and fumed; provisions were running low and the dignity of Venice and of the Pope were flouted by this strange remissness on the part of the Admiral of the Emperor. At last, furious with impatience, Grimani made a raid into the Gulf of Arta, which was defended at the entrance by the fortress of Prevesa. The only result of this ill-timed attack was that two Papal captains and a number of soldiers were killed. Grimani then returned to Corfu, to find Capello irritated to the last extent by the non-appearance of Doria.

At last, on September 5th, the Imperial fleet hove in sight. It was composed of forty-nine galleys, but these were supplemented by a great number of sailing ships; the sailing craft, however, did not arrive till September 22nd. These vessels were gradually making way among the Spaniards since the discovery of the new world.

At this time the Venetians possessed fourteen *nefs*. Doria had augmented these by twenty-two of his own, and the total number of thirty-six was commanded by Franco Doria, a nephew of the admiral. The Venetian *nefs* were commanded by Alessandro Condalmiero, captain of the *Galleon of Venice*. This was the most formidable fighting vessel in the Mediterranean; she was reckoned an excellent sailor, she was by far the most heavily armed sailing ship then afloat; in fact, in the opinion of contemporary seamen, she was "an invincible fortress."

Doria, Grimani, and Capello had now nearly 200 ships carrying nearly 60,000 men. Such a force, in all ages, has been considered great. William the Conqueror conquered Britain with a less number; it is almost half the total of the personnel of the British fleet in the present day which has to defend a country with 40,000,000 inhabitants, and all this force had been raised, armed, and equipped to combat with a Moslem corsair.

Barbarossa had succeeded in assembling 122 ships. He was accompanied by all the most famous corsairs of the day, among whom was Dragut, who fell at the siege of Malta, and of whom we shall have more to say in due time. Far and wide ranged the swift galleys of the Ottoman fleet, for the plan of the commander of the Moslems was to locate and destroy his enemies in detail if possible. At last news came to him that Grimani's ships had been sighted in the Gulf of Arta. Not one moment did he lose; he would fall upon the Papal contingent with his whole force and destroy it utterly. Such, at least, was his plan when he sailed for Prevesa; but, notwithstanding his haste, he was too late. Happily for himself, Grimani had returned to Corfu before the arrival of his enemy.

At this juncture Barbarossa hesitated; had he not done so, and had he followed Grimani to Corfu, he might have destroyed both him and Vincenzo Capello in detail before the arrival of Doria. The Prevesa campaign is a curious study of hesitation on both sides, and the idea naturally occurs were not the corsair and the Christian commanders-in-chief too old for the work on which they were engaged? Men of over seventy are not impetuous, but grave and deliberate as a rule; but there is no rule without its exceptions, and Doria and Barbarossa were not as other leaders. Up to the present their dash and initiative had been unimpaired. There was no question that Barbarossa not only made a mistake in hesitating, but that by it he lost the game. Instead of striking at once he did what he had never done before in the whole of his career, which was to send to Constantinople for instructions. Some of his galleys had captured a fishing-boat off Corfu, the crew of which had seen Doria's fleet. The Moslem leader sent the fishermen themselves to report to Soliman exactly what they had seen, and to ask for and bring back instructions from that potentate. What Barbarossa had discovered was that the odds were very much against him; so much, in fact, that he would have to act on the defensive. In consequence, he steered for Prevesa and entered the Gulf of Arta, which is approached by a long narrow strait, dominated by the castle of Prevesa. Once inside he anchored his galleys in such a position that they could fire direct out to sea, thus overwhelming with their fire any vessel attempting to enter.

Barbarossa now occupied the same position as did Octavius in his combat with Antony. The role of the latter general was now taken by Doria. Antony, like Doria, had heavy ships which could not advance to the attack owing to their too great draught. Octavius, with his light-draught ships, could both attack and retreat into safety if overmatched.

On September 22nd Doria, having collected all his ships, gave orders to fill up with wood, water, and fresh provisions. On the 25th, to the sound of the trumpet, the Commander-in-Chief, with his fleet of two hundred sail, weighed anchor and sped before the wind rapidly southwards. Grimani commanded the advance-guard, Doria was in the centre, Vincenzo Capello, with his Venetians, brought up the rear. Formed in two columns, the *nefs* followed the galleys; the *Galleon of Venice*, commanded by Condalmiero, a squadron in herself, preceded them.

From the anchorage at Corfu to the entrance of the Gulf of Arta is about fifty-eight miles, and, traversing this distance during the hours of daylight, the fleet anchored, as night fell, under Cape Prevesa. The Galleon which acted as what we should now call the guide of the fleet, anchored in sixteen feet of water, which was barely sufficient to keep her afloat.

The Gulf of Arta, in which, as we have said, the fleet of the Moslems were now anchored, presents very curious physical peculiarities: it is twenty-two miles in length from east to west, and fifteen miles in breadth from north to south. This sheet of water is formed into an immense bay by the configuration of the land, and its depth, in places, is from one hundred and thirty to two hundred feet. Inside it all the navies in the world might ride at anchor, were it not for the fact that the entrance is closed by a bar upon which the depth varies from six and a half to thirteen feet. With his light-draught ships Barbarossa occupied the interior position, while the heavy ships of Doria must in any event

Galeasse under sail

remain outside. A strong sea-breeze was blowing on shore; all night the *nefs* and the galleys were nearly rolling their gunwales under. In these packed and crowded vessels the misery and discomfort of their crews may be imagined. On the morning of the 26th, however, the west wind dropped, and a light wind sprang up from the northward.

The position at this time was one of surpassing interest. Here at long last the two most renowned sea-captains of the time were face to face. Each was aware that his antagonist was worthy of his steel, also that great issues, political and national, hung upon this conflict; which was no mere affair of outposts, but a struggle to the death as to whether the Crescent or the Cross was in time to come to be supreme in the tideless sea. And yet—such is the irony of fate—this battle proved indecisive, and it was not until thirty years later, at the battle of Lepanto, that this momentous question was set at rest for a time.

Would Doria, greatly daring, go in and risk all in attacking a fortified position; or would Barbarossa make a sally and fight it out to the death on the element on which he was so supremely at home?

But Doria had no mind to attack a fleet anchored under the guns of a fortress; Barbarossa would not risk all in an encounter with a foe possessed of great numerical superiority without orders from Constantinople. On Doria's side nothing but a disembarkation and a land-attack would offer a fair security for success, Kheyr-ed-Din, who held, as we have said, the interior position, was well aware of this fact, and in this supreme moment of his career was not disposed to give away any advantage. The situation occupied by Kheyr-ed-Din at the battle of Prevesa was, in a sense, different from any which he had held before, as he was in this case hampered by his sense of responsibility as *Admiralissimo* to the Grand Turk. What happened on the distant shores of Africa mattered but little to that monarch, and he had been content to allow his admiral an entirely free hand; here in Europe, on the shores of Greece, so close relatively to his own capital city, it was a very different matter, and Soliman was kept in touch with the happenings of his fleet as far as was possible in those days. But if the great corsair did not add to his reputation in this eventful campaign he still displayed an aptitude in realising the situation which, it is safe to say, was shown by none of those under his command.

Prevesa illustrates for us more than any other action the difficulties with which the path of the partisan leader in these days must always have been filled; and how it was that personal ascendancy was the only force to which such a leader had to trust Sheer dominance of the minds, the wills, and the bodies of others had placed Kheyr-ed-Din where he was; all his life he had commanded undisciplined pirates, and yet now, when he was the properly accredited officer of a mighty monarch, when he might have expected far more discipline and subordination than had ever been his lot in the past, he was met with a contumaciousness which he was unable to quell, and was forced into taking steps which, in his own unequalled knowledge of war, he knew to be doomed to disaster.

Around him the Reis, or captains of the Moslem galleys, clamorously demanded that he should take precautions against a land-attack. It was true that the raid which had been made by Grimani had been easily repulsed, but in present circumstances there was no question of a mere raid, as, should the Christian admiral so decide, he could land twenty thousand men. Sinan Reis, an old Osmanli warrior, furious with jealousy that the chief command should be in the hands of a corsair, sustained his opinion in a manner which augured ill for the hearty co-operation of all the Turkish forces. Sinan was just one of those blindly valiant fighters from whom the politic Ibrahim had desired to deliver his master when he had urged the appointment of Kheyr-ed-Din: brave as a lion, keen as the edge of his own good *scimitar*, fanatical, as became a Hodja who had visited the Holy Places, Sinan was a type of the Turkish sea-officer: devoid of strategical instinct and tactical training, his one idea was a headlong attack, then victory or the *houris* of Paradise. It will be seen that Barbarossa had not only Doria and the Christian fleet and army against which to contend on this occasion.

The peril conjured up by Sinan Reis on this occasion was not altogether an imaginary one: the idea of a disembarkation had, in point of fact, been seriously discussed that very morning by Andrea Doria and his council of war, at which Hernando de Gonzaga, Generalissimo of the troops embarked, had advised a landing. His argument, embodied in a long and technical harangue, may be reduced to the following:

> If we cannot go straight at the enemy and force our way through the entrance under his cannon why should we not reduce the fortress of Prevesa by a siege? Once masters of this height, we could close the strait by sinking in it vessels laden with stones, and we then have the Ottoman fleet at our mercy.

But Doria the sailor was not to be led by Gonzaga the soldier. He said:

> The advice seems sound, but in reality it would prove most dangerous if followed. Barbarossa must have landed some of his men,

the cavalry which defeated Grimani's raid will no doubt come again from the interior, if necessary. If we deprive our ships of their soldiers we expose ourselves to a sea-fight under most disadvantageous conditions. But most, important of all is the fact that time presses; the season is far advanced; at any time the fleet may be driven off these shores by a storm, in which case what would become of the troops left on shore? Again, if it comes on to blow a tempest from the westward we may lose not only our troops, but our ships, in fact the whole expedition.

At the battle of Actium, Octavius occupied the shore upon which Hernando Gonzaga wished to land and assault; but notwithstanding this fact Octavius did not attempt the passage of the gulf but waited for his enemy outside. Doria was therefore all the more justified in not sacrificing ships and men in attempting to force an entrance now that this same shore was in the hands of the enemy. He was asked, he said, to thrust his head into the mouth of the wolf, and this he was determined not to do.

In the meanwhile Barbarossa was using much the same language to his captains as was Doria.

> My brothers, you wish to transport cannon and raise redoubts on this uncovered shore because you think that the Christians will disembark and seize it: if you attempt this I tell you that the guns of the enemy will annoy you terribly. Not only this, supposing that Doria, profiting by the moment that our vessels are empty of troops, should attack in force, we cannot with five thousand men repulse twenty thousand. The fort of Prevesa will defend itself quite sufficiently well with its own garrison; our business is to think of the fleet and not to weaken in any way our means of attack and defence, If the infidels force, or attempt to force, an entry into the port, they will be most likely merely losing time and ammunition in cannonading us. You know that it is principally in this that these accursed dogs do trust, whereas we, O men of Islam, will place our confidence in God, in Mahomet his Prophet, in the strength of our right arms, in the keenness of our scimitars; we will carry them by boarding, therefore we must keep our crews on board.

But Barbarossa had not that absolute domination of the forces under his command which should be the prescriptive right of any leader. Sinan-Reis, the implacable be-turbaned old Osmanli, held him in bitter scorn. "Your advice may be good," he retorted, "but we think our plan the better."

The admiral suggested a reconnaissance of the site, which was merely a ruse to gain time. This was carried out under his own supervision, and confirmed him in the idea that disembarkation was folly; but Sinan-Reis and the Janissaries held obstinately to their opinion, while the "Joldaks," or Turkish soldiers in the galleys, grumbled among themselves that Kheyr-ed-Din must indeed be full of vanity to reject the counsels of one like Sinan-Reis. Both commanders-in-chief, Christian and Moslem, seem on this occasion to have taken an absolutely correct view of the problem as it was presented; but whereas Andrea Doria was a real commander-in-chief, Barbarossa was forced to consider and to defer to the opinions of men whom he knew to be in the wrong.

It was against his better judgment that Kheyr-ed-Din at last yielded; the men were backing up their officers, a spirit of disaffection was abroad in the armada: such a thing as this a wise chief must gauge at its true value, and stop before it goes too far. The Osmanli were murmuring against "the corsair"; it was time to let them see whether they or their war-worn leader possessed the greater wisdom.

According to Moslem chroniclers the valour of Kheyr-ed-Din was only equalled by his piety; consequently he murmured a prayer into that famous beard of his, which was now so much nearer to white than red, and gave orders that the cannon shall be immediately disembarked. "Let the will of God and of His Prophet be accomplished; that which is written is that which will take place," exclaimed this pious man as he watched the preparations being carried out under the supervision of Mourad-Reis.

That which "took place" was precisely and exactly what the Commander-in- Chief had predicted from the first: no sooner had Mourad-Reis landed upon the exposed beach, and attempted to open a trench, than he was met by a furious and concentrated fire from the galleys and *nefs* of the Christian fleet. To entrench themselves was impossible in the circumstances, as they had been told by the Admiral before they started on this harebrained adventure. There could be only one result, which was that, after a cruel and perfectly useless slaughter, the soldiers of Mourad-Reis had to retreat before the hail of shot poured upon them, and to return ignominiously to their vessels.

It is not on record what Kheyr-ed-Din said to Sinan, Mourad, and those other tacticians who had recommended the landing; which perhaps is a pity.

Doria then made a tentative movement against the strait by a detachment of galleys; Barbarossa told off an equal number to oppose them, and they mutually cannonaded and skirmished during the day. There was much noise and excitement, but practically no advantage was gained by either side, as Doria's men could not risk passing the guns of the fort, nor could those of Barbarossa the chance of being cannonaded by the heavy vessels lying in wait-for them outside. And so the day closed down with no success on either side, but with a decisive demonstration to the Moslems that, if they desired victory, to their admiral had better be left the organisation by which it was to be obtained.

Whether Doria really desired a pitched battle can never be known; that which is certain is that, during the whole time the fleets were in touch, all his dispositions make it appear there was nothing of which he was so much afraid. And yet it was the opportunity of his life; he had superiority in numbers, he had valiant and experienced leaders, and sixty thousand men thirsting for battle, under his command. Also he had his opportunity, which, had he seized upon, must have ended in victory, did those who were under his orders only fight as he had every reason to believe that they would. As it was, he threw away the gift of fortune, and left to the Osmanli the practical dominance of the Mediterranean Sea until that great day in 1571 when Don John of Austria, the natural son of Charles V., proved to the world at Lepanto that the Turk was not invincible upon the waters.

It is true that Doria was awkwardly situated; Kheyr-ed-Din held the interior position, and that leader was a great believer in the adage that "if Brag is a good dog, Holdfast is a better." He was well aware of his numerical inferiority, and in consequence refused to listen to the frenzied appeals of the excited Moslems to be led against the Christian dogs. It may seem a contradiction in terms to speak of the moral courage of a pirate; but if ever that quality were displayed to its fullest extent it was exhibited by Barbarossa in the Prevesa campaign. In his intellectual outlook on all that was passing, both inside and outside of the Gulf of Arta, in this September of 1538, we see Kheyr-ed-Din at his best. Ever a fighter, he knew when to give battle and when to refrain, when to sweep headlong upon the foe, but also when to hold back and to baffle by waiting till the psychological moment should arrive. Around him Sinan-Reis, Mourad-Reis, and half a hundred others of their kidney were clamouring; they hurled insults at his head, they heaped opprobrium on "the corsair," they practically incited their troops to mutiny in their mad appeals to be led against the foe.

But "the corsair" kept his head, and kept his temper, and saved the Ottoman fleet for his master from his great rival, Doria. That noble Genoese seaman was for once in his life "letting I dare not wait upon I would"; he would not order the attack for which his men were waiting, and no provocation, apparently, could tempt Barbarossa to play Antony to the Octavius of Doria; the Christian admiral was tempting Providence at that advanced season of the year in keeping the sea on an hostile coast on which at any time he might be driven by a tempest. His old and experienced antagonist was well aware that the winds and the waves might save him the trouble of destroying the fleet of the enemy; an equinoctial gale would do that far more effectually than could he. If Doria had an uneasy consciousness that he might at any time see the shore littered with oarless galleys and dismasted *nefs*, while the sea was filled with drowning men, the same vision had been vouchsafed to his imperturbable adversary. Had it been left to the entire initiative of Barbarossa, his Fabian tactics would assuredly have prevailed in the end; but as it was he was surrounded by a clamouring host of men, soldiers by trade, who, understanding nothing of the happenings of the sea, merely derided as cowardice any postponement of what they regarded as the inevitable battle. The admiral of the Sultan held out as long as it was possible, but at last, owing to a new factor in the case, was forced, against his better judgment, to offer the battle which it was in his power to have withheld.

CHAPTER 13

The Battle of Prevesa

How Alessandro Condalmiero fought the Galleon of Venice—
"The King of the Sea is dead."

There is something almost pathetic in the spectacle of a really great leader badgered and importuned by lesser men to adopt a course which he, with a superior insight, knows to be unsound. In the matter of the landing Barbarossa had demonstrated that it was he whose knowledge of war was superior to those who were so ready to thrust upon him their opinions; this, however, did not content them, and they now desired to close with the foe waiting for them outside. If ever a commander was justified in waiting on events it was Barbarossa at this juncture; the business of a commander-in-chief is to ensure victory, and if he sees, as did the Moslem admiral on this occasion, that more is to be gained by delay than by fighting, then he is justified in refusing battle: particularly is this the case when the enemy is in greatly superior force blockading on an open and dangerous coast at an inclement season of the year. Every day that Doria was kept at sea added to his difficulties, as fresh water and provisions would be running short, and the energies of the human engines by which his galleys were propelled would be weakened; naked men chained to a bench were suffering from the blazing heat of the days, the cold and drenching dews of the nights. All these things had the veteran seaman weighed in his mind, they all inclined him to wait still longer in that secure anchorage where he could not be touched by his foe.

There was one counsellor, however, whom even Kheyr-ed-Din could not resist, and who had hitherto kept silence; this was the eunuch Monuc, legal counsellor to Soliman, who had accompanied the armada. He now brought the weight of his influence to bear upon the side of Sinan-Reis and his colleagues.

"Are you going," he asked the admiral, "to allow the infidels to escape without a battle? Soliman can find plenty of wood to build new fleets, plenty of captains to command them; he will pardon you if this fleet is destroyed: that which he will never pardon is that you should allow Doria to escape without fighting. You have brave men in plenty; why not lead them to the attack?"

The patience of the veteran gave way at last; none who knew Barbarossa had ever seen him shrink from fighting—to this his whole career bore witness. He had delayed the issue from the soundest of strategical reasons, which those under his command were too stupid and too prejudiced to understand: what cared they for reason in their blind valour?—they wished only to do or die heedless of the fact that their lives might be spent in vain. Truly it was no thanks to the subordinates of Kheyr-ed-Din that this campaign did not end in disaster to the arms of the Ottoman Porte. Such backing as the admiral had came from among his own men, the corsairs whose lives had been spent at sea, but their opinions were but dust in the balance once the all-powerful Monuc ranged himself on the side of the malcontents.

"Let us then fight," said the admiral to Saleh-Reis, "or this fine talker who is neither man nor woman will accuse us before the Grand Turk and we shall all probably be hanged."

The Christian fleet during the night of September 26-7th had made some thirty miles to the southward; just before daybreak the wind freshened and drew right ahead; Doria approached the island of Santa Maura and anchored under the small islet of Sessola.

Barbarossa had now decided to leave his anchorage, but the veteran seaman did not disguise from himself the risks which he ran: a greater sea captain than he once said "only numbers can annihilate," and it was at annihilation that both the Moslem and the Christian aimed: in this case, however, he knew that he could but hope for a hard-won victory, and only that if Allah and his Prophet were unusually favourable to his cause. He assembled his captains, many of whom had served with him during long periods of his career, and directed them to form line: he said, "I have but one order to give, follow my movements attentively and regulate your own accordingly."

With *fustas*, brigantines, *galleots*, and galleys, the Ottoman fleet amounted in all to one hundred and forty sail. With shouts of joy the soldiers hailed the command to weigh the anchors, and in a very short time all were slowly moving seaward.

The die was cast: Doria from his anchorage at Sessola saw the sea white with the sails of the enemy, the blue water churning to foam beneath the strokes of his oars; the Ottoman fleet was issuing from the Gulf of Arta manoeuvring with precision and deploying into a single line abreast; which line being slightly concave, either from accident or design, resembled the form of a crescent. In advance came six great *fustas* commanded by Dragut; the left wing hugged the shore as closely as possible; the Ottoman commander-in-chief intended to commence operations on the first principles of strategy by flinging his whole force on a portion of that of the enemy.

Andrea Doria remained undecided: he was on a lee shore, and that shore was the coast of the enemy; although his foes were advancing to the attack it seemed as if he had no mind to fight: whether he had or had not he displayed a most remarkable sluggishness, hesitating for three hours before getting up his anchors; these he only weighed at last under pressure from the bellicose Patriarch of Aquilea, Vincenzo Capello, and the Papal captain, Antonio Grimani. Doria had counted on the support of the *Galleon of Venice* and the *nefs*; but the galleon was becalmed four miles from the land and ten miles from Sessola, where Doria was at the beginning of the action.

Condalmiero sent a light skiff from the *Galleon of Venice* to the commander-in-chief demanding orders and help from the galleys.

"Begin the fight," answered the admiral, "you will be succoured."

The position of Condalmiero was that of a modern battleship which is disabled and surrounded by foes in full possession of their motive power; the great galleon floated inert upon the waters while the galleys could fight or fly as they wished. The captain of the galleon, however, had no alternative save to surrender or fight; but there was no hesitation on his part, for a more gallant officer never trod the decks of a warship of the proud Republic to which he belonged.

The Moslem galleys were now close upon him, although as yet out of gun-shot; around him they wheeled and circled like a flight of great sea-birds, their ferocious crews shouting their war-cries calling upon Allah and the Prophet to give them the victory for which they craved; many a brave Venetian who heard for the first time the name of Barbarossa shouted in battle must have braced himself for the coming conflict, knowing all that was imported by that terrible name. The sun shone in a cloudless sky, the galleon lay becalmed in the middle of furious and ravening foes, the succour promised by Doria was ten miles away; they saw no movement which indicated help, and the odds against them were heavy indeed. But all the nervousness was not on one side, for the *Galleon of Venice* was something new in the naval warfare of the time; she carried engines of destruction in the shape of great guns which the corsairs could by no means equal. Of this they were well aware, and the attack was delayed while the oarsmen in the galleys rested on their oars out of range to allow them breathing time before the supreme moment arrived. But the hounds were only held in leash; there came a signal which was answered by a concentrated yell of fury and of hate; then from right ahead, right astern, on the port side and the starboard, the galleys were launched to the attack. But all on board the great Venetian vessel was as still as that death which awaited so many of the combatants in this supreme struggle.

Condalmiero had caused the crew of the galleon to lie down upon her decks, and stood himself, a gallant solitary figure in his shining armour, a mark for the hail of shot so soon to be discharged. It came, and with it the mast of the galleon bearing the Lion Standard of St. Mark crashed over the side into the water; renewed yells of triumph came from the Moslems, but still that ominous silence reigned on board the galleon. Untouched, unharmed, the Osmanlis came on firing as rapidly as possible until they were absolutely within *arquebus* range. Closer they came and closer; then the sides of the galleon burst into sheeted flame, and the guns levelled at point-blank range tore through the attacking host. Condalmiero was throwing away no chances; he had directed his gunners to allow their balls to ricochet before striking rather than to throw them away by allowing them to fly over the heads of the enemy.

The first broadside did terrible execution; a ball one hundred and twenty pounds in weight, fired by the chief bombardier, Francisco d'Arba in person, burst in the prow of a galley so effectually that all her people flew aft to the poop to prevent the water rushing in; but the vessel was practically split in twain, and sank in a few moments. All around were dead and dying men, disabled galleys, floating wreckage; the *Galleon of Venice* had taken a terrible toll of the Osmanli; the order to retreat out of range was given, and never was order obeyed with greater alacrity.

With accuracy and precision the galleon played upon such vessels as remained within range, doing great execution. But she was now to be subjected to an even severer test than the first headlong attack. She had demonstrated to the Moslem leaders that here was no vessel to be carried by mere reckless valour; a disciplined and ordered offensive was the only plan which promised success; the Osmanli must use their brain as well as their courage if that tattered flag, rescued from the water, and nailed to the stump of the mast of the galleon, was ever to be torn down. There was something daunting in the very aspect of the solid bulk of the huge Venetian, something weird in the manner in which her crew never showed, save only the steadfast figure of her captain immovable as a statue of bronze, where he stood on her shot-torn poop.

This Homeric conflict was a triumph of discipline and gunnery on the part of the Venetians; alert, accurate, and cool, the gunners of the galleon threw away none of their ammunition: inspired by the heroic spirit of their captain, great was the honour which they did on this stricken field to the noble traditions of their forbears and the service to which they belonged.

The first attack had been most brilliantly repulsed, but this was only preliminary to a conflict which was to last all through the day; the Moslem galleys withdrew out of gunshot and re-formed; then a squadron of twenty advanced, delivered their fire, and retired; their place was then taken by a second squadron, which went through the same performance, and then came on a third. In this manner the attack, which began one hour after noon, and which was continued until sunset, was conducted. The galleon had thirteen men killed, and forty wounded; no doubt the slaughter would have been much greater had it not been for the enormous thickness of her sides and for the fact that the guns carried by the galleys were necessarily light. Notwithstanding, the galleon suffered terribly, she was a mass of wreckage; twice fire had broken out on board of her, she was cumbered by fallen masts, battered almost out of recognition, but still Condalmiero and her gallant crew fought on imperturbably with no thought of surrender. Covered with blood, wounded in the face and the right leg by flying splinters, her captain preserved his magnificent coolness, and his decimated crew responded nobly to his call. At eventide the fire from the galleon was almost as deadly as it had been at the first onslaught, and many galleys of the Turks were only saved from sinking by the activity and bravery of their carpenters, who, slung over their sides in "boatswains' chairs," drove home huge plugs of wood with their mallets into the shot-holes made by the Venetian guns.

At the hour when the sun dipped below the horizon all the Turkish fleet seemed assembled to assault the colossus which so long had resisted their attack; there was a pause in the combat, and the firing died down. Condalmiero and his men braced themselves for the assault which they felt to be inevitable: for now the darkness was swiftly coming, in which they could no longer see to shoot, and under cover of which their numerous foes could assail them by boarding in comparative safety. Now the moment had come for the last act in this terrible drama of the sea. They had held their own at long odds throughout the whole of a hot September day, and as the level beams of the setting sun shone on their shattered ship they were prepared to die, fighting to the last man for the honour of Venice and the glory of St. Mark.

Stiff and worn, wearied almost to the breaking strain, there was no man on board who even dreamt of surrender; all the guns were charged to the muzzle with bullets and broken stone, the artillerists match in hand stood grimly awaiting the order to fire, straining their eyes and their ears in the gathering darkness; in a few minutes at most they knew that the fate of the *Galleon of Venice* must be decided.

On board his galley, decorated for this occasion with scarlet banners, Barbarossa himself directed the assaulting line. Never before when the battle was joined had the gallant corsair been known to draw back; and yet on this occasion he not only hesitated but actually hauled off. The Venetians saw to their amazement that the expected attack was not to be pushed home; for Barbarossa and his captains fell upon some lesser vessels: the *Galleon of Venice* was victorious.

Meanwhile Doria was displaying his mastery of tactics when it was hard fighting that was wanted; he pretended that he wished to draw the Ottoman fleet into the high seas in order that he might destroy their galleys by means of the broadsides of his *nefs*; consequently he executed useless parade movements when he should by all the rules of warfare have closed with his enemy who was in distinctly inferior force; as he had a fair wind there is only one conclusion to be drawn, and that is that he did not want to fight.

His manoeuvres certainly mystified the Turks, who viewed his tactics with mistrust, thinking them the outset of some deeply laid scheme; it never entered into their calculations for one moment that the great Andrea Doria, the terror of the Mediterranean sea, and the victor in scores of desperate engagements, was anxious to avoid a fight.

Grimani and Capello, docile to the orders of their admiral, followed him full of uneasiness and distrust; they were fighting men of the most fiery description; to them the issue seemed of the simplest: there was the enemy in inferior force to themselves, they had the weather gauge, why delay the attack?

"For much less than this," says Admiral Jurien de la Gravière, "the English shot Admiral Byng in 1756." The conduct of Doria on this occasion has certainly never been explained; the two other leaders went on board and remonstrated with their commander-in-chief; they were neither of them men who could be treated as negligible quantities on the field of battle; both belonged to that brilliant Venetian nobility so renowned in commerce and in war. Marco Grimani was in command of the Papal galleys, in itself a mark of the highest esteem and confidence from a potentate second to none in his influence in the civilised world. To Vincenzo Capello, Henry the Seventh of England confided his royal person and the command of his fleet when he crossed the Channel to encounter Richard the Second at Bosworth Field. Five times had he filled the office of Providiteur in Venice, twice had he been commander-in-chief of her fleet, he was in perpetuity Procureur of St. Mark, to him Venice owed her naval discipline. He wore on this day the mantle of crimson silk with which the Republic invested her generals. Bitter was the rage in his heart, and bitterly must he have spoken to Doria, who, in spite of all remonstrances, continued his futile manoeuvrings.

There was glory won on this day, but it was gained neither by Andrea Doria nor Kheyr-ed-Din Barbarossa. The *Galleon of Venice* with Alessandro Condalmiero and his gallant crew had shown to all a splendid example of disciplined valour unexcelled in sixteenth-century annals.

Barbarossa had captured a Venetian galley, a Papal galley, and five Spanish *nefs*, but he had recoiled from the assault on Condalmiero when the prize was actually within his grasp. For the rest it was a day of manoeuvring and tactics; tactics when sixty thousand men had been embarked on board two hundred ships for a specific and definite object on the side of the Christians and under the command of their most celebrated admiral; and yet the balance of advantage was actually gained by the inferior force. No subsequent glories can ever wipe this stain from the scutcheon of Doria, or can excuse the fact that at the most supreme moment of his career he failed to fight the battle that he was in honour, in conscience, and in duty bound to deliver. Next day the wind came fair for Corfu, and Doria, his ships untouched, unscathed, unharmed, put his helm up and sailed away followed by his fleet.

Sandoval records the fact that Barbarossa, roaring with laughter the while, was accustomed to say that Doria had even put out his lanterns in order that no one might see whither he had fled. This was an allusion to the fact—or supposition—that Doria extinguished on that night the great poop lantern carried by him as admiral.

When Soliman the Magnificent heard of the result of this battle he caused the town of Yamboli, where he was at the time, to be illuminated, and in the excess of his joy he added one hundred thousand *aspres* to the revenues of the conqueror; there were processions to the Grand Mosque, and all Islam rejoiced and sang the praises of the invincible admiral who had humbled to the dust the pride of the Christian and caused the dreaded Doria to fly from before the fleet of the Sultan.

This, the most historical, if not the greatest feat in the life of Kheyr-ed-Din Barbarossa, was for him a triumph indeed; with a vastly inferior force he had driven from the field of battle his "rival in glory," as he himself had denominated Andrea Doria, and he had accomplished this feat notwithstanding the almost mutinous condition of his own forces. In spite of this it is with Condalmiero and with him alone that the glory of this day must rest; alone, absolutely unsupported as we have seen, he fought one of those fights which bring the heart into the mouth when we read of them; the stern pride of the Venetian noble, who despised as canaille the pirate hosts by whom he was assailed, had its counterpart in the sturdy valour of Chief Bombardier Francisco d'Arba and the other nameless heroes of which that good company was composed; to them we render that homage which so justly is their due.

The whole campaign of Prevesa, as we have said, is a curious study in hesitation, in dilatoriness, in absolute lack of initiative and virility on the part of the two chief actors in the drama: that Doria should fly from the field of battle in an untouched ship is only one degree less incredible than that Barbarossa should have relinquished his attack on the *Galleon of Venice*. It would almost seem as if on this occasion each of the great rivals was hypnotised by the presence of the other; all their lives they had been seeking honour and riches on the sea, they knew, of course, that all men in both the world of Islam and that of Christendom looked upon them in the light of the special champions of the opposing sects, that the eyes of the entire world were fastened on this meeting of theirs in the classic waters of the Ambracian Gulf. In consequence neither man was at his best; indeed, we might go further than this, and say that on this occasion both lamentably failed. There is no fault to be found with the strategic preliminaries to the final conflict, each admiral acting with prudence and wisdom in the situation in which he found himself placed. That the perfectly correct idea of not giving battle to a superior force when he held so strong an interior position was given up by Barbarossa, was, as we have seen, not his fault; and when he issued from his anchorage, in deference to a sentiment among those under his command which he could no longer resist, his dispositions seem to have been made with his usual skill. Where he failed, however, was where, from all his previous history, we should least have expected failure, in his abandonment of the attack on the *Galleon of Venice*; this, of course, was inexcusable, and can only be set down to failure of nerve at the supreme moment. The ship had been battered by artillery all day long, a huge percentage of her company were dead and wounded, and the remainder worn out with fatigue. On the Moslem side we have seen that there were squadrons of galleys able to relieve one another with no interference from Doria, who was persisting in his futile manoeuvring miles away. Had the galleon been boarded, as she might and should have been, at nightfall, nothing could have saved Condalmiero and his crew: so strenuous, however, had been their resistance, that the Turkish seamen feared the issue; in consequence the battle between them and the Venetians was a drawn one, with all the honours on the Christian side.

It is here that we shall take leave of Kheyr-ed-Din Barbarossa, as although he was yet to live another eight years before he died in his bed at Constantinople in July, 1548, there are no further happenings of any great importance in his career.

"Valorous, yet prudent, furious in attack, far-seeing in preparation, he ranks as the first sea-captain of his time;"[1] as the story of his life has unfolded itself in these pages we have seen what manner of man it was who terrified Europe, who made for himself a reputation which stands out clear and distinct among all the great men of which this century was so prolific. One of the surest methods of estimating a strenuous man of action is to seek for the names of those by whom he was surrounded: the men selected by him to assist in the carrying out of the work of his life; thus in reading of Napoleon Bonaparte we interest ourselves in his marshals, in reading of Nelson we note the captains by whom he was supported. In the case of Kheyr-ed-Din Barbarossa, a great man of action if one ever lived, we find no trace of devoted adherents on that high plane of command we have indicated in the cases cited above. That he had devoted followers enough is absolutely certain, but of high officers we very seldom find a trace, and these he treated with contumely and offence on many occasions; witness the treatment meted out to Hassan and to Venalcadi. There is practically no trace of his domestic life to be found, we cannot discover that he possessed any intimate friend. There is none other in all history to whom he can be satisfactorily compared; there are few who in their generation have wielded such enormous powers, who have climbed so high from the sheer unassisted force of their own intellect and their own character.

---

1. Stanley Lane Poole.

Physical strength such as is vouchsafed to one man in a million, a constitution nothing could impair, endurance incomparable, were his bodily attributes: an intellect cold, clear, and penetrating was his, joined to an imperturbability of temperament which enabled him to accept with a cheerful philosophy blows by which weaker men were absolutely prostrated; his outlook on life was not dimmed by any affections, and pity was a sensation which to him was entirely alien. In this record of his deeds the reader has been spared all mention of the atrocious tortures he was in the habit of inflicting on his victims for any or no provocation, and many of them are as incomprehensible as they are sickening. That in which he was supreme was his craft as a seaman in an age when real seamen were rare; on land he was frequently defeated, at sea there seems to be no record of such an occurrence. To sum up, he appears to us in the light of history as a body, a brain, and an intellect, without any trace of a heart. His path through life was one unending trail of blood and fire, moistened by the tears of his countless victims, followed by the curses of those whom he despoiled. Yet, in spite of this, it is impossible not to admire the man who, by his own superhuman energy, ever swept all obstacles from his path, and caused the whole of the civilised world to quail at the name of Barbarossa.

He died peacefully in his bed at Constantinople in July, 1546, to the grief of the world of Islam and the inexpressible joy of Christendom. "The king of the sea is dead," expressed in three Arabic words, gives the numerical value 953, the year of the Hegira in which he died.

For many years after his death no Turkish ship ever left the Golden Horn without her crew repeating a prayer and firing a salute over the tomb of Beshiktsah, where lie the bones of the first and greatest of Turkish admirals, the corsair who was at one and the same time admiral, pirate, and king.

CHAPTER 14

The Galley, the Galeasse and the Nef

In the sixteenth century the vessel of war in the Mediterranean was essentially that oar-propelled craft known to us as the galley. As time went on she was gradually superseded by the sailing man-of-war which was able to carry that heavy ordnance which the light scantling of the galley did not permit of her mounting; but for the use of the corsairs who lived by means of raids and surprise attacks, whose business it was to lie *perdu* on the trade routes, the mobility of the galley was of prime importance, and they could not afford to trust to the wind alone as a motive power. The galley was analogous to the steam vessel in that it was independent of the wind to a large extent: human bone and muscle supplied the part of engines, and those who fought upon the sea caused themselves to be moved over the face of the waters by the exertions of their enemies. It is true that upon one occasion, as we have seen, Kheyred-Din Barbarossa did possess a fleet of galleys the rowers of which were all Moslems, which crew upon battle being joined dropped their oars, seized their weapons and assisted in the conquest of the foe. But this was an isolated instance, as it was almost impossible at any time and in any circumstances to procure free men ready to undertake a life of such intolerable suffering as that of a rower on board a galley; in consequence these men were almost invariably slaves, or else in later times condemned felons whose judges had sent them to work out their sentences upon the rowers' bench. The great characteristic of the galley was her mobility, and in a comparative degree her speed, as for a short burst, when her crew of rowers were fresh, their trained muscles were capable of tremendous exertion; for any length of time, however, it is obvious that her speed must have declined as the rowers became exhausted. She was long, narrow, of extremely low freeboard, and slight depth of hold; a galley of 125 feet between perpendiculars would perhaps be 180 feet over

Galley under oars

all taking in the poop and the prow. A galley of this length would only have a beam of 19 feet and a depth of hold of 7 feet 6 inches. The sailing ship of contemporary times would for the same length have had a beam of about 40 feet and an extremely high freeboard; she was in consequence necessarily slow and incapable of sailing on a wind.

So distinct at this time was the line drawn between the sailing vessel and the galley that the actual terminology used was entirely different; that is to say, the names of such things as masts, sails, rudder, tiller, stern, stempost, cutwater, etc., were not the same words; the sailor who used sails could not understand his brother mariner who used oars, and *vice versa*.

What was necessary of course in the galley was many oars and many hands to use them; the vessel was most skilfully constructed for this purpose so as to get the fullest power from her human engines; the result was that men were crowded on board of her to such an extent that there was scarcely room to breathe, such a craft as the one of which the dimensions have been given having on board some four hundred men.

Barras de la Penne, a French officer who in 1713 first went on board a galley, thus describes what he saw:

> Those who see a galley for the first time are astonished to see so many persons; there are an infinite number of villages in Europe which do not contain an equal number of inhabitants; however, this is not the principal cause of one's surprise, but that so many men can be assembled in so small a space. It is truth that many of them have not room to sleep at full length, for they put seven men on one bench; that is to say, on a space about ten feet long and four broad; at the bows one sees some thirty sailors who have for their lodging the floor space of the *rambades* (this is the platform at the prow of the galley) which consists of a rectangular space ten feet long by eight in width. The captain and officers who live on the poop are scarcely better lodged, and one is tempted to compare their grandeur with that of Diogenes in his tub.
>
> When the unpitying Libyan Sea surprises these galleys upon the Roman coasts, when the Norther lashes to foam the Gulf of Lyons, when the humid east wind of Syria is driving them off shore, everything combines to make life on board a modern galley a hell of misery and discomfort. The creaking of the blocks and cordage, the loud cries of the sailors, the horrible

maledictions of the galley slaves, the groaning of the timbers, mingled with the clank of chains and the bellowings of the tempest, produce sentiments of affright in the most intrepid breasts. The rain, the hail, the lightning, habitual accompaniments of these terrific storms, the waves which dash over the vessel, all add to the horror of the situation, and although devotion is not as a rule very strongly marked on board a galley, you will hear these folk praying to God, and others making vows to the Saints; these would do much better not to forget God and his Saints when the danger is past.

Calm itself has also its inconveniences, as the evil smells which arise from the galley are then so strong that one cannot get away from them in spite of the tobacco with which one is obliged to plug one's nostrils from morning till night.

The gallant officer here goes into further details concerning the vermin on board which it will be as well to spare the reader.

Jean Marteille de Bergeraq, who died at Culenbourg in 1777, was condemned to serve on board the galleys in 1707 "in his quality of Protestant"; he must indeed have been a man of iron constitution as he lived to the age of ninety-five. This is his description of the life of a *forçat*:

> They are chained six to a bench; the benches are four feet wide covered with sacking stuffed with wool over which are thrown sheepskins which reach to the floor. The officer who is master of the galley slaves remains aft with the captain to receive his orders; there are two under officers, one amidships and one at the prow; all of these are armed with whips, with which they flog the absolutely naked bodies of the slaves. When the captain gives the order to row, the officer gives the signal with a silver whistle which hangs on a cord round his neck; the signal is repeated by the under officers and very soon all the fifty oars strike the water as one. Imagine six men chained to a bench as naked as they were born, one foot on the stretcher the other raised and placed on the bench in front of them, holding in their hands an oar of enormous weight, stretching their bodies towards the after part of the galley with arms extended to push the loom of the oar clear of the backs of those in front of them who are in the same attitude. They plunge the blades of the oars into the water and throw themselves back, falling on to the seat which bends beneath their weight. Sometimes the galley slaves row thus ten, twelve, even twenty hours at a stretch, without

the slightest relapse or rest, and on these occasions the officer will go round putting into the mouths of the wretched rowers pieces of bread soaked in wine to prevent them from fainting. Then the captain will call upon the officers to redouble their blows, and if one of the slaves falls fainting upon his oar, which is a common occurrence, he is flogged until he appears to be dead and is then flung overboard without ceremony.

The Italian captain, Pantero Pantera, of the *Santa Lucia* galley, in his work on *L'Armata Navale* published in 1614, gives it as his opinion that although soldiers and sailors could be obtained for service in the galleys if good pay were given, still no money could tempt any free man to adventure himself as a rower for any length of time owing to the intolerable sufferings which the *"gallerian"* was called upon to endure. As, however, in the opinion of the captain it was most necessary that the galleys should be manned, he thought that all judges should in future send criminals aboard; those who had committed murder as "lifers," those who had committed lesser crimes *pro rata*. Those who by the nobility of their birth or their physical incompetence were unable to handle the oar should be called upon to pay for substitutes to act for them; these were called "*Buone-Voglie.*"

There was not much difference after all between the methods used by the seventeenth-century Italian to those actually in force in England at a much later date when the Press Gang swept the honest and the dishonest into its net in its midnight raids. Pantera observes:

> The galley slaves cherish repose and sincerely wish to avoid fatigue; in order to incite them to do their duty it is necessary to use the whip as well as the whistle; by using it with severity the officers will find that they are better obeyed, and it will in consequence be good for the service, for fear of the whip is the principal cause of good behaviour among the *gallerians*.

Further on he observes that it is well not to flog them too severely and without reason:

> .... for this irritates the *gallerians*, as I have frequently observed: this may cause them to despair and to wish for death as the only sure way out of their troubles.

The excellent Pantera a little later on even says that he cannot agree that the attempt to cure a sick *gallerian* "is all nonsense, as is maintained by some persons," as sick men are a source of danger on board. He apparently was not prepared to throw them overboard alive, but urges that the best way to avoid such pestilences among them as killed forty thousand Venetians at the port of Zara in 1570 is to embark sound and good victuals.

It is interesting to have a contemporary view of the correct treatment of the galley slave from those who had to do with him. In the case of the corsairs and their adversaries the *gallerians* were as a rule prisoners of war, but as time went on and wars became less frequent than they were throughout the sixteenth century, another source of supply was tapped by sending to the galleys the criminals of any country which desired to fill up the rowers' benches. In consequence there was always one thing which was feared above all others on board a galley, and that was a rising of the slaves.

If they were not your enemies officially, they were a set of desperate criminals ripe for any mischief should they get loose, and chained, starved, beaten, frozen with the cold, baked by the summer heats, tortured, murdered, they had nothing earthly for which to hope except escape. If in the heat of battle there should occur a rising of the slaves, then their masters knew that victory would declare itself surely on the side of the enemy. Therefore that they should be securely chained was the first and most important thing to which the boatswain of a galley and his mates had to see. If by a bold stroke they once freed themselves from their shackles it was a fight to the death for those who erstwhile had been in command, as the *gallerians*, outnumbering them and caring nought for their lives in comparison to their liberties, were far the most formidable foes that they could be called upon to encounter. When men are so treated that their daily life is one long martyrdom they become the most dangerous force in existence, and on the occasions which sometimes happened that the slaves got the upper hand, there were none left of the fighting men of the galley to tell the tale of their discomfiture.

In time of battle the *gallerians* were of course equally exposed to death and wounds from the projectiles of the enemy as were the orthodox fighting men; but to them came no rejoicing at the sound of victory; rather they prayed for the defeat of their masters, as it frequently happened that those against whom they were arrayed were their own countrymen and friends by whom they hoped for release. Thus at Lepanto, the Christian slaves, seeing the right wing of the Turkish fleet thrown into disorder by the galleys of the Allies, broke out into furious mutiny, succeeded in shattering their fetters and chains, attacked their masters the Turks in the rear with incredible energy with any weapons upon which they could lay their hands, and thus contributed in no small measure to the ultimate triumph of the Christian arms.

The Captain Pantero Pantera and Barras de la Peine have written exhaustively on the galley, her crew, her armament, her manner of provisioning, her masts, sails, rigging, etc., and Admiral Jurien de la Gravière has given a most painstaking exposition concerning the technicalities of these craft. But to enter into too much detail would be to weary the reader unnecessarily, who, it is apprehended, merely desires that a general idea should be given of the way in which these vessels were handled and fought.

It would appear that during the whole time that oar-propelled vessels were used as warships their form did not differ to any material extent, as certain limitations of size were obviously imposed on them by the mere fact that they had to be moved by so finite and feeble a force as human muscles, hearts, and lungs. No cruelty, however ghastly, could extract from the *gallerians* more than a certain amount of work, and the Captain Pantero Pantera, as we have seen, even advocates that a certain minimum of consideration should be shown to them in order that better work might be obtained. It was probable, however, that in the case of the Christian slaves captured by the corsairs even this minimum was to seek, as the numbers swept off by them were so enormous that they could be used up and replaced without inconveniencing these rovers of the sea, to whom compassion for suffering was absolutely unknown.

The Knights of St. John of Jerusalem, or the Knights of Malta as they were also called, used the galley in their unceasing warfare with the Moslem. The General of the Galleys was a Grand Cross of the order; the captains were knights, and the second officer, or first lieutenant, was known as the Patron. The crew of a galley of the knights had twenty-six rowing benches and carried two hundred and eighty rowers and two hundred and eighty combatants; the armament consisted of one bow cannon which discharged a forty-eight pound ball, four other small guns, eight pounders, and fourteen others which discharged stones.

"The Religion," as the Knights were in the habit of describing themselves, had certain definite stations assigned to each knight, seaman, or officer during action. It is to be imagined, however, that these were merely for the preliminary stages of the fight, as it was seldom that time allowed for more than one discharge, or at the most two, of the artillery, before the opposing galleys met in a hand-to-hand conflict which must have immediately become an indiscriminate melee.

The manner in which the galley should engage is thus contained in an answer to a question of Don John of Austria, the victor of Lepanto. He wrote to Garcia de Toledo, fourth Marquis of Villafranca, and General of the Galleys of Sicily, to ask his opinion as to what distance it was most efficacious to open fire in a naval action. Toledo replied:

> .... one cannot fire more than twice before the galleys close. I should therefore recommend that the *arquebussiers* should hold their fire until they are so close to the enemy that his blood will leap into the face of him who discharges his piece. have always heard it said, and this by captains who are well skilled in the art of war, that the last discharge of the cannon should be coincident with the noise made by the breaking of the spurs carried in the prows of the galleys; in fact that the two noises should be as one; some propose to fire before the enemy does: this is by no means my advice.

Artillery, it will be seen from this, played a comparatively unimportant part in the combats between galley and galley; that in these craft men still relied on the strength of their right arm and the edge of their swords; there was still a certain contempt for villainous *saltpetre*, which was looked upon as a somewhat cowardly substance, preventing the warrior from settling his disputes in the good old fashion of his forbears. In any case, when you practically had to push the muzzle of your gun against your enemy's body in order to hit him, it was not a weapon upon which much reliance was to be placed.

There were, in addition to the galley, the *nef* and the *galeasse*; the former of these was a sailing vessel pure and simple like those remarkable caravels in which Columbus discovered America.

What these caravels were exactly like it was the good fortune of the writer to see in the year 1893. This was the date of the great exhibition of Chicago, and the American Government were most anxious to have, and to exhibit if possible, an exact replica of these historic craft. They accordingly communicated with the Spanish Government and inquired if by any chance they possessed the plans and specifications of the caravels of Columbus? Search was made in the archives of Cadiz Dockyard and these priceless documents were discovered. From them the ships were built in every respect the same as the wonderful originals and then towed across the Atlantic by the United States cruiser *Lancaster*. On their way they were brought to Gibraltar, where the writer's ship was then stationed, and were anchored inside the New Mole. The *Santa Maria*, the flagship of Columbus, was a three-masted vessel with a very high "forecastle" and "sterncastle" and very deep in the waist; she had three masts, the foremast carrying one square sail, the mainmast having both mainsail and main-topsail, the mizzen was rigged with a lateen sail, on the mainsail was painted the Maltese and on the foresail the Papal cross, and on deck she carried a brick-built cooking galley. A most beautiful model of this vessel is to be seen in the Science and Art Department of the South Kensington Museum.

The *nef* in its later manifestations became a much more seaworthy vessel than this, with four masts, the two foremost ones square-rigged and carrying courses and topsails, the two after ones carrying lateen sails; the latter from their small size and their proximity to one another could not have had much effect on the sailing qualities of the ship. The *nefs* in the fleet of Don John of Austria in 1571 were rigged in this fashion and comprised vessels of eight hundred, nine hundred, and even one thousand tons, while a contemporary English vessel, the *Great Harry* or *Henri Grace à Dieu*, was as much as fifteen hundred tons, and carried no less than one hundred and eighty-four pieces of ordnance. It was from the *nef* and the *galeasse* that the sailing man-of-war arrived by the process of evolution. The galley in the first instance was the vessel of men who fought hand to hand, the men in whom personal strength and desperate valour were blended, who desired nothing so much as to come to close grips with their enemy. Such rude engines of war as the *pierriers*, or short cannons which discharged some forty or fifty pounds of broken stone upon the enemy, were first mounted in the galley; these were followed by improved artillery as time went on. But although the galleys eventually carried quite big guns, as instanced by the forty-eight pounder in the galleys of the Knights of St. John, still it soon became apparent that the limit was reached by guns of this weight; the galley was essentially a light vessel and was not built to withstand those rude shocks caused by firing heavy charges of powder.

The *galeasse* was the connecting link between the navy of oars and the navy of sails. The navy of oars was in its generation apt for warlike purposes; but it was in its essence a force analogous to the light cavalry of the land; useful for a raid, a sudden dash, but without that great strength and solidity which came in later years to the building of the sailing line of battleship.

The *galeasse* was really a magnified galley, one which used both sails and oars, on board of which the rowers were under cover; she was built with a forecastle and a sterncastle which were elevated some six feet above the benches of the rowers, and her very long and immensely heavy oars were of course proportionate to the size of the vessel. The description of a *galeasse* of nearly one thousand tons burden is set forth as follows by Jurien de la Gravière:

> Her draught of water was about 18 feet 6 inches, she was propelled by 52 oars, 48 feet in length, each oar being worked by 9 men. Her crew consisted of 452 rowers, 350 soldiers, 60 marines, 12 steersmen, 40 ordinary seamen, 86 cannoneers, 12 petty officers, 4 boatswains' mates, 3 pilots, 2 sub-pilots, 4 counsellors, 2 surgeons, 4 writers, 2 sergeants, 2 carpenters, 2 caulkers, 2 coopers, 2 bakers, 10 servants, a captain, a lieutenant, a purser. In all some thousand men, or about the same number as the crew of a three-decker of a later date.

The fleet of the "Holy League" at the battle of Lepanto had in it six *galeasses* from the arsenal of Venice; and whereas an average galley carried 110 soldiers and 222 galley slaves, the crews of these *galeasses* comprised 270 soldiers, 130 sailors, and 300 galley slaves.

The speed of the galley was calculated by the French engineer Forfait to be in the most favourable circumstances, that is to say in a flat calm, but four and a half knots for the first hour, and two and a quarter to one and a half miles per hour for subsequent hours; the exhaustion of the rowers consequent on their arduous toil would not admit of a greater speed than this. The studies of Forfait were made when the invasion of England by rowing boats was a topic of burning interest. It is evident from this that long voyages, trusting to the oar alone, could not be undertaken; but as we have seen, the galley was also provided with motive power in the shape of two masts carrying the lateen sail, which may be still seen in so many Mediterranean craft.

That the galley was no vessel in which to embark in bad weather is instanced for us by the disasters which befell a Spanish fleet of these craft in 1567 under the Grand Commander of Castile, Don Luiz de Requesens. A revolt of the Moors in Granada had caused Philip the Second to wish to withdraw a certain number of Spanish troops from Italy. Requesens was sent to Genoa with twenty-four galleys to embark a detachment of an army corps then stationed in Piedmont. Each galley embarked one hundred and fifty soldiers; they then got under way and reached the island of Hyères, where they anchored, the weather being too bad to proceed. At the end of their eighth day in port a number of vessels were seen flying to the eastward before the wind; it was a squadron of Genoese.

Requesens, who was no seaman, was furious. Here were the Genoese at sea, and he wasting his time in harbour; if they could keep the sea why could not he, he demanded? He instantly ordered the anchors to be weighed. The commander of the Tuscan galleys, of which there were ten in the fleet, immediately went on board the galley in which Requesens was embarked and represented that the wind was foul and that should they leave their anchorage they could make no headway once they got clear of the land. But Requesens was obstinate: "if others can go on their way it is shameful that I should not proceed on mine," he protested. Alfonso d'Aragona argued with him in vain, representing that his master, the Duke of Tuscany, would hold the Grand Commander responsible for damage to his galleys. It was all in vain, as the Grand Commander was too arrogant and stupid to listen to advice from anybody. The fleet put to sea and struggled out a mile from the land; when they got thus far Requesens discovered his mistake and regretted that he had not taken the advice of the mariners; but it was now too late, they had drifted to leeward of their anchorage and could not get back again.

One galley, a new vessel, ran into another which was an old one, and sank her on the spot, carrying all her luckless crew to the bottom. The remaining vessels scattered far and wide; Alfonso d'Aragona found refuge in the Bay of Alghieri, two more of his galleys reached an anchorage in the Isle of St. Pierre, another sheltered in the Gulf of Oristano; three galleys were shipwrecked on the coast in this neighbourhood and lost many of their men; yet another, called the *Florence*, was twice nearly wrecked on the coast of Barbary, and eventually reached the Bay of Cagliari. A Genoese captain found himself as far afield as the Island of Pantellaria, two galleys were never heard of again, and the Grand Commander himself anchored eventually in the Bay of Palamos on the Spanish coast. Of the twenty-four galleys which left their anchorage twelve were lost and the twelve which remained were practically valueless until large sums had been spent in repairs.

It is small wonder in the light of these events that the seamen who ranged the Mediterranean in vessels propelled by oars regarded the winter as a close season and laid up their galleys in harbour. They were seaworthy enough for ordinary weather, but could not withstand such a tempest as the one in which Requesens put to sea. The whole story is only a further proof of the folly of putting supreme command of a sea-going venture in the hands of a man totally ignorant of the hazards he was called upon to encounter. In the sixteenth and even in the seventeenth centuries this was done perpetually, and if no disaster occurred it was because no bad weather was encountered.

Brigantine chasing a felucca

As time went on the sailing ship became larger and larger and was able to mount more and more powerful ordnance; this had the effect of discounting the value of the galley as a fighting ship; in consequence she became practically obsolete, for the line of battle, after the combat at Lepanto. In spite of this she was to linger on for many long years to come as the weapon of the corsairs who had established themselves on the coast of Africa. The "long ship" was still to be the cause of many an awful sea tragedy, whether the actors therein were the pirates who hailed from the Barbary coast or their most capable imitators the notorious rovers of Sallee.

Chapter 15
Dragut-Reis

In character, in capability, in strategic insight, in tactical ability, not one of the predecessors or the successors of Kheyr-ed-Din Barbarossa can be compared to him; he was the greatest and most outstanding figure of all those corsairs of whose deeds we hear so much during the sixteenth century, the man above all others who was feared and hated by his contemporaries in Christendom. He lived, as we have said, for another eight years after the battle of Prevesa, but his great age prevented him from pursuing a very active career. There were, however, other and younger men, trained in the terrible school of hardship in which his life had been passed, who proved themselves to be his very worthy successors, even if they did not display the same genius in war and statecraft. The conditions of this period are somewhat remarkable when we come to consider them; Europe, which had been sunk in a rude and uncultured barbarism during the middle ages, was emerging under the influence of the Renaissance into a somewhat higher and nobler conception of life. It is true that the awakening was slow, that morally the plane on which the peoples stood was far from being an elevated one, that altruism was far from being the note of the lives lived by the rulers of the so-called civilised nations. For all this they had emerged from that cimmerian darkness in which they had lived so long, and the dawn of better things, of more stable government, of some elementary recognition of the rights of those governed, was beginning to show above the murky horizon.

But if the sun of European progress was slowly and painfully struggling through the clouds, the light which had shone brightly for over seven centuries of Moslem advance was certainly and surely dying. Beneath the mail-clad heel of the Christian warrior the torch of learning which had burned so brightly in Cordova and Granada had been extinguished and ground into the dust, and the descendants of the alumni of those universities were seeking their bread in the Mediterranean Sea in the guise of bloodthirsty and desperate pirates.

There were no longer among the Moors of Andalusia learned philosophers, expert mathematicians, wise astronomers, and practical agriculturists; there was among them but one art, one science, one means of gaining a livelihood—the practice of war—and their very existence depended on the spoils which could be reft from the hereditary enemy. The corsair who grew to man's estate, brought up in Algiers, Tunis, Tenes, Jerba, or any other of the lurking places in which the sea-wolves congregated, had as a rule no chance but to follow the sea, to exist as his father had existed before him; he must fight or starve, and in a fighting age no youngster was likely to be backward in taking to the life of wild excitement led by his elders. Unless following in the train of one of the leaders, such as Barbarossa, the Moslems were apt to take to the sea in a private capacity; a certain number of them joining together to man a small craft which was known as a brigantine. As has been said in a previous chapter, this word must not be understood in the light of the terminology of the modern seaman: the brigantines of the Moslem corsairs were really large rowing boats, carrying fourteen to twenty-six oars, and made as seaworthy as the small size of such craft would allow. Should the venture of the crew of a brigantine prove successful, then the *reis*, or captain, might blossom out into the command of a galley, in which his oars would be manned by his slaves; but, in the first instance, he would man his brigantine with a crew of Moslem desperadoes working on the share system and dividing anything that they could pick up; in this manner most of those corsairs who became famous commenced their careers, and rose as we have seen from the thwart of a brigantine to the unstable eminence of a throne in Algiers, Tunis, or Tlemcen.

This life which they led made of them what they were, namely desperate swordsmen, efficient men at arms, incomparably skilful in the management of the craft in which they put to sea; but it did nothing else for them in the way of education; in consequence he who would rise to the top, who aspired to be a leader amongst them and not to remain a mere swash-buckling swordsman all his life, was bound to acquire that dominance necessary for control of the wild spirits of the age. Nor was this ascendancy by any means easy to obtain, as the rank and file led lives of incredible bitterness, almost inconceivable to modern ideas. What they suffered they alone knew, but it was compounded of hunger, thirst, heat, cold, sickness unrelieved by care or tending, wounds which festered for lack of medicaments, death which ever stared them in the face, and last, and worst of all, the risk of capture by some Christian foe, by whom they would be chained to the rowers' bench and taste of a bitterness absolutely unimaginable. As a set-off to this the man who aspired to lead must offer to his followers at least a record of success in small things; also he had to be something of an enthusiast, something of an orator, some one subtly persuasive. Against all the disagreeables of the strenuous life of the corsair he had to hold before the dazzled eyes of Selim, Ali, or Mahomet the promise of fat captures of the merchant vessels of the foe; when they had but to slit a few throats and to return with their brigantines laden to the gunwale with desirable plunder. Again he had to hearten them for possible encounters with Spaniards, with the terrible Doria, or worst of all with the dreaded Knights of St. John themselves; to point out that to die in conflict with the *infidel* was a sure passport to heaven and its *houris*, and to invoke great names, such as that of Barbarossa to show to what dizzy heights the fighting Moslem could climb. In such an age and among such men as these it was no mean feat to become a leader by whom men swore and to whom they yielded a ready obedience.

Fashioned by the hammer of misfortune on the anvil of racial expropriation, such leaders arose among the Moslems, men of iron, before whom all who worshipped at the altars of Islam bowed the knee. These men, whose fame extended throughout all the length and breadth of the Mediterranean, taught to European rulers something of the value of that great force which is known to us under the modern name of "Sea Power."

Next in importance to Kheyr-ed-Din Barbarossa himself and in many ways his very worthy successor, was Dragut Reis. We have it on the authority of Messire Pierre de Bourdeille, the Seigneur de Brantôme, that Dragut was born at a small village in Asia Minor called Charabulac, opposite to the island of Rhodes, and that his parents were Mahommedans. Being born within sight and sound of the sea, the youthful Dragut naturally graduated in the school of the brigantine and completed his education on board of a galley. His training was that which makes the best of fighting seamen, as from contemporary records he appears to have passed all his life actively engaged on board ship. At a very early age he entered the service of a master gunner who served on board the galleys of the Grand Turk. Under his auspices the youngster became an expert pilot in his own home waters, and likewise a most excellent gunner. Dragut was evidently a youth of ability and determination, as almost before he reached man's estate he had succeeded in buying a share in a cruising brigantine where his venture prospered so exceedingly that he was soon able to become sole proprietor of a *galeasse*. Here again fortune favoured the enterprising young man; his name began to be known as a formidable corsair in the Levant, where he was remarkable for his knowledge of that portion of the Mediterranean.

To better his condition he offered his services to Barbarossa at Algiers, who accepted this new subordinate with joy, delighted to have so valiant and capable a man under his orders.

"During some years," says J. Morgan in his *Compleat History of Algiers*, 1728:

> .... he was by that *basha* entrusted in the direction of sundry momentous expeditions; in which he acquitted himself much to the satisfaction of his principal: as having never once been unsuccessful.

When we remember the treatment meted out by Barbarossa to some of his unsuccessful lieutenants, Dragut must be esteemed a very fortunate man. His master, we are told, advanced him to all the military offices of the State—it would be interesting to know what these were in a purely piratical confederation ruled by a pirate! In the end Dragut was appointed to be *kayia*, or lieutenant, and given entire command of twelve galleys.

> From thenceforward this redoubtable corsair passed not one summer without ravaging the coasts of Naples and Sicily; nor durst any Christian vessel attempt to pass between Spain and Italy; for if they offered it he infallibly snapped them up, and when he missed his prey at sea, he made himself amends by making descents along the coasts plundering villages and towns and dragging away multitudes of inhabitants into captivity.

That "no vessel durst pass from Spain to Italy" is no doubt a picturesque form of exaggeration on the part of the historian; at the same time, when Dragut was at the height of his activities there is no doubt that any one passing through those seas ran a great risk of capture; so much so in fact that at this period, from 1538, the date of the battle of Prevesa, until Lepanto in 1571, all maritime commerce in the Mediterranean was greatly circumscribed. At the beginning of this epoch, which saw the rise of the Moslem corsairs, these robbers perforce confined themselves more to the North African coast than was the case later on. The pioneers of the piratical movement, after the fatal date 1492, which saw the wholesale expulsion of the Moors from Spain, were comparatively speaking inexpert practitioners in the art and mystery of piracy; they had not the habit of the sea, and in consequence confined their depredations to the neighbourhood of their own selected ports in Africa, which dominated that sea lane running east and west through the Mediterranean, which then, as now, was one of the greatest highways of commerce of the world. Gradually, as we have seen, under the able guidance of the two Barbarossas, but particularly that of the second and greater of the two, piracy became a commonplace in the north, as well as in the south, of the tideless sea; the corsairs, as time went on, even devoting more time and attention to the coast of Italy and the islands of the archipelago than they did to the recognised trade routes. These latter had become by 1540 similar to an estate which has been shot over too frequently; birds had become both wild and scarce, it was hardly worth while to go over the ground, except now and again on the chance of picking up a straggler. Towns and islands, on the other hand, even if they did not yield much in the way of actual plunder, were always good cover to beat for slaves, which had a certain value in the markets of Algiers and Tunis. Another circumstance which had led to the now frequent raids on the littoral of the European countries was the countenance and support accorded to the corsairs by the Grand Turk: so admirably did they fit into the scheme of his ambitions, that by the time Dragut arrived at a commanding position they were, so to speak, officially recognised as a fighting asset of the Sublime Porte; and, as we have seen, the Sultan did not hesitate to lend his picked troops, the Janissaries, to the corsairs when engaged in their ordinary piratical business. To the Grand Turk the corsairs were Moslems who were prepared to fight on his side, and who, taking it all in all, really cost him hardly anything; in fact, at this date, owing to the magnificent gifts made to the Sultan by Kheyr-ed-Din, the Padishah must have made something out of his association with the sea-wolves.

By the year 1540 Dragut had distinctly "arrived"; that is to say, he had succeeded in making himself so dreaded that Charles V. ordered Andrea Doria to seek him out and destroy him at any cost. The Christian admiral was "to endeavour by all possible means to purge the sea of so insufferable a nuisance."

Andrea got ready a fleet, which he entrusted, together with the care and management of this affair, to his nephew Jannetin Doria. This was the nephew who, in the disastrous attack by Charles on

Hassan Aga at Algiers in the following year, was so nearly lost in the storm which destroyed the fleet of the emperor; and of whom Andrea Doria is reported to have said, "It was decreed that Jannetin should be reduced to such an extremity purposely to convince the world that it was not impossible for Andrea Doria to shed a tear." Certainly from what we know of the celebrated Genoese admiral it is hard to imagine him in a tearful mood. Jannetin Doria put to sea, and, after a long hunt, found the object of his quest at Andior on the coast of Corsica; Dragut was at anchor in the road of Goialatta, under a castle situated between Cabri and Liazzo. The corsair knew nothing of his enemies being at sea, and was in consequence keeping no particular look-out. Although we are not told the composition of the fleet of Jannetin Doria, it must have been a large one, as Dragut had under his orders thirteen galleys, and was unable to withstand the attack to which he was subject. He was also assailed from the shore, as well as the sea, as the castle under which he was at anchor opened fire upon him as soon as it was discovered by its garrison that the new arrivals were Christians. The fire was too hot for the corsair to withstand, and, to add to his embarrassments, the beach soon became lined by hundreds of the fierce Corsi, awaiting the inevitable end when they should be able to fall upon the defeated Moslems and wipe them from off the face of the earth; it was a warfare in which there was no mercy, and if the pirates were to fall into the hands of the islanders they knew well that they would be exterminated.

In all his venturesome life things had never gone so badly with Dragut as upon this occasion. On the one side, should he and his men land they would be massacred; on the other hand, his road to the open sea was barred by an immensely superior force. Recognising the logic of circumstances, and seeing no way of escape, the white flag was hung out by the Moslem leader. The only terms, however, which he could obtain were immediate surrender or instant death. It must have been a moment of anguish to the man who hitherto had always ridden on the crest of the wave of success and achievement to be thus trapped like a rat; and to have the added bitterness of the thought that had he exercised seamanlike care and precaution in keeping a good look-out he might have escaped. As it was, he was allowed no time for reflection, but had to decide on the instant: he did the only thing possible in the circumstances, which was to haul down his flag and to become the thrall of his lifelong foes.

The principal captives were made to pass before young Doria. When

Dragut beheld him he cried out in a fury: "What! Am I a slave to that effeminate Caramite?" for Doria was but a beardless youth. These opprobrious epithets being interpreted to the young nobleman:

> . . . . highly incensed he flew at Dragut, tore out his beard and moustaches, and buffeted him most outrageously: nay his passion was so great it is said that had he not been prevented, he certainly would have sheathed his sword in the bowels of that assuming prisoner.

For four long years Dragut rowed in Doria's galley. No distinctions were made in those days, and knight or noble, companion or grand master, *basha* or boy, was, if caught, condemned to the rowers' bench to slave at the oar beneath the boatswain's lash, perchance alongside some degraded criminal, filthy and swarming with vermin. While Dragut was employed as a galley slave there came on board the craft in which he rowed Monsieur Parisot, grand master of the Knights of Malta. This high officer, recognising his old enemy, called out to him in Spanish:

"*Hola, Señor Dragut, usanza de guerra*" ("The usage of war, Señor Dragut").

To which the undaunted corsair merely replied with a laugh:

"*Y mudanza de fortuna*" ("And a change of luck").

The grand master, who had known the chain and lash himself, smiled and passed on—there was no pity in those days.

But Dragut was not destined to end his life as a galley slave, for, when indeed hope must have died within him, after more than four years of this veritable hell upon earth, there sailed one day into the harbour of Genoa the great Kheyr-ed-Din himself. The *Admiralissimo* of the Grand Turk, full of years, honours, and booty, was on his last cruise, and one of the last acts of his active life was the rescue of Dragut, the man who had served him so well, and for whom he had so high a regard as a resourceful mariner, from the degrading servitude into which he had fallen. The Spanish historian, Marmol, recounts that the sum of three thousand ducats was paid by Kheyr-ed-Din Barbarossa for the redemption of Dragut. As this history was published in 1573, we must conclude that the author who wrote of these events so soon after they had happened is correct; at the same time, Barbarossa was in command of one hundred galleys of the Grand Turk, and it was never his custom to pay for anything which he could take by force. However this may have been, and the point is not one of very great importance, the Genoese Senate was terrified lest their territory should be ravaged; they wrote accordingly to their Grand Admiral, requesting that Dragut might be released and sent on board of the galley of the admiral *basha*. This was immediately done, and the man who for four years had tugged at the Christian oar was once again in a position to make war on those who had been for that period his masters.

Not only had he tugged at the Christian oar, but also he had tasted of the Christian whip—and of very little else, as the food of the rower was as scanty as it was disgusting; in consequence, if he had been an implacable foe to Christendom before this event, he was not likely to have become less so while toiling in the Genoese galley.

The practical retirement of Barbarossa from that sphere of activity in which his life had been passed now left Dragut-Reis the most feared and the most formidable of all the Moslem corsairs in the Mediterranean. From the time of his release by Barbarossa until the day of his death at the siege of Malta in 1565, he followed the example shown him by that prince among pirates with so much assiduity as to render him only second to Kheyr-ed-Din in the detestation in which he was held. Says Morgan: "The ill-treatment he had met with during his four years' captivity was no small addition to the Innate Rapaciousness of his Disposition."

In the year 1546, Kheyr-ed-Din Barbarossa died, and to replace him the Sultan Soliman ordered all the mariners in his dominions to acknowledge Dragut-Reis as their admiral, and to obey him in the same manner as they had obeyed his predecessor. From this date he was the foremost corsair in the Mediterranean, and the feats which were performed by him showed that the Padishah had not erred in his selection.

The ambition of Dragut increased with his power, and he determined, following the example of the Barbarossas, to seize and hold some strong place of arms possessed of a commodious port in which he might be the supreme ruler. Accordingly, in the depth of winter in the year 1548, at a time which was, as we have pointed out, a close season for piratical enterprises, and during which attack from the sea was not expected, he collected all the corsairs whom he could gather, and fell upon the Spaniards on the coast of Tunis, at Susa, at Sfax, and at Monastir. These places had been taken from the corsairs in the previous summer by Andrea Doria; they formed a sort of regular battle-ground when the combatants were in want of something to do, and were held alternately by the King of Tunis, the Spaniards, and the corsairs.

Dragut was well aware that as soon as the spring arrived he would be attacked; he also knew that the attack would come in sufficient force to drive him out, as none of these towns was really strong or easily defended; in consequence he concentrated his attention on the town of "Africa," otherwise known as Mehedia, and in the Roman histories as Adrumentum.

This great city lay some leagues to the east of Tunis on a tongue of land projecting into the sea; its fortifications were regular, its walls of great thickness, height, and solidity, and were strengthened by many towers and bulwarks; the guns were large, numerous, and in good condition. At the back of the town, on an eminence, stood a large fortress, the citadel of the place; the harbour was large and secure, with an inner basin forming a port for galleys; the entrance to this was closed by a strong chain. The sea washed the walls of the city; indeed, it was entirely surrounded, except where by a narrow neck of land it joined the shore.

The inhabitants, natives of the place, had shaken off the yoke of the King of Tunis, and had formed themselves into a kind of independent republic. They admitted neither Turk nor Christian within their walls, trusting neither party, and fearing from them the fate which befell Susa, Sfax, and Monastir.

"Africa" was the goal of the desires of Dragut-Reis: once in possession of this, by far the strongest city on the littoral of Northern Africa, he thought that he might abide secure against the attacks of Charles and of Andrea Doria. He had seen the enormous expedition of 1541 against Algiers come to naught on account of the wholesale wrecking of the fleet in which it had sailed by a tempest of unexampled violence. But he was too level-headed a man to think that a miracle like this would be likely to come to pass a second time for his own special behoof, and preferred to act the part of the strong man armed who keepeth his goods in peace. He had, however, first to gain over the inhabitants of "Africa" to his views, and they proved anything but anxious to listen to his blandishments. The more he tried to ingratiate himself the less inclined did these people seem to listen.

"My ambition," said the silver-tongued corsair, "is to become a citizen of your great and beautiful city. If you will admit me to its privileges it shall be my business to render you the richest people in the whole Mediterranean, and your city the most dreaded place in the world."

The "Africans," however, were obdurate; they knew a pirate when they saw him quite as well as any one else, and they were quite aware that, should they open their gates to Dragut, sooner or later they would have to stand a siege from the Christian forces, which was a thing they by no means desired.

But Dragut was not yet at the end of his resources; he was rich, and he spent money freely in order to gain over to his side those men of importance by whom such a question as this was bound to be decided. By rich presents and other blandishments he succeeded in securing the friendship of one Ibrahim Amburac, who was not only a leader among the inhabitants, but also governor of one of the towers by which the city was surrounded. Through him he approached the Council by which the town was ruled, only to receive a very decided negative: the Council observed the outward forms of politeness to this formidable person who was speaking them so fair: in reality, they hated and feared the corsairs only one degree less than they did Andrea Doria and his Christians. To admit the one was to bring upon themselves the vengeance of the other; therefore if they could keep them both out they intended so to do. The ill-omened courtesy of the corsair filled their hearts with apprehension, and they viewed his immediate departure, after the refusal of the council had been conveyed to him, with undisguised relief. Had they but known their man a little better, their uneasiness would have been far greater than their joy at his temporary absence. Those things desired by Dragut which he could not obtain by fair means he usually seized by the strong hand; and when he left so hurriedly, and at the same time so unostentatiously, he had already entered into a plot with Ibrahim Amburac. This leader, furious at the rebuff which he had received at the hands of his fellow councillors on the subject of the admittance of Dragut to the citizenship of "Africa," was now ready to deliver that city into the hands of the corsairs by treachery.

Chapter 16

The Town of "Africa"

Dragut had made it a practice never to appear in the harbour of "Africa" in any great force, as he had no desire to frighten the birds whom he desired to snare; on the occasion of which we are now speaking he had but two galleys, and their departure from the outer harbour passed almost unnoticed, as the ruck of the population were accustomed to visits from the corsairs, who came to fill up with provisions and fresh water. Swiftly as hawks his vessels swept along the coast collecting the garrisons of Susa, Sfax, and Monastir to aid him in his latest design; they were all picked men and singularly apt for the stern business which their leader destined them to undertake. In this manner he soon collected five hundred of the stoutest and most reckless fighters who sailed out of the ports of Northern Africa, and, when it became noised abroad among them what the service was for which they were required, there was universal joy and eagerness. True the adventure was a formidable one: to capture "Africa" was no light task, even for such men as these under so renowned a leader; there was further the difficulty that the persons against whom they went up to fight were no Christians but Moslems like themselves. But against this was the declaration of Dragut, who represented to his following that there was really no choice in the matter; that to these stiff necked and singularly ungrateful people he had offered the protection of the corsairs, that they had refused in the most contumelious manner, and in consequence there was nothing for it but the strong hand. They—that is to say the corsairs—knew right well that some strong place of arms in which to shelter themselves and their vessels was an absolute necessity for their continued existence, as at any moment Doria or the Knights of Malta might be on their track in superior force, and then what was their fate likely to be if they had no harbour under their lee in which to shelter? Further it was hinted that "Africa" would provide very nice pickings in the way of loot, and when this came to be generally understood the promptings of the Mahommedan conscience yielded easily to the sophistries with which it was lulled.

The council of the town of "Africa" troubled themselves but little more concerning Dragut, his ships, and his corsairs; he had departed, and as the days wore on and no further tidings of him came to hand, these simple folk thanked God that they were rid of a knave and went about their usual avocations as unconcernedly as if no sea-wolves lurked under the shadowed headlands of that continent in which their homes were situated. They were a people essentially of the land; although they dwelt on the confines of the ocean the ways and habits of those who earned a precarious living on the waters were a sealed book to them, and with the "Africans" it was a case of "out of sight out of mind" so far as the corsairs were concerned. But that black-hearted traitor Ibrahim Amburac and the few others who had been gained over by the gold of Dragut watched and waited for the attack which they knew to be impending.

The inhabitants of the doomed city never saw their assailants until they were actually upon them, so well had the surprise attack been planned by the leader of the corsairs. He had collected five hundred men, and this was but a small number with which to assail so strong a place; but Dragut knew exactly what he was doing and the effect likely to be produced by the introduction of this number of highly trained men-at-arms among a population which, although brave and warlike, lacked the elements of organisation for the defence of their city.

So it was that, all preparations being completed, he stood along the coast anchoring out of sight of his objective, but close enough to reach it by midnight after darkness had fallen. He had every confidence in himself, an absolute trust in the hard-bitten fighters whom he was about to lead; success or failure now rested in the hands of traitors within the city.

"Faith unfaithful kept them falsely true," for when Dragut and his followers arrived at a certain rendezvous outside the walls which had been agreed upon previously, there they found Ibrahim Amburac and his men ready to assist them in scaling this obstacle. It will be remembered that Ibrahim Amburac was personally in charge of one of the towers with which the walls were guarded, and thus his task of aiding those who came from without was a singularly easy one. But even at midnight the passage of five hundred men could not remain long undiscovered as they clambered in over the walls. Soon an alarm was raised and the "Africans" rushed to arms and hurried to the quarter from which danger threatened. The townsmen were well armed and brave, also they were numerous; but it was the old story of the break-up of undisciplined valour by highly organised attack.

In the choking heat of the African night townsmen and corsairs wrestled in deadly conflict hand to hand and foot to foot; but these untrained landsmen stood but a poor chance against the picked fighting men of the Moslem galleys who had been inured to bloodshed from their earliest youth and trained by such a master in the art of war as Dragut. That warrior, his great curved *scimitar* red to the hilt, the blood dripping from a gash in his cheek, his clothing torn and in disarray, followed by a gigantic negro bearing a flaming torch, was ever in the thickest of the fray. Behind him his lieutenants Othman and Selim strove to emulate his prowess, while all around surged his devoted band of fanatics.

"Allah! Allah!" and "Dragut! Dragut!" pealed the war-cry of the corsairs; foot by foot and yard by yard that spearhead of dauntless dare-devils pressed onwards into the packed masses of the "Africans," who, fighting stubbornly, nevertheless were borne back by the fury of the terrible onslaught. Torch-bearers among the pirates leaped into houses and set them ablaze, the flames volleyed and crackled, the dense smoke rolled upwards to the stainless sky, the night was a hell of blood and fire.

There was a sharp order repeated and passed on, the corsairs drew back, and the "Africans" shouted that the triumph was theirs; but they little knew Dragut, the sea-hawk who poised to strike anew. A blazing beam dropped across the street, the townsfolk shouted in insult and derision; but the joy which they had experienced at seeing their adversaries recoil was but a short and fleeting emotion. Giving himself and those who had hitherto been engaged time to breathe and recover themselves, Dragut waited while the noise of the strife died down, and nought was heard but the roar of the flames and the crash of the burning buildings.

The leader turned to his followers, among whom dwelt an ominous silence. "Dost remember Prevesa," he cried, "when Andrea Doria and the best of the Christian warriors fled before you like sheep before a dog: are these miserable townsmen to stay your onward march?"

There remained for an appreciable period after he had spoken a tense silence; the red light from the burning houses shone on the lean faces alight with the fierce fire of fanaticism, with an inextinguishable lust of slaughter. There came an answering frenetic roar, "Lead! Lead! Dragut! Dragut! Dragut!" It was enough: the corsair had tried the temper of the steel, he had now but to use the edge. There was an ordered movement on the part of the pirates: a fresh hundred men, who had hitherto taken no part in the combat, now pressed to the front and formed the advance, those who had been before engaged now forming the supports; that which had been the shaft of the spear now forming its head. With Dragut leading, these fresh unwounded men swept forward over the burning beam; irresistible as some mighty river in spate, these disciplined ruffians, headed by this master spirit, burst through the ill-organised resistance opposed to them, and slew and slew and slew.

Behind them, alert and wary, came the supports, asking no quarter and giving none, cutting up the wounded, trampling under foot friend and foe alike who fell in the weltering shambles which marked the onward path of their leader and the advanced party. Very soon the broken hosts of the "Africans" cried piteously for mercy; the fight was over, and Dragut-Reis, wounded, breathless, but victorious, stood master of the strongest place of arms in all the continent of Africa. It is true that treachery had given him his opportunity, but once that was obtained the rest he had done for himself: the stealthy advance by sea, the midnight march to the exact spot on the walls where he was awaited by Ibrahim Amburac, the marshalling of his five hundred for the conflict, and the actual conduct of the fight itself, were all to the credit of this apt pupil of the great Kheyr-ed-Din Barbarossa, As warriors his followers were worthy of their leader: defeated the corsairs frequently were, but, in the combats in which they engaged, they were frequently, as we have seen in the course of this story, largely dependent upon auxiliaries in whom no trust could be placed; and at Prevesa, at the siege of Malta, and later on at the battle of Lepanto, the spot on which they fought, were it on the land or on the sea, was ever the one which formed the nucleus of resistance. It was not only that fighting was their particular trade; that, of course, might be said also of any man who trailed a pike or carried an *arquebus* and marched in the ranks of Spain, France, Genoa, or Venice. In the case of the sea-wolves it was the perpetual practice in the art of war, as it was then understood, that caused them to be the men that they were. Much of their fighting could hardly be dignified by such a name, as in their everlasting raids on villages and undefended places they seldom lost many of their number: when, however, it came to the real thing, as it did on the occasion we have just recounted, the long years of training told, and opposition had to be strong indeed if it were not to be beaten down by such a leader as Dragut, by such men as his picked five hundred.

What passed between Dragut and the council of "Africa," who in so unqualified a manner had refused that warrior as a citizen, is not on record; all that we know is that the Moslem leader dispensed with their services, and did not invite his new fellow-townsmen to share with him the burden of government. There was hurry in the administration of the corsair states, as the form of rule which they adopted was apt to irk the rulers in Christendom. In this particular instance Dragut, having expelled the Spaniards from the coast towns, knew that a reckoning with the Emperor and his militant admiral, Andrea Doria, was but a matter of time, and, in all probability, of a very short time.

Promptly, hurriedly, but efficiently, the corsair organised his new possession: such laws as he decreed did not err on the side of tenderness towards a people so ungrateful as to have refused his protection in the first instance, and who had only accepted the gift at the point of the sword. His nephew Aisa, a man young in years but a past-graduate in the school of his terrible uncle, was left in charge, while Dragut himself sailed once more with his fleet, for, as it is put by the Spanish historian Marmol, "truly the sea was his element."

Once again had a Moslem corsair bid defiance to that ruler whom Sandoval and Marmol in their histories greet by the name of the "Modern Caesar." It was told to Charles that Susa, Sfax, and Monastir had fallen, that "Africa" was in the hands of the corsairs; "was he never to be free from these pestilent knaves," he demanded of his trembling courtiers? Hot-foot came the couriers from Charles to Andrea Doria, with orders to take Dragut dead or alive, but alive for choice; and up and down the tideless sea in the summer of 1549 did the great Genoese seaman range in search of the bold corsair. Doria was getting a very old man now, but his eye was undimmed, his strength yet tireless, his vigilance and zeal in the service of his master unabated.

Dead or alive, great was the reward offered for the capture of Dragut, but the veteran admiral required no stimulus of this sort to urge him to put forth his utmost endeavours, to strain every nerve and sinew in the chase. All his life he had been fighting the corsairs, mostly with conspicuous success; but what Andrea could never forget—and what his enemies never allowed him to forget even had he been so inclined—was the fact that, at the supreme crisis of his valiant life, when he met with Kheyr-ed-Din Barbarossa at the battle of Prevesa, he had come off so badly that his under officers of the Papal and Venetian fleets had made representations, on their return to their respective headquarters, which had detracted from his fame, and lowered him in the estimation of Europe. Further than this, he knew that Barbarossa had laughed at and made game of him among his wild followers: this to the aristocrat, the Prince of Oneglia, the admiral who treated on almost equal terms with such men as the Pope, Charles of Spain, and Francis of France, was an insult hard to be borne; the next corsair with whom he should meet should not escape so easily as had Kheyr-ed-Din, that the admiral had sworn.

Personal pique and vanity, racial detestation, and religious fanaticism were in his case all allied together to spur him on in the chase of this the last of the Emperor's foes; but, search as he might, during that summer Doria could never get on to the track of Dragut. The corsairs, as we have just remarked, were fine fighters on occasion when it was necessary for the purposes of loot, or of escape from those who, like Doria, interfered with their particular method of gaining a livelihood; but, on the other hand, they were no fools, they did not covet hard knocks and the possibility of defeat from such a one as the admiral of the Emperor, when by the exercise of a little ingenuity they could keep out of his way. Dragut was not going to fight a general action at sea merely to please Doria; in this summer his luck stood to him, and he never came across this man, who, with a sombre hatred in his heart, was seeking him high and low. If the corsair were bold as a lion when occasion offered, he was no less as slippery as an eel when he desired to escape; to face twenty-two royal galleys with Doria in command was no part of his programme. An occasion might arise when he would be forced to action; should this happen Dragut had not forgotten his four years in the galley of Jannetin Doria, the nephew of the admiral, and next time he intended to fight to win. Just at present the Christian admiral was in too great strength for him to do aught but keep out of his way, and much to Andrea's annoyance this was what he succeeded in doing.

Doria got information that Dragut was at Monastir, information that was perfectly correct; but by this time the corsair knew that not only had he raised all Christendom, but that the admiral was on his track. In consequence, he slipped out of Monastir, "for," as it is pithily put by Marmol, "our corsair cared not to be shut up in so defenceless a port; he had good heels and loved sea-room."

Dragut did not fear for his new possession, "Africa," as he knew that Doria had not sufficient force to attack so formidable a place; therefore, leaving it to its destiny and the valour and conduct of his nephew Aisa, on whom he knew that he could rely, "he went," according to the chronicler, "on his old trade making Horrid Devastations on the coast of Spain and its islands."

While Dragut was pursuing his "Horrid Devastations," Doria was not idle, but was ranging the northern coast of Africa in his fruitless search; in the course of this he landed at Cape Bona, on which was the castle of Calibia, held by the corsairs; these men, who were a portion of Dragut's following, made a most valiant defence; they were, however, few in number, and when their captain was killed by the ball from an *arquebus* they surrendered. Encouraged by this success, the Christian fleet then stood along the coast to inspect "Africa." Sailing quite close to the shore they came within range of the guns of the garrison, who, under the direction of Aisa, were very much on the alert. As the admiral's galley at the head of the line passed the walls of the town, she was received with a hot fire, and one large cannonball struck the stern of Doria's ship, doing considerable structural damage, and killing five of his men. This occurrence took place in broad daylight in full view of all the garrison, who signalled their delight at the discomfiture of their foes by the noise of cymbals and *atambours*, and by wild and ferocious yells. Doria, who was in no position to land and make reprisals, fell into the greatest paroxysm of fury, and we are told that "he swore the destruction of that detested city."

The season being now advanced, Doria returned home, where he found orders awaiting him from Charles that preparation was to be made for the capture of "Africa". While the admiral was in harbour, Dragut, finding the seas open to him once more, returned from his "Horrid Devastations," and employed his time profitably in throwing provisions and men into the city, which he knew would be beleaguered in the following year.

During the ensuing winter Doria, in conjunction with the viceroys of Naples and Sicily, prepared the expedition which was to accomplish not only the capture of "Africa," but what was, in his opinion, equally important, the destruction of Dragut-Reis, Early in the spring of 1550, all was in readiness, and the armada of Charles sailed from Palermo to Trapani, where it met with the forces of Don Juan de Vega, Viceroy of Sicily, those of Don Garcia de Toledo, the son of the Viceroy of Naples, and likewise the Maltese squadron. The galleys, accompanied by a fleet of transports, set sail early in June, and on the 20th of that month landed an army a little to the east of Mehedia or "Africa."

It must be remembered that the inhabitants of Mehedia were by no means enamoured of Dragut-Reis and his piratical followers: King Stork had succeeded to King Log, the part of the former monarch being taken by that singularly capable and ferocious person, Aisa, whose rule was far from being to the liking of the richer and more respectable portion of the townsfolk.

When, therefore, Andrea Doria and his captains laid siege to the city, they murmured against its defence, desiring ardently to enter into some sort of treaty with the besiegers; they had had enough of war, they said, and wished to end their days in peace if possible.

Aisa Reis, however, would hear no word of surrender, telling those who murmured against the defence that "if he heard a word more of these plots he would infallibly sacrifice every mother's son amongst them, and then lay the town in ashes." Having already had a taste of the quality of this redoubtable corsair, and feeling perfectly certain that should the occasion arise he would be as good as his word, there was no more disaffection among the inhabitants, who had to put up with their native place being made a cockpit for Doria and Dragut to fight out their quarrel. It is permissible to sympathise very sincerely with these unfortunates, who, having been betrayed in the first instance, were compelled to stand a siege in the second.

Aisa had a picked force of his uncle's men, some seventeen hundred foot and six hundred horse, all seasoned and formidable veterans, inured to warfare by land and sea. On these of course he could rely to the death. The common folk of the town were inclined to make common cause with the corsairs in resistance to their hereditary enemy the Christians; but the magistrates and members of the council, the grave and reverend *seigniors*, held so conspicuously aloof that Aisa was constrained into forcing them to aid in the defence when he had time to attend to the matter. As Dragut was not actually present at the siege it falls outside the scope of this chronicle; he was without the walls when the besiegers arrived, but all that he could do, that he did. With a body of his own men reinforced by a rabble rout of Berber tribesmen, he harassed the Christian army; they were, however, in far too great numbers for him to make any impression, and after several desperate skirmishes he recognised that the day was lost, and re-embarking in his galleys sailed away. The town after a desperate and prolonged resistance was at last taken by storm; and Doria captured Aisa, a Turkish *alcaid*, and ten thousand prisoners of the baser sort. Of these, however, there was scarce one who owed allegiance to Dragut; the warriors of this chief neither gave nor accepted quarter, as they feared the wrath of the terrible corsair even more than death itself.

Don Juan de Vega put his son Don Alvaro in command of the city and set out in search of Dragut with twenty galleys, but the sea leaves no traces by which a fugitive can be tracked, and his search proved as fruitless as had been that of Doria in the previous year. The rage and the disappointment of the admiral were beyond all bounds; what to him was the value of the capture of Aisa, of the Turkish *alcaid*, of the ten thousand of the baser sort; nay, what to him was the value of "Africa" itself when once again like a mocking spirit Dragut had glided beyond the sea horizon to devastate, to plunder, and to slay once more, the scourge and the menace of Christendom.

It will be interesting to record briefly the fate of this city which we have seen taken and retaken. Don Alvaro de Vega remained as governor till the end of July, 1551, when his place was taken by Don Sancho de Leyva; at which time there took place one of those curious military mutinies so characteristic of the sixteenth century. The soldiers, unpaid for months, possibly for years, mutinied, expelled the governor and other officers, even the sergeants, from the city, and placed themselves under the direction of a stout soldier called Antonio de Aponte, to whom they gave the title of "Electo Mayor."

Don Sancho repaired to Brussels to report matters to the Emperor, and during his absence a circumstance which is also singularly characteristic of this faithless epoch took place, for the Prior of Capua, then general of the French galleys, entered into negotiations with the mutineers for the surrender of the city to the French King.

Bluff Antonio de Aponte would have none of this treachery; he held the city for the Emperor Charles and only wanted his pay. Eventually a mutiny within a mutiny was fomented from without, and with the mutineers divided the Emperor regained possession of the city; some of the mutineers were hanged, and Aponte, who had been captured by the Turks, died at Constantinople.

The Emperor offered "Africa" to the Knights of Malta with a yearly allowance of twenty-four thousand ducats; the Knights refused, much to the chagrin of Charles, who gave orders for its complete destruction. This was accomplished by blowing up with gunpowder the walls, towers, and fortifications which Al-Mehedi, after whom the city had been named, "had erected with such art and strength, and had his mind so fixed upon that work that he used to say, 'If I thought building these fortifications with iron and brass would render them more durable, I would certainly do it.'"

Chapter 17
Dragut-Reis and the Knights of Malta

Charles V. had "smoked out the fox," but his admiral in so doing had not succeeded in capturing that remarkably wily animal; for Dragut was not only still at liberty, but was burning for revenge on those by whom he had been dispossessed. He had lost "his city," as he called "Africa"; he had lost two thousand five hundred men—among them some of the fiercest and most experienced of his corsairs; he had lost ten thousand slaves, representing a large sum of money, and much wealth besides. The corsair, however, was not one of those who merely sit down and repine; for him strenuous and continued action was the law of his being, and he at once repaired to Constantinople. Here he was well known as an adroit and skilful seaman and a most determined enemy of the Christians, and, in consequence, was not only certain of a welcome, but of substantial help as well, if he could but win over the Grand Turk to take the same view of his grievances as he did himself. In reality, the corsairs, as we have seen, played the game of the Padishah, as a rule, at no expense to that potentate; when they were in trouble he was therefore by no means indisposed to render them assistance.

Dragut, like all the sea-wolves, was fond of money, fonder still of what money could buy; he now hankered after revenge as the sweetest morsel that his hoarded ducats could procure for him. That the Sultan was well disposed to him he had every reason to think; none the less did he spend royally among the venal favourites of the court in order that nothing might be left undone to inflame the ardour of Soliman against those whom he considered to be his hereditary foes.

With such skill and address did the corsair manage his suit that he prevailed upon the Sultan to address a letter to Charles demanding the immediate return of the towns of Susa, Sfax, Monastir, and "Africa." This, of course, meant war; as Charles immediately replied that these places were dependencies of the King of Tunis, and that that ruler was under his special protection; further that they were his by right of conquest; finally that the matter was no concern whatever of the Sultan of Constantinople. The stern and imperious Christian Emperor was in no mood to brook interference, the more so that he discerned plainly that though the demand was that of Soliman, the mover in the affair was none other than Dragut. He therefore by way of a rider to his answer to the Sultan informed that monarch that these places which he had taken on the coast of Africa had been reft by him "from one Dragut, a corsair odious to both God and man"; that without in any way departing from the treaty which he had made with Soliman "he intended to pursue this pirate whithersoever he might go."

Whether or no this denunciation of Dragut had any influence on the Sultan it is impossible to say; he was in the habit of employing the corsairs, and apparently cared nothing about their piratical reputation, so long as their depredations were confined to Christian vessels. Shortly after the receipt of the answer of Charles, however, the Sultan conferred upon Dragut the title of *sandjak* or governor of the island of Santa Maura, thus constituting him a Turkish official.

Once again was Andrea Doria ordered to put to sea to fight against neither small nor great save Dragut alone; he was to take him dead or alive, but alive for choice, in order that he might be made to answer at the bar of Christian justice for all the atrocities committed by him both by land and sea. The corsair had returned in the meanwhile to Jerbah, an island on the east coast of Tunis much affected by the sea-wolves, and which in contemporary histories is known as Jerbah, as Los Gelues (by the Spanish writers), as Gelves, and various other names which greatly confuse its identity.

Doria put to sea with twenty-two royal galleys before Dragut was aware of the fact. The Genoese admiral heard that his prey was at Jerbah; he repaired thither without losing a moment, found that he had been correctly informed, and anchored at the mouth of the harbour, at a place known as La Bocca de Cantara. Dragut was completely hemmed in, Doria was in such strength that he could not, reckless as he was, attempt to force the passage. But as the hour came the spirit of the corsair rose to answer the challenge: it was one thing to get Dragut-Reis into a trap, it was quite another to keep him there. Accordingly, he assembled all his troops, dragged cannon to the mouth of the harbour, and opened so brisk a foe on the Christian ships as to compel them to haul out of range. These tactics left Doria unaffected; there was but one way out of the harbour, and he felt quite convinced that when Dragut had had enough of starvation he would either surrender or else fight a hopeless action. The admiral surveyed his anchored fleet with a contented mind; his enemy had been delivered into his hand, he had nothing to do now but wait for that final triumph of appearing before his master the Emperor with the famous corsair as his prisoner. He saw a great fort rising before his very eyes at the mouth of the harbour, and merely smiled serenely; he sent off to Sicily and Naples for reinforcements in order that when the psychological moment should arise he might crush the corsair stronghold so thoroughly that it should never rise again. In the despatches which he sent he said "the fox is trapped"—"which news rejoiced all parts of Christendom, and most powerful succours came daily flocking to the seaports from every quarter; so eager were the sufferers to revenge themselves on this so much dreaded corsair."

The history of what now happened is given by Don Luys de Marmol Caravajal in his *Descripcion general de Affrica*, which was printed in Granada, "*en casa de Rene Rabat impresor de libros año de 1573*," or only some twenty years or so after these occurrences; it is set forth in his chapter entitled "*Como Andrea Doria fue en buscar de Dragut Arraez.*" We have also the authority of that eminent historian, M. L'Abé de Vertot.

Captain Juan Vasquez Coronado journeyed to Naples carrying with him letters from Andrea Doria to Don Pedro de Toledo, requesting that the Viceroy would send him all the galleys in Naples, carrying as many soldiers as possible, pointing out that he had Dragut in a trap, from which he could not possibly escape, but that this time he wished to make security doubly secure. Letters to the same purport were also sent to Don Juan de Vega, the Viceroy of Sicily, and to Marco Centurion at the admiral's own city of Genoa. Doria was leaving nothing to chance this time. Meanwhile, great earthworks had been thrown up at the Bocca de Cantara at the entrance of the harbour by Dragut, and any ship which approached within range was most furiously bombarded. This served to amuse Andrea Doria, who, confident that the jaws of the trap had closed, kept a sharp look-out for vessels issuing from the harbour, but otherwise concerned himself not at all about the entrenchments. Was not Naples humming with the note of preparation? Would not the Genoese come in their thousands to the summons of their renowned chieftain? Could not the Viceroy of Sicily be trusted to work his best to gain the favour of his Imperial master?

"Time and I are two" was the favourite expression of King Philip II. of Spain; the same idea might have crossed the mind of Doria on this memorable occasion. He had only to wait; the longer he waited the more secure he would be of success, the more certain would he be of the complete undoing of his enemy. But even yet the admiral did not know the man to whom he was opposed; in all the years in which he had done battle against Dragut, he had never gauged the limitless resource and calculated audacity of this lineal successor of Kheyr-ed-Din Barbarossa. While the admiral had been sending his despatches, and idly watching that which he considered to be the futile construction of earthworks on the shore at the Bocca de Cantara, his enemy was preparing for him that surprise which was shortly afterwards to make of him the laughing-stock of the whole of Europe. Dragut was in a trap, and he was quite aware of the fact; by way of the Bocca de Cantara escape was impossible, and neither a tame surrender nor complete annihilation was by any means to the taste of the pirate leader. Had Doria gone in and attacked at once, the fate of the corsair had been sealed; the policy of delay adopted by the Christian admiral was his salvation.

A man less able, less determined, than Dragut, might well have despaired; but he brought to bear on the problem with which he was confronted all the subtlety of his nature, all the resourcefulness of the born seaman that he was. His mind had been made up from the very beginning: the earthworks at the Bocca de Cantara, the movements of troops, the furious cannonading, had all been nothing but a blind to hide the real design which he had in view. In addition to his fighting men he had at his command some two thousand islanders, stout Mohammedans to a man, ready and willing to assist him in his design of cheating the Christians of their prey. Day and night, with ceaseless silent toil, had garrison and islanders been at work on the scheme which the leader had devised. From the head of the harbour Dragut had caused a road to be made right across the island to the sea on the opposite side: on this road he caused planks to be laid, bolted to sleepers and then thickly greased. The vessels of the day were of course comparatively speaking light, and capable of being manhandled, supposing that you had sufficient hands. At dead of night Dragut assembled his forces, and before morning every galley, *galeasse*, and brigantine had been dragged across the island and launched in the sea on the opposite side. There was then nothing left to do but to embark stores, guns, and ammunition and to sail quietly away, and this was what happened. Once again Dragut faded away beyond the skyline, "leaving Andrea Doria with the dog to hold," in the quaint language of the chronicler of these events, Don Luys de Marmol Caravajal.

Not only did the indefatigable corsair get clear away without any suspicion on the part of the admiral, but his first act on gaining the open sea was to capture the *Patrona* galley sent from Sicily by Don Juan de Vega to say that reinforcements were on the road. In this ill-fated craft was Buguer, the son of Muley Hassan, King of Tunis, who was sent as prize to Soliman at Constantinople, where the Sultan caused him to be shut up in the "Torre del Mar Negro." Here he remained till he died, as a punishment for that he, a Mussulman, had aided the Christians.

Never again was Dragut to be in such sore straits as he was on this occasion at the island of Jerbah, when, by sheer wit and cunning, he escaped from the trap in which he had been held by Doria. What the emotions of the admiral must have been when he found that once again he had been fooled, it is not difficult to imagine, as by no possible means could the story be hushed up; and, in spite of the annoyance of Christendom generally at the escape of Dragut, no one could help admiring his extraordinary cleverness, or roaring with laughter at the discomfiture of Doria and the viceroys of Naples and Sicily.

Dragut now returned to Constantinople to receive congratulations upon his escape, and to take part in a fresh design of stirring up the Sultan against the Christians. All who professed this faith were naturally obnoxious to the corsair; but his private and personal hatred was entirely directed against the Knights of Malta, with whom he had been at war all his life. The present preoccupation of the Sultan was to regain the towns on the coast of Africa which had been taken by the Spaniards; but it was represented to him by Dragut that "until he had smoked out this nest of vipers he could do no good anywhere." The *bashaws* and the *divan*, heavily bribed by the corsair, held the same language, until Soliman heard of nothing from morning till night but the ill deeds of the Knights of Malta. They were represented to him as corsairs who ruined his commerce and defeated his armadas, who let slip no opportunity of harrying the Moslem wheresoever he was to be found. In this there was more than a grain of truth, as we shall see when we come to the next chapter, which will be devoted to a sketch of this militant order. Suffice it to say here that the Knights fought for what they termed "the Religion" (it was in this manner they designated their confederacy), and to harry and enslave the Mussulman, to destroy him as a noxious animal wherever he was to be found, was the reason for which they existed. It is true that they plundered not for individual gain, but many was the rich prize towed into Malta past St. Elmo and the ominously named "Punta delle Forche" (the "Point of the Gallows," where all captured pirates were hanged), the proceeds of which went to the enrichment of the order; to buy themselves the wherewithal to fight with the Mahommedan again.

The abuse of the Knights fell upon sympathetic ears; in his early days Soliman the Magnificent had expelled the Knights from Rhodes; since then Charles V. had given them the islands of Malta and Gozo, and the town of Tripoli in Barbary as their abiding place; from Malta they had never ceased their warfare against the corsairs, and incidentally against the Sultan and his subjects. Therefore, in this year 1551, Soliman ordained that an expedition should be prepared with the object of crushing once and for all these troublers of the peace of Islam. The preparations were on so large a scale that very soon it became noised abroad in Europe that something really serious was in the wind: in Constantinople, however, men kept their own counsel; it was ill talking of the affairs of the *padishah*, and, further than that, beyond Dragut and the proposed leaders of the expedition, the Sultan took no one into his confidence. Charles V., well served as he was by his spies, was as much in the dark as to the destination of this new armada as were humbler folk; in it he recognised the hand of Dragut again, and Doria had standing orders to catch that mischievous person if he could. At present, however, there was no chance of so desirable a thing happening, as Dragut was superintending the fitting out of the new expedition at Constantinople.

Anxious and suspicious of the designs of the Turks, Charles ordered a concentration of his fleet at Messina.

The grand master of the Knights of Malta at this time was a Spaniard, one Juan d'Omedes; he was, says de Vertot, "*un Grand Maître Espagnol,*" meaning by this that he was completely under the domination of the Emperor and ready at any time to place the galleys of "the Religion" under the orders of that monarch. The Knights, like every one else, had watched with anxiety the preparation of this great expedition in Constantinople, and when the grand master proposed to send the galleys of the order to join forces with Doria at Messina, there was great dissatisfaction at the Council Board. That which it behoved them to do, the members informed the grand master, was not to help a great potentate like Charles, but to make provision for their own security by attending to their fortifications, which were in anything but a satisfactory condition. D'Omedes maintained that this expedition was destined to serve with the King of France against the Emperor, and that Malta was not the objective. He accordingly sent away the galleys of "the Religion" under the Chevalier "Iron-Foot," the General of the Galleys, to join the fleet which had its rendezvous at Messina. Hardly had he done so when news came from the Levant that the fleet of the Grand Turk was at sea heading for Sicily. The fleet was composed of one hundred and twelve royal galleys, two great *galeasses*, and a host of brigantines and transport vessels. Sinan-Reis was in command with twelve thousand Janissaries, numerous pioneers and engineers, and all the necessary appliances for a siege.

The embarkation of so large a number of Janissaries was the measure of the serious purpose of the expedition, as the Sultan did not readily part with the men of this *corps d'élite* unless he was in person taking the command. It may be as well to explain here exactly what the Janissaries were, and it cannot be better done than by an extract from the famous historian Prescott:

> The most remarkable of the Turkish institutions, the one which may be said to have formed the keystone of the system, was that relating to the Christian population of the Empire. Once in five years a general conscription was made by means of which all the children of Christian parents who had reached the age of seven and gave promise of excellence in mind or body were taken from their homes and brought to the capital. They were then removed to different quarters and placed in seminaries where they might receive such instruction as would fit them for the duties of life. Those giving greatest promise of strength and endurance were sent to places prepared for them in Asia Minor. Here they were subjected to a severe training, to abstinence, to privations of every kind, and to the strict discipline which should fit them for the profession of a soldier. From this body was formed the famous corps of the Janissaries.... Their whole life may be said to have been passed in war or in preparation for it. Forbidden to marry, they had no families to engage their affections, which, as with the monks and friars of Christian countries, were concentrated in their own order, whose prosperity was inseparably connected with that of the State. Proud of the privileges which distinguished them from the rest of the army, they seemed desirous to prove their title to them by their thorough discipline and by their promptness to execute the most dangerous and difficult services. Clad in their flowing robes, so little suited to war, armed with the *arquebus* and the *scimitar*—in their hands more than a match for the pike or sword of the European—with the heron's plume

waving above their head, their dense array might ever be seen bearing down in the thickest of the fight; and more than once when the fate of the Empire trembled in the balance it was this invincible corps which turned the scale, and by their intrepid conduct decided the fortune of the day. Gathering fresh reputation with age, so long as their discipline remained unimpaired they were a match for the best soldiers in Europe. But in time this admirable organisation experienced a change. One Sultan allowed them to marry; another to bring their sons into the corps; a third opened the ranks to Turks as well as Christians; until, forfeiting their peculiar character, the Janissaries became confounded with the militia of the Empire. These changes occurred in the time of Philip the Second.

But to resume: just before the sailing of the galleys of "the Religion" from Malta there had arrived in that island from France the famous Chevalier, the Commandeur de Villegagnon. This great noble told the grand master to his face that he was neglecting his duty, that the expedition of the Grand Turk was bound for Malta and Tripoli: further, that he was charged by Anne de Montmorency, Constable and First Minister of France, to advise the grand master that this armament was directed against "the Religion." The interview between the grand master and de Villegagnon took place at a chapter of the Grand Crosses of the order; when the Commandeur had finished speaking, he was coldly thanked by D'Omedes, who then bowed him out. Turning to the Knights Grand Cross he said with a sneer, "Either this Frenchman is the dupe of the Constable or he wishes to make us his." He then proceeded to give at length the reasons why Soliman would not direct so huge an expedition against "the Religion." Many of the Knights dissented vehemently from his conclusions, but D'Omedes refused to listen to their arguments. Even advices which arrived on July 13th, representing that the armada was moving southwards devastating the Italian ports, did not move him from his obstinate pre-occupation; till on July 16th the arrival of the Ottoman fleet put an end to all speculation.

The armada which had sailed from Constantinople was under the command of Sinan Basha: but he had explicit orders that he was to take no important step without first consulting Dragut, who was nominally his lieutenant. It was well for the Knights that on this occasion the corsair was not in supreme command; had this been the case the islands must have been taken, as no preparations had been made to repulse an attack in force, and Juan D'Omedes was a grand master who excited little enthusiasm either among the Knights or the inhabitants. The choice of Sinan was not one which did great credit to the penetration of the Sultan. Let us explain. We are all of us conscious at one time or another of a desire to express some fact in the fewest possible words; to place the transaction or the circumstance which we wish to describe in the searchlight of truth in so undeniable a fashion that the illumination consequent upon this mental effort of our own shall throw up our meaning in immediate relief on the intelligences of those whom we address. This attribute is possessed by but few even among great writers—indeed, some historic sayings which have come down to us have not emanated from the writing fraternity at all, but from soldiers, sailors, statesmen, and other busy men of affairs. The quality which distinguishes a man of action above all others is fearlessness of responsibility; the possession of sufficient greatness of soul and of moral fibre to seize upon an opportunity and to make the most thereof when an occasion arises which has not been foreseen by those in authority over him. But far more often in the history of the world has it happened that brave and capable leaders have failed for the lack of the indefinable quality that separated their sterling merits from that absolute and real supremacy which marks the first-class man.

How then is it possible to differentiate, to describe where and in what manner this luck occurs?

Fortunately, this has been done for us in seven words by Seignelay, the Minister of Marine to Louis Quatorze in 1692. Speaking of Admiral de Tourville, who defeated the English and Dutch at the Battle of Beachy Head, July 10th, 1690, Seignelay says of him that he was *"poltron de tête mais pas de coeur."* The judgment was just: de Tourville, as recklessly gallant as any French noble of them all, failed to live up to his responsibilities two years later at the Battle of La Hogue. Mahan says:

> The caution in his pursuit of the Allies after Beachy Head, though so different in appearance, came from the same trait which impelled him two years later to lead his fleet to almost certain destruction at La Hogue because he had the King's order in his pocket. He was brave enough to do anything, but not strong enough to bear the heaviest burdens.

We see the application of this truth in the period which we are considering; particularly is it borne in upon us in the case of the leaders of the Ottoman Turks. Serving as they did a despot of unlimited powers, failure in the success of his arms was apt to lead to the immediate and violent death of the man in command. If, therefore, precise instructions were issued, they were, as a rule, carried out to the letter; as in case of defeat an effort could be made to shift responsibility on to the shoulders of the *padishah*. Failure owing to initiative was certain of prompt retribution; success complete and absolute would be the only justification for a departure from orders.

Far otherwise was it with the sea-wolves, who were a law to themselves and to themselves alone. Should they care "to place it on the hazard of a die to win or lose it all," there was none to say them nay, there was no punishment save that of defeat. This it was that so often conduced to their success. Despots as were such men as Kheyr-ed-Din Barbarossa and Dragut, they were none the less dependent on the goodwill of their followers. If, therefore, they decided on a desperate enterprise, they appealed to the fighting instincts, the cupidity, and the fanaticism of these men. Should they succeed in gaining their good will for the attempt which they meditated, then all was well with them, and behind them was no grim sinister figure whose word was death and whose breath was destruction.

Freed from all the trammels which bound the ordinary warrior of the day in which they lived, they were able, as we have seen, to go far; for the man in whom supreme ability is united to absolute unscrupulousness is the most dangerous foe of the human race. The despotism of the leaders among the sea-wolves was not theirs by right divine, as men considered it to be in the case of the Padishah; none the less in its practical application it was but little inferior to that wielded by the Sultan. For reasons of policy, the sea-wolves allied themselves to the Grand Turk; for reasons of policy that monarch employed them and entrusted them with the conduct of important affairs. The bargain was really a good one on both sides; as to the sea-wolves was extended the aegis of one of the mightiest empires of the earth; while to the *sultan* came "veritable men of the sea," hardened in conflict, as fearless of responsibility as of aught else; capable in a sense that hardly any man could be capable who had grown up in the atmosphere of the court at Constantinople. To Kheyr-ed-Din the Sultan had extended his fullest confidence; he had been rewarded by seeing the renowned Doria forsake the field of battle at Prevesa, and by the perpetual slights and insults put upon his Christian foes by that great corsair. To Dragut he had now turned, and, as we have said, when Sinan Basha sailed from the Golden Horn he had orders to attempt nothing important without the advice of the corsair. It is impossible to say why the command-in-chief had not been entrusted to him, as the Sultan had the precedent of Kheyr-ed-Din upon which to go. It can only be conjectured that Soliman, having discovered how unpopular that appointment had been amongst his high officers, did not care to risk the experiment the second time; and in consequence employed Sinan. To this officer the aphorism of Seignelay applies in its fullest force. He was as brave a man as ever drew a sword in the service of his master; he was, however, a hesitating and incompetent leader, with one eye ever fixed on that distant palace on the shores of the Golden Horn in which dwelt the arbiter of his destiny and of all those who sailed beneath the banner of the Crescent.

Chapter 18

The Knights of St. John

Amongst all those principalities and powers against which Dragut contended during the whole of his strenuous existence, there was no one among them which he held in so much detestation as the famous Knights of Saint John, known in the sixteenth century as the Knights of Malta. This militant religious organisation had its origin in Jerusalem in peculiar and interesting circumstances. After the death of Mahomet, his followers, burning with zeal, put forward the tenets of their religion by means of fire and sword; during the years which followed the Hegira, 622 A.D., the arms of the Moslems were everywhere successful, and amongst other places conquered by them was Palestine. So great was the renown acquired by the Emperor Charlemagne that his fame passed even into Asia, and Eginard states that the Caliph Haroun Raschid permitted the French nation to maintain a house in Jerusalem for the reception of pilgrims visiting the holy places, and that, further, the Prince permitted the Patriarch of Jerusalem to send to the Christian Emperor, on his behalf, the keys of the Holy Sepulchre and those of the Church of Calvary, together with a standard which was the sign of the power and authority delegated by the Moslem ruler to his mighty contemporary. In the middle of the eleventh century Italian merchants coming from Amalfi, who had experienced the hard lot of the Christian pilgrims in reaching the Holy City, secured from the Caliph Moustafa-Billah a concession of land, on which they built a chapel known as St. Mary of the Latins, to distinguish it from the Greek church already established at Jerusalem, and also constructed a hospice in which to receive the pilgrims, whether in sickness or in health, known as the Hospice of St. John.

In 1093 the untiring efforts of Peter the Hermit, with the support of Pope Urban II., brought about the first Crusade, and in 1099 we first hear of Gerard, the founder of the order of St. John.

Gerard was a French monk who, seeing the good work done by the Hospice of St. John, had attached himself to it, and had at this time been working in the cause of charity, and devoting himself to the pilgrims for many years.

Godfrey de Bouillon, having defeated the Saracens outside the walls of Jerusalem, entered that city and visited the Hospice of St. John; he there found many of the Crusaders who had been wounded during the siege, and who had been carried thither after the taking of the place: all of these men were loud in their praises of the loving kindness with which they had been received and tended.

Great was the honour and reverence in which these simple monks were held ever after by the Crusaders; for was it not common talk that these holy men had themselves subsisted on the coarsest and most repulsive fare in order that the food in the hospice should be both pure and abundant? Fired by this fine example of Christian charity, several noble gentlemen who had been tended in the hospice gave up the idea of returning to their own countries, and consecrated themselves to the Hospice of St. John, and to the service of the pilgrims, the poor, and the sick. Among these was Raimond Dupuy.

The great Prince Godfrey de Bouillon fully approved of the steps taken by these gentlemen, and for his own part contributed to the upkeep of the hospice the *seigneurie* of Montbirre, with all its dependencies, which formed a part of his domain in Brabant. His example was widely copied by the Christian princes and great nobles among the Crusaders, who enriched the hospice with many lands and *seigneuries*, both in Palestine and in Europe. All these lands and properties were placed unreservedly in the hands of the saintly Gerard to do with as he would for the advancement of his work. In 1118 Gerard died in extreme old age; "he died in the arms of the brothers, almost without sickness, falling, as it may be said, like a fruit ripe for eternity."

The choice of the Hospitallers as his successor was Raimond Dupuy, a nobleman of illustrious descent from the Province of Dauphiny, and it is he who first held rule under the title of grand master. In all charity and loving kindness the life of Gerard had been passed, the brethren of St. John occupying themselves merely in tending the sick, in helping the poor and the pilgrims; but Raimond Dupuy was a soldier of the Cross, and he laid before the order a scheme by which, from among the members thereof, a military corps should be formed, vowed to a perpetual crusade against the *Infidel*. This, in full conclave, was carried by acclamation, and the most remarkable body of religious warriors that the world has ever seen then came existence.

This pact against the *Infidel* was in the first instance directed against the barbarians who swarmed around the Holy City, and the Hospitallers, who nearly all had been knights and soldiers of Godfrey de Bouillon, joyfully took up their arms again to employ them in the defence of this locality which they cherished, and in defence of the pilgrims who were robbed, murdered, and maltreated in all the surrounding country. In becoming warriors once more, they vowed to turn their arms against the *Infidel*, and against him alone; to neither make nor meddle with arms in their hands in any dispute between men of their own faith. The composition of the order as it was arranged by Raimond Dupuy caused it to consist of three classes. In the first were placed men of high birth and rank who, having been bred to arms, were capable of taking command. In the second came priests and chaplains, who, besides the ordinary duties attached to their religious profession, were obliged, each in his turn, to accompany the fighting men in their wars. Those who were neither of noble houses nor belonging to the ecclesiastical profession were known as "serving brothers": they were employed indifferently in following the knights into battle or in tending the sick in the hospital, and were distinguished by a coat-of-arms of a different colour from that worn by the knights.

As the order prospered amazingly, and as to it repaired numbers of the young noblesse from all parts of Europe to enrol themselves under its banner, it was accordingly divided into seven "Languages"; those of Provence, Auvergne, France, Italy, Arragon, Germany, and England. To the Language of Arragon was in later years allotted those of Castile and of Portugal. The dress consisted of a black robe, with a mantle of the same colour, the whole being called *manteau à bec*, having upon the left side thereof a white cross in cloth, with light points. The eight-pointed cross, or the Maltese Cross, as it came to be known in subsequent centuries, will be seen upon the armour, engraven on the breastplate, of all the pictures of the grand masters.

In the year 1259 the Pope, Alexander IV., finding that men of noble birth objected to be habited as were the "serving brothers," ordained that the knights on a campaign should wear a *"sopraveste"* of scarlet embroidered with the cross in white; further, that should any knight abandon the ranks, and fly from the battle, he should be deprived of his order and his habit. The form of government was purely aristocratic, all authority being vested in the Council, of which the grand master was the chief, the case of an equal division of opinion being provided for by giving to the grand master the casting vote. There were in the order certain aged knights who were called "Preceptors," who, under authority delegated to them by the Council, administered the estates and funds accruing, and also paid for the hire of such soldiers or "seculars" whom the Knights took into their service.

Incidentally, it may be mentioned that the establishment of the Knights of St. John led to the foundation of the famous order of the Knights Templars. In 1118 Hugues de Payens, Geoffrey de St. Aldemar, and seven other French noblemen, whose hearts were touched by the sufferings which the pilgrims underwent in their journey to Jerusalem, formed themselves into a society with the object of the protection of these inoffensive persons on their transit from the coast inland. Hugues de Payens, received in audience by Pope Honoré II., was sent by the Pontiff to the Peers of the Council, then assembled at Troyes in Champagne; the Council approving of so charitable an enterprise, the order was formed, and Bernard, known as "Saint" Bernard, drew up the code of regulations by which it was to be governed. The movement spread, and many princes and nobles returned to the Holy Land in the train of de Payens and his companions.

So famous did the order of St. John become, that in 1133 Alfonzo, King of Navarre and Arragon, who called himself Emperor of Spain, carried his zeal so far as to bequeath to the knights his kingdoms of Navarre and Arragon: this, however, was naturally and hotly contested in these places, and Raimond Dupuy, who attended a Council to regulate the matter, was content to compromise on certain lands and benefits being allocated to those whom he represented.

On August 15th, 1310, the knights, under the grand master, Fulke de Villaret, conquered the Island of Rhodes and established themselves there, and from this time onward, while they held the island, were known as the Knights of Rhodes. No sooner were the knights firmly established in Rhodes and the fortifications placed in a proper state of repair, than a tower was built on the highest point of the island, of great height, from which a view could be obtained of the sea and the surrounding islands, and from which information could be signalled as to the movements of any vessels which were observed. It was then decided to fortify the small island of Cos or Lango in the vicinity, as it contained an excellent harbour; a fortress, planned by the grand master himself, was erected on the island, a knight was left in command, and we are told that under the successors of de Villaret—himself twenty-fourth grand master—the island, which was very fertile, flourished exceedingly, producing much fruit and some most excellent wine.

There was reigning in Bithynia, at the time when the knights seized upon Rhodes, that Ottoman whose name has come down to us when we speak of the Ottoman Empire; it is a somewhat strange coincidence that the Christian warriors, sworn foes of the Mussulman, should have so established themselves just when the tide of the Mohammedan conquest was about to rise and sweep away Byzantium; that they should arrive upon the scene just as the curtain was about to rise on the tragedy which, in its onward march, was to make of the church of St. Sophia a mosque for the worship of the Ottoman Turks.

Ottoman—the descendant of one Soliman, the chief of a nomadic tribe of Tartars who had been chased from the Empire of Persia in the year 1214—was not only a soldier and a conqueror, but also a great and beneficent ruler in those regions in which he held sway. Approached by those of his co-religionists who had been driven out of Rhodes by the Knights, Ottoman embarked an army and attacked the place, assuring himself of an easy conquest. In spite, however, of the fortifications having been hastily constructed, his troops were defeated with great loss, and he was obliged to raise the siege. In this manner did the indomitable champions of Christendom begin that long and bloodthirsty war between the Cross and the Crescent in the Mediterranean which was to endure for nearly another five centuries.

In the long, chequered, and glorious history of the Knights there are many strange and semi-miraculous deeds recounted of them in the wars and adventures in which they took so prominent a part; the following, which is gravely set out by the historians of the time, may be left to the judgment of the reader. In 1324 Fulke de Villaret was succeeded in the grand mastership by Helion de Villeneuve, a knight of exemplary piety and a strict disciplinarian. Under his rule the order regained those habits of severe simplicity from which they had been allowed to lapse by his predecessor. In 1329 Rhodes was greatly agitated by the fact that a crocodile or serpent—as it is indifferently described—had taken up its abode in the marshes at the foot of Mount St. Etienne, some two miles from the town. This ferocious creature devoured sheep and cattle; also several of the inhabitants had lost their lives by approaching the neighbourhood in which it dwelt. Several attacks were made upon it, but, as there were no firearms, all the missiles projected against it rebounded harmlessly from the scales with which it was covered. So dangerous had it become, that the grand master thought it his duty to forbid any of the knights to attempt its destruction; an order which was obeyed with a right good will. There was, however, a knight of the Language of Provence called Gozon de Dieu-Donné, who secretly determined that he would slay the serpent,

Gozon de Dieu-Donné slaying the great serpent of Rhodes

and he accordingly made it his occupation to observe as closely as possible the habits of the monster. Having satisfied himself on certain points, he then returned to his chateau of Gozon in the province of Languedoc. The point which Gozon had wished to determine was in what portion of its body was the serpent vulnerable; and he had convinced himself that the belly of the creature was unprotected by scales. He accordingly modelled in wood as exact a representation of the serpent as he could accomplish, colouring it the same as the original; the belly of the model was constructed of leather. He then trained some large and ferocious hounds, at a certain signal, to dash in under the model and fix their teeth in its leathern underpart. For months did the ingenious knight persevere with the training of his dogs, himself on horseback in full armour cheering them to the assault. At last he considered them to be perfect in their parts, and, taking two servants and the hounds with him, returned to Rhodes. Avoiding everybody, he caused his arms to be carried to a small church in the neighbourhood of Mount St. Etienne by his servants. The knight went into the church, where he passed some time in prayer, recommending his soul to God in the enterprise which he was about to undertake.

He then donned his armour and mounted his horse, ordering his servants, if he were killed, to return to France but if he succeeded in killing the serpent to come at once to him, or to aid him if he were wounded. He then rode off in the direction of the marsh accompanied by his hounds. No sooner did the serpent hear the ring of bit and stirrup-iron, the trampling of the charger and the baying of the hounds, than it issued forth with wide-open slavering jaws and terrible burning eyes to slay and to devour. Gozon, recommending his soul to his Maker, put spurs to his horse and charged. But his lance shivered on the hide of the serpent as though it had struck a stone wall. His horse, mad with terror at the sight and the foul odour of the serpent, plunged so furiously as to unseat him. He fell to the ground, uttering as he did so his call to the hounds; had it not been for these faithful auxiliaries he would instantly have been slain, but they rushed in and, fastening their teeth in the belly of the serpent, caused it to writhe and twist in its anguish. Instantly Gozon was upon his feet again, and, watching his opportunity, plunged his sword into the exposed vitals of his enemy. Mortally wounded, the serpent flung itself high in the air with a convulsive effort, and falling backwards pinned the knight to the ground beneath its enormous bulk. The servants, who had been the horrified spectators of this terrific conflict, now rushed to the assistance of their master, and succeeded in freeing him from his unpleasant predicament. Gozon, they thought, was dead, but upon dashing some water in his face he opened his eyes, to behold the pleasing spectacle of his monstrous enemy lying by his side a corpse.

Naturally elated, he returned to Rhodes, where he became on the instant the popular hero; for who could say or do enough for the man who had slain the serpent. He was conducted in triumph to the palace of the grand master by his fellow knights, but here a remarkably unpleasant surprise was in store for him. Very austerely did Helion de Villeneuve regard the triumphant warrior, and stern and uncompromising was the voice in which he asked him how he had dared to contravene the express order of his grand master by going forth to combat with the serpent? Calling a Council immediately the implacable de Villeneuve, in spite of all entreaties, deprived Gozon de Dieu-Donné of the habit of a knight. "What," said this just and severe disciplinarian, "is the death of this monster, what indeed do the deaths of the islanders matter, compared with the maintenance of the discipline of this order of which I am the unworthy chief?"

But Helion de Villeneuve was of too wise and kindly a nature to make his decree absolute, and having thus vindicated his authority he shortly afterwards released Gozon and made him happy by his praises and more material benefits.

The Abbè de Vertot tells us that the learned Bochart argues that the Phoenicians gave to this island the name of Gefirath-Rod (from whence the name "Rhodes"), or the Isle of the Serpents, and that when the Romans were at war with the Carthaginians Attilius Regulus slew a monster in the island of Rhodes the skin of which measured one hundred feet. Thevenot, in his *Travels* published in 1637, states that he saw the head of Gozon's serpent still attached to one of the gates of the town of Rhodes, and that it was as large as the head of a horse.

Upon the death of Helion de Villeneuve in 1346, a Chapter of the order was held as usual to elect his successor. When it came to the turn of the Commander Gozon de Dieu-Donné to speak, he said:

> In entering this conclave I made a solemn vow not to propose any knight whom I did not consider to be most worthy of this exalted office, and animated by the best intentions for the glory and well-being of the order. After considering carefully the state of the Christian world, of the wars which we are perpetually obliged to wage against the *infidel*, the firmness and vigour necessary for the maintenance of discipline, I declare that I find no person so capable of governing our 'Religion' as myself.

He then proceeded to speak in a purely impersonal tone of the magnificent services which he had rendered, not forgetting the famous episode of the serpent, and drew their attention to the fact that the late grand master had constituted him, Gozon, his principal lieutenant. He ended: "You have already tried my government, you know well that which you may hope to expect. I believe that in all justice I shall receive your suffrages."

Naturally the assemblage was stupefied at hearing a man thus recommend himself; on reflection, however, they decided that he had spoken no less than the truth, and Gozon de Dieu-Donné, "the hero of the serpent," became twenty-sixth grand master of the order. He died in 1353, when he was succeeded by Pierre de Cornillan, and upon his tomb were graven these words:

Cy Gist le Vainqueur du Dragon.

In the years 1480 and 1485 under the grand master Pierre D'Aubusson, Rhodes withstood two great sieges from the Turks. The first of these is described at length by the knight Merri Dupuis *"temoin oculaire"* who sets down:

Je, Mary Dupuis gros et rude de sens et de entendement je veuille parler et desscrire au plus bref que je pourray et au plus pres de la verite selon que je pen voir a lueil.

The description of that of 1485 is written by another eye-witness, the Commandeur de Bourbon, to whom. . . .

. . . . ma semble bon et condecent a raison declairer premierement les causes qui out incite mon poure et petit entendement a faire cest petit oeuvre.

But we have no space to follow these gallant Knights, and it must suffice to say that on both occasions, after incredible exertions and terrible slaughter on both sides, the attacks of the Turks were eventually repulsed.

It was reserved for Soliman the Magnificent to finally vanquish the Knights and to expel them from Rhodes; from July 1522 until January 1523 the Knights under the heroic Villiers de L'Isle Adam maintained an all unequal struggle against the vast hosts of the Crescent, which were perpetually reinforced. At last, on January 1st, 1523, the Knights, by virtue of a treaty with Soliman, which was honourably observed on both sides, evacuated the island in which they had been established for nearly two hundred and twenty years.

By favour of Charles V. the Knights on October 26th, 1530, took charge of the islands of Malta and Gozo, and established themselves therein; still under the grand mastership of L'Isle Adam, whose sword and helmet are still religiously kept in a small church in Vittoriosa, just at the back of the Admiral Superintendent's house in the present dockyard.

The knights fortified the islands and there abode, until in 1565 the Ottoman returned once more to the attack.

It may be said that heroism is a relative term, that it has many uses and applications all equally truthful. On the side of mere physical courage almost every man who took part in that memorable siege of Malta in the year 1565 may have been said to have earned the title of hero. No man's foot went back; no man's courage quailed; no man's face blanched when called upon to face perils so appalling that they meant an almost inevitable and speedy death; this was true or Christian and Moslem alike. The death-roll on either side was so tremendous as to prove this contention up to the hilt. From May 18th to September 8th, 1565—that is to say, in one hundred and thirteen days—thirty thousand Moslems and eight thousand Christians perished—an average of some three hundred and thirty-six persons per day. In that blazing torrid heat the sufferings of those who survived from day to day must have been accentuated beyond bearing by the myriads of unburied corpses by which they lived surrounded; and that the contending forces were not swept away by pestilence is an extraordinary marvel.

In many, nay, in most campaigns, personal feeling enters but little into the contest. Nationality strikes against nationality, army against army, or navy against navy; but no burning hatred of his adversary animates the breast of the combatant on either side; it may even be said that frequently some pity for the vanquished is felt, when all is over, by the side which has conquered. At Malta the element of actual personal individual hatred was the mainspring by which the combatants on both sides were moved; each regarded the other as an *infidel*, the slaying of whom was the sacrifice most acceptable to the God they worshipped. "*Infidel*" was the term which each hurled at the other; to destroy the *infidel*, root and branch, was the act imposed upon those whose faith was the one only passport to a blessed eternity, and those who fell in the strife, whether Christian or Moslem, felt assured that for them the gates of heaven stood wide open. Great as were those others who perished, faithful to the death as were those noble knights who died to a man in the culminating agony of St. Elmo, adroit,

CARRACK IN WHICH THE KNIGHTS ARRIVED AT MALTA, 1530

resourceful, master of himself and others as was the famous Dragut, there is one name and one alone that shines like a beacon light upon a hill-top when we think of the siege of Malta. Jean Parisot de la Valette, whose name is enshrined for ever in that noble city which crowns Mount Sceberass at the present day, was the forty-eighth grand master of the Noble order of the Knights of Saint John of Jerusalem the charter for which, contained in the original Bull of Pope Paschal II., dated 1113 (in which the Holy Father took the order under his special protection), may be seen to this day in the armoury of the palace at Valetta. At the time when the supreme honour was conferred upon him, in the year 1557, he had passed through every grade of the order: as soldier, captain, general, Counsellor, Grand Cross: in all of them displaying a valour, a piety, a self-abnegation beyond all praise, A man of somewhat austere manner, he exacted from others that which he gave himself—a whole-hearted devotion to the order to which he had consecrated his life. Fearing no man in the Council Chamber, even as he feared no foe in the field, he ever spoke his mind in defence of that which he deemed to be right. Proud, with the dignity becoming a man of his ancient lineage, he merged all personal haughtiness in the zeal he felt in upholding the rights and privileges of that splendid confederation of knights of the best blood in Europe over which he had been called upon to preside at the mature age of sixty-three. There is no instance in history of any man more absolutely single-minded than La Valette; that in which he believed he cherished with an ardour almost incredible in these days, and that the sword of the Lord had been confided into his hand for the utter extermination and extirpation of the Moslem heresy was the leading feature in his creed. That he had been advanced to a dignity but little less than royal in achieving the grand mastership was but as dust in the balance to him compared with the opportunities which it gave him to harry his life-long foes; and he who had known so well how to obey throughout all his youth and manhood was now to prove, in the most emphatic manner, that he had learned how to command. In all those terrible hundred and thirteen days during which the siege lasted there was none to be compared to him. As occasion occurred this man's soul rose higher and ever higher; beseeching, imploring, commanding, by sheer force of example did he point out the way to the weaker spirits by whom he was surrounded.

To speak of weaker spirits in connection with the siege of Malta seems almost an insult; these gallant knights and soldiers were only so in comparison with their leader. Twice during the siege of St, Elmo did the garrison send to La Valette and represent that the place was no longer tenable; but Garcia de Toledo, Viceroy of Sicily for Philip of Spain, was writing specious letters instead of sending reinforcements, and every moment gained was of importance. Coldly did La Valette remind the Knights of their vows to the order, and when renewed assurances came that it was only a matter of a few hours before they should be overwhelmed he replied that others could be found to take their places, that he, as grand master, would come in person to show them how to die. A passion of remorse overcame these noble gentlemen, who, thus nerved by the indomitable spirit of their chief, died to the last man in the tumbled ruins of that charnel-house which had once been a fortress.

La Valette was ready to die; there was no man in all that garrison so ready. With pike and sword this veteran of seventy-one years of age was ever at the post of the greatest danger, repelling the assaults of Janissaries and corsairs, fighting with the spirit of the youngest among the Knights in the breaches rent in the walls of Il Borgo. In vain did his comrades try to prevent him from this perpetual exposure; in vain did they point out that the value of his life outnumbered that of an army. He was very gentle with these remonstrances, but quite firm. There were plenty as good as he to take his place should he fall, he insisted; till that time came it was his duty to inspire all by his example, to show to the simplest soldier that he was cared for by his grand master.

As things went from bad to worse, when Il Borgo became in little better case than had St. Elmo before it, La Valette never hesitated, never looked back, never ceased to hope that the sluggard Garcia de Toledo might send relief; and, if he did not, then would they all perish with arms in their hands, as had their brethren across that narrow strip of water who had held St. Elmo to the last man. What man or woman can read without something of a lump coming in their throat of those noble words of the grand master in the last few days of the siege when all had utterly abandoned hope?

Grimed, emaciated, covered with sweat and blood and dust, did La Valette move from post to post exhorting and encouraging his soldiers. So few had the gallant company of the Knights become that command was necessarily delegated to the under-officers; yet who among them did not find fresh courage and renewed strength when that great noble, the head of the order, stood by their sides and spoke thus to them as man to man?—

"My brothers, we are all servants of Jesus Christ; and I feel assured that if I and all these in command should fall you will still fight on for the honour of the order and the love of our Holy Church."

We have to think of what it all meant, we have dimly to try and realise the burden which was laid upon this man, before we come to a right conception, not only of what he endured but the terrible sacrifices he was called upon to make. Here was no man of iron lusting for blood and greedy of conquest for the sake of the vain applause of men; but one full of human love and affection for those among whom he had lived all the days of his life. Upon him was laid the charge of upholding the honour of the order, the majesty of the God whom he served. To this end he doomed to certain death those brethren of his in St. Elmo, his own familiar friends, reminding them that it was their duty so to die, while his heart was breaking with the agony of this terrible decision, which no weaker man could have given. When his beloved nephew was slain, together with another gallant youth, he smiled sadly and said that they had only travelled the road which they all had to tread in a few days; that he grieved as much for the one as for the other. In speaking of this man, it may truly be said that there is no character in history more elevated; there is none which shows us the picture of a more perfect, gentle, and valiant knight.

CHAPTER 19

A Great Armada

Great must have been the consternation of the Knights when the armada, commanded by Sinan Basha, appeared off their coasts, and bitter must have been the reflections of Juan d'Omedes, the grand master, who had all along contended that so formidable an expedition could not possibly be directed against Malta. The inhabitants of that island were, however, not left long in doubt, as Sinan, immediately on his arrival, entered the Grand Harbour, or "the Great Port," as it was called in those days. Sinan, in his royal galley, led the way in, contemptuously assured of an easy victory over so insignificant a place of arms. He had his first rude awakening before he had traversed some quarter of a mile of the placid waters of the Great Port. The harbour, as is well known, though long, is very narrow, and, on the starboard hand of the Turkish galleys as they entered, the Commandeur de Guimeran, a Spanish Knight, had ambushed three hundred *arquebusiers*. As the galley of Sinan came abreast of the ambush, the Commandeur gave the order to fire. The volley at so close a range had a terrible effect, especially among the *"chiourme,"* or the slaves who rowed the galley, some hundred of whom were placed *hors de combat*. Sinan, in a furious rage, ordered an immediate disembarkment; but when his men landed and scaled the heights of Mount Sceberras (the elevated land on which the city of Valetta now stands) there was no one to be found, the Commandeur and the men who had formed the ambush having disappeared. Gazing from the heights at Il Borgo, the fortress on the opposite side of the harbour where the Knights then dwelt, Sinan demanded of Dragut, "If that," pointing to the fortress, "was the place which he had told the Sultan could easily be taken?"

Dragut, whom no peril ever daunted, coolly replied:

"Certainly, no eagle ever built his nest on a rock more easy of access."

A corsair, who had been slave to the Knights, now approached Sinan, and told him that he had assisted at the building of the fortress; which, he averred, was so strong that if the admiral delayed until he had taken it that the winter would be upon them, although it was then only the month of July. Sinan, as we have said, was a hesitating commander. He had the ever-present fear of the Grand Turk before his eyes, and was not inclined for so difficult and dangerous an enterprise as this was represented to be. Leaving the fortress in his rear, he marched off to the high land in the centre of the island, on which was situated the Città Notabile, the capital of Malta, some seven miles distant from the sea. On their march through the island the Turks committed their usual atrocities, murdering the wretched inhabitants, firing their dwellings, destroying their crops, and carrying off their women. Had the siege of Notabile been pressed, the city must have fallen; but Sinan declared to Dragut that the principal object of the expedition was the reduction of Tripoli, and, in consequence, he had not the time to devote to its reduction. Dragut, furious at this temporising policy, urged an immediate assault, and, while the contention was waxing sharp between the two leaders, a letter was brought to Sinan which had been captured in a Sicilian galley. It was from the "Receiver" of the order, who dwelt at Messina, to the grand master, informing him that he had expressly sent this ship to inform him that Andrea Doria had just returned from Spain and was hastening with a large fleet to attack the Turks. The letter was a ruse on the part of the "Receiver," and contained not a particle of truth. It was, however, quite enough for Sinan, who immediately called a council of war and imparted this alarming news to its members. The council, after the invariable fashion of such bodies, decided to take the safest and easiest course: the name of the terrible Andrea was one of evil omen to the Ottomans, and, as one man, they voted for prosecuting their voyage to Tripoli before the Genoese seaman should put in an appearance. In vain was the fury of Dragut, who had counted on a full revenge on his ancient enemies the Knights. The armada sailed to the adjacent island of Gozo, which was thoroughly sacked with every refinement of cruelty. Every house on the island was burned, and six thousand of its inhabitants carried off to slavery. One incident is deserving of record. In Gozo dwelt a certain Sicilian with his wife and two daughters: sooner than that they should fall into the hands of the Turks this man stabbed his wife and daughters and then threw himself, sword in hand, into the ranks of his enemies, where he slew two of them, wounded several others, and was then hacked to pieces. The fleet then proceeded to Tripoli, which was taken almost without opposition, as it was defended by a mere handful of the Knights and some utterly unreliable Calabrian infantry, who had never before seen a shot fired: these men very soon mutinied and refused to fight any longer. Dragut became the autocrat of Tripoli, as his great predecessor Kheyr-ed-Din Barbarossa had been of Algiers: from hence, in the years that were to come before his death, he carried on his sleepless and unending warfare with his Christian foes, on whom he was destined to inflict another terrible defeat when they attacked this stronghold which he had made his own.

Claude de la Sangle dying on August 18th, 1557, Jean Parisot de la Valette was chosen grand master of the Knights of Malta in his stead on August 21st of the same year. He was, as we have said before, in succession, soldier, captain, councillor, general, and Grand Cross; he was as wise in council as he was terrible in battle; he was as much esteemed by his brethren as he was feared by the *infidel*. Under his governorship "the Religion" regained the ancient authority which it had once possessed, especially in some of the German Provinces and in the Republic of Venice. So great was the influence of La Valette that he succeeded in making the "Languages" (or confederations of Knights) of Germany and Venice pay their *"responsions,"* which had been allowed to get into arrear. These *"responsions"* were a tax levied on the "Languages" exclusively for the purpose of combating the *infidel*, and La Valette brought all the firmness of his high character to bear, in order to induce these Knights to do what, he reminded them, was their simple and obvious duty. Fired by the highest conception of the office he had been called upon to execute, La Valette allowed none of those under his command to be slack in their performance of their duties. In him dwelt the real old crusading spirit. He saw life with the single eye, for that which was paramount was the utter destruction of the *infidel*. There are many men who have a high conception of duty; there are but few who can inspire those with whom they are brought in contact. Of these latter was Jean Parisot de la Valette; in him the pure flame of religious enthusiasm burnt with so clear a light as to act as an illuminant for the paths of others. In him dwelt that rare quality of lifting others almost to that plane on which he dwelt himself, of making men nobler and better almost in spite of themselves. So it was that, when La Valette stooped to remind others of his brother Knights that they owed money to the order, that money was paid at once.

Having thus restored order to the finances, the grand master turned his attention to the state of affairs (as he had received them from his predecessor) connected with the territorial possessions of the Knights. For long years now the fortress of Tripoli had been in the hands of the renowned Dragut, who was the scourge and the terror of the Christians. The corsair dwelt in his stronghold in insolent defiance of the Knights, whose property it once had been. Years before he had wrested it from them by the strong hand: what, then, more necessary in the eyes of such an one as La Valette than to expel this audacious pirate? The grand master invited the co-operation of Juan la Cerda (a Spanish Grandee, Duke of Medina-Celi, and Viceroy of Sicily for the King of Spain) in this enterprise. The Viceroy joyfully acceded to the request, and informed his master. Philip II. approved the project, and sent orders to the Duke of Sesse, Governor of Milan, to the Duke of Alcala, Governor of Naples, and to John Andrea Doria, General of the Galleys, to join forces and to repair to Sicily, placing themselves under the orders of the Duke of Medina-Celi, who was expressly charged to take no action save by the advice of the grand master. The expedition assembled, the Duke took it to Malta, where it wintered, and in the spring it sailed and attacked Tripoli.

They found this fortress, however, in a very different state from that which they expected. Dragut, says De Vertot, "*avoit faire terasser les murailles de cette place.*" Bastions had been constructed, and every advantage taken for defence which was permitted by the terrain, or that the art of fortification admitted at this epoch. The castle, which was not advantageously placed, was, notwithstanding, put in a state of defence by an enormous expenditure of money. Great towers, in which were mounted many big guns, defended the entrance to the port, which had become the headquarters of the vessels owned by Dragut, and also of those corsairs who sailed their craft under the crescent flag of the Sultan of Constantinople. It was against such a fortress as this that the Duke of Medina-Celi went up: we have no space to deal here with the details of this attack, which ended in the hopeless and irremediable defeat of the Christian forces. The Duke was an incompetent commander; he was opposed to one of the greatest leaders of the age—an expert in almost every branch of the science of war, in command of a large body of the fiercest fighters of the day, who ever feared the wrath of Dragut more than the swords of the enemy.

La Valette, though he mourned over the repulse of the Christian forces from Tripoli, did not on that account allow his pursuit of the *infidel* to grow faint; the galleys of "the Religion" were always at sea, and both the corsairs and the Ottoman Turks were perpetually losing valuable ships and costly merchandise. Under the General of the Galleys, the Commandeur Gozon de Melac, and that celebrated chevalier, the Commandeur de Romegas, the sea forces of the Knights were everywhere in evidence. Into the hands of the Christians fell the Penon de Velez, situated on the northern coast of Africa opposite to Malaga—a fortress much frequented by the corsairs; the Goletta at Tunis was also taken, and the pirates became so much alarmed that they demanded succour from Constantinople. They represented to Soliman that, at this rate, the whole of Northern Africa would soon be in the hands of the Christians to the total exclusion of the true believer.

Soliman listened to their complaints and promised that soon he would send forth an armament which should put an end to the misfortunes from which they were suffering. Once again preparations were begun in the arsenals of Constantinople, and while these were in progress an event took place which had an important bearing on the situation. Just after the taking of the Penon de Velez seven galleys of "the Religion," under the command of the chevaliers de Giou and De Romegas, which were cruising in the neighbourhood of Zante and Cephalonia, fell in with "a puissant galleon" filled with the richest merchandise of the East, armed with "twenty great cannons of bronze," and a number of smaller guns, under the command of the Reis Bairan-Ogli, having on board "excellent officers of artillery," as well as two hundred Janissaries for her defence. This great ship was the property of Kustir-Aga, the chief Eunuch of the Seraglio of the Sultan, and many of the ladies of the harem were interested in a pecuniary sense in the safe arrival of this vessel at Constantinople. The galleys of "the Religion" attacked, and, after a most obstinate resistance, in which one hundred and twenty of the Christians and an even larger number of the Turks were killed, the galleon was captured. If there had been an outcry in Constantinople before this occurrence it was all as nothing to that which now arose. Kustir-Aga and the Odalisques of the Harem prostrated themselves at the feet of Soliman the Magnificent, and with streaming eyes, dishevelled hair, and frantic gestures, demanded the instant despatch of an expedition to utterly exterminate these barbarian corsairs, the Knights of Malta, who had thus injured them and lacerated their tenderest susceptibilities. The Grand Turk, autocrat as he was, had no peace day or night; he was surrounded by wailing women and sullen officials, all of whom had lost heavily by the capture of the puissant galleon. The Imaum, or preacher in the principal mosque, called upon the Sultan in his discourse to fall upon the audacious *infidel* and smite him hip and thigh. He reminded the Padishah that, in the dungeons of the

Knights, true believers were languishing; that on the rowers' benches of the galleys of "the Religion" Moslems were being flogged like dogs. In a furious peroration he concluded:

> It is only thy invincible sword which can shatter the chains of these unfortunates, whose cries are rising to heaven and afflicting the ears of the Prophet of God: the son is demanding his father, the wife her husband and her children. All, therefore, wait upon thee, upon thy justice, and thy power, for vengeance upon their cruel and implacable enemies.

Contrary to all precedent, which enjoins the most perfect silence in the mosque, these bold utterances were received with something more than murmurs of applause: never in all his long and glorious reign had the great and magnificent despot heard so plainly the voice of his people. Apart, however, from eunuchs, women, and Mullahs, Soliman had long been importuned by Dragut to take the course which was now being urged upon him with so much insistence. There was at this time no warrior in all his entourage for whose opinion the Sultan had the same respect as he had for that of the ruler of Tripoli. Dragut had more than a tincture of learning: he was first of all an incomparable leader of men and an entirely competent seaman. He was also a scientific artillerist, and was learned in the technique of the fortification of his time. Added to this he was—albeit by no means so cruel as most of his contemporaries—one of those men before whom all trembled: as we have seen in the case of the corsairs who defended "Africa," "they feared the wrath of Dragut more than death itself."

It was this renowned leader who warned Soliman against the Knights; he pointed out that they were far more dangerous now than they had been in 1523, the year of their expulsion from Rhodes. When established there they were, so to speak, surrounded by the Turkish Empire; in Malta, on the contrary, they were easily succoured from Sicily, which belonged to Spain, another implacable enemy of the Moslem; that Malta lay right on the route which all the ships of the Sultan must take on passage from the East to Constantinople; and in consequence the order was a standing and perpetual menace to the trade of the Empire. All this was so undeniably true that so shrewd a man and so competent a ruler as Soliman could not fail to be impressed by the soundness of the reasoning.

Besides all this, he knew quite well that now he could not hold back, had it been even against his inclination—which was by no means the case; for there had arisen one of those storms of popular opinion—all the more formidable because of their infrequency—before which even the most hardened of despots must bend. Accordingly the Sultan called a conference of his fighting men, which was held on horseback in the open-air. The inclination of the Sultan being known, most of the generals, like good courtiers, voted for immediate war with the Knights. At this conference was present that Ali Basha, or Occhiali, or Uluchali, as he was indifferently called, of whom we shall have more to say later on. Upon this occasion he was present as the representative of Dragut, and urged, on behalf of his master, that the time was not yet ripe for an attack on Malta. First, he contended, it was necessary to recapture the Goletta and the Peñon de Velez, and to defeat the Moors of Tunis, who were feudatories of the Spanish king and avowed enemies of the Ottoman Empire. Ali was supported by one Mahomet, an old warrior who had grown white in the service of the Sultan, who strongly opposed the contemplated campaign on the ground that the Knights would in all probability have the full strength of Europe at their backs.

Numbers, however, added to the personal inclination of the Sultan, carried the day. The die was cast, the memorable expedition was decided upon, and all the Sultan's vast Empire soon rang with the note of preparation. The Capitan Basha, Piali, was in command of the fleet, and the direction of the land forces was confided to Mustafa, an old officer sixty-five years of age, a severe disciplinarian, and of a sanguinary and cruel disposition to any of his enemies who had the misfortune to fall into his hands.

Once again did Europe lose itself in speculation: against whom, all men were asking, was this new expedition to be directed? Spain feared for her African possessions, as the Goletta was the key to the kingdom of Tunis, while the Peñon de Velez was one of the bulwarks of Algeria. In consequence Don Garcia de Toledo passed over from Sicily to confer with the grand master of the Knights. Garcia de Toledo was by no means a favourable specimen of the illustrious race from which he sprang, and was a complete antithesis to La Valette; he was to prove himself in the terrible days that were to come to be sluggish, incompetent, a ruler who could not rule, a person for ever letting "I dare not wait upon I would." Just as long as Spain considered this new expedition was directed against herself considerable activity was shown; when the attack developed and it was seen that the objective of the Turks was Malta, the procrastinating Spanish king and his incompetent viceroy allowed matters so to drift that, had any other man than La Valette been in command at Malta, the fall of that island had been inevitable.

We have seen how Juan d'Omedes had dealt with a previous crisis in the affairs of the order; very different was it in the opening months of the year 1565. La Valette was well served by his spies in Constantinople, and the grand master was under no illusions from the very first as to what the destination of the army of the Sultan would be. He recognised that against the small islands of Malta and Gozo all the strength of the mightiest Empire in the world was about to be directed, and with serene confidence set about the task of preparation. His first care was to send out "a general citation" to those Knights living in their own homes in different countries in Europe, commanding them to repair at once to Malta and take part in the defence of that order to which they had vowed to consecrate their lives. The agents of the order in Italy succeeded in raising two thousand infantry, and the Viceroy of Sicily sent over two companies of Spanish infantry which he had promised. All the galleys of "the Religion" were called in from distant service and were set to work importing ammunition, stores, provisions, and all requisites for the withstanding of a siege. As the galleys passed backwards and forwards to Sicily, in each returning vessel came noble gentlemen of every country in Europe, in answer to the summons of their grand master. They were received with the tenderest affection by him and by those others already assembled; never in all its long and glorious history had the order assembled in circumstances more grave; never in its history, either in the past or in the future, did it quit itself with so supreme a heroism as in those days of 1565 which were yet to come. In Malta the orderly bustle of preparation went on ceaselessly; the Italian and Spanish troops and the inhabitants of the island, for the most part hardy mariners well accustomed to the ceaseless *guerre de course* of the Knights, were formed into companies, officered by the members of the order, and assigned to different posts.

Meanwhile the grand master caused copies of the letters which he had received from Constantinople to be sent to all the great princes of Europe; showing them the straits to which the order was shortly to be reduced and imploring of them to send timely succour. But it was not upon outside aid that La Valette counted overmuch; he was preparing to confront the Turks with such forces as he had at his own disposal; content, if necessary, to leave the issue in the hands of the God in whom he trusted. As the chevaliers came flocking to the standard of St. John he received them, we are told, "as a kind father receives his beloved children, having provided in advance for their food and lodging." He personally entered into the most minute details of his charge; he reviewed his infantry, he instructed his artillery, he planned sites for hospitals, he sketched out new fortifications, and then went among the humblest of his followers and wielded the pick and shovel in the burning sun. Everywhere his cheering presence was felt, his equable and serene temperament diffused confidence and hope.

All things being thus in train he assembled his brethren and addressed them in the following terms:

> A formidable army, composed of audacious barbarians, is descending on this island; these persons, my brothers, are the enemies of Jesus Christ. To-day it is a question of the defence of our faith as to whether the book of the Evangelist is to be superseded by that of the Koran? God on this occasion demands of us our lives, already vowed to His service. Happy will those be who first consummate this sacrifice. But that we may indeed be worthy to render it come, my dear brothers, to the foot of the altar, where we may renew our vows. Let each one rely on the blood of the Saviour of men and in the faithful practice of the sacraments; in them we shall find so generous a contempt for death that we shall indeed be rendered invincible.

The Knights then, headed by the grand master, took themselves in procession to the church. Here they confessed and received the sacrament. "They went out from thence as men who had received a new birth." The Knights, we are then told, tenderly embraced one another in all solemnity; vowing to shed the last drop of their blood in defence of their religion and its holy altars. It was in this lofty frame of mind that the Knights of Malta awaited the coming of their hereditary foe. Into the hearts and minds of these gallant gentlemen of the best blood in the world the grand master had instilled some leaven of the greatness by which he himself was inspired. When belief is so wholehearted as it was in the case of La Valette; when it is allied to a genius for war, and a supreme gift for the inspiration of others, then that man and the force which he commands are as near to invincibility as it is permitted to fallible human beings to attain. There were two things in which the Knights were supremely fortunate on this occasion: the first was that they had La Valette as grand master, the second that Dragut was not in supreme command of the Turks, and that the siege had opened before he arrived upon the scene. In this expedition, as in previous ones, the Turkish commanders had orders to attempt nothing really important without the advice of Dragut. They found themselves without him when they arrived and made an initial mistake. With La Valette in command there was no room for blundering; the ultimate result of their blunder was the defeat which they sustained.

Grand master, Knight, and noble, soldier, peasant, and mariner, strove valiantly with the task of putting the island into a state of defence, and when at last the long-expected armada of their foes rose above that distant blue horizon in the north all had been done that skill and experience could dictate.

It was upon May 18th in the year 1565 that the Turkish fleet arrived at Malta. It was composed of one hundred and fifty-nine galleys and vessels propelled by oars: on board of these was an army for disembarkation of thirty thousand men, composed of Janissaries and Spahis, the very pick and flower of the Turkish army. Soliman the Magnificent was leaving as little to chance as was possible on this occasion; he well knew the temper of the Knights, and that this expedition had before it a task which would try both the army and its leaders to the very utmost of their strength. Behind the main body of the fleet came a host of vessels, charged with provisions, the horses of the Spahis, the siege-train of the artillery, all the innumerable appliances and engines of war which were in use at that day. The initial mistake on the part of the Turks was in embarking cavalry for a siege; they knew, or they should have known, of the extreme smallness of the island which they were about to attack, and that they were by no means likely to be met with armies in the field owing to the enormous preponderance of numbers which they had assured to themselves.

Piali, as we have said, was in command of the fleet, and Mustafa of the army; the corsairs did not arrive on the scene till some days afterwards.

The Turks landed some men who encountered the Chevalier La Riviere and some Maltese troops, with whom they had some lively skirmishes. Unfortunately, in one of these the Chevalier was captured, put to the torture, and eventually beheaded for having wilfully misled the Turks. A council of war was held by Piali, Mustafa, and their principal officers, to deliberate on the best manner of prosecuting the enterprise on which they were engaged. The admiral, wishing to conform strictly with the instructions of Soliman, voted to delay all initiative until the arrival of the famous corsair. Mustafa, however, held a different opinion: the unfortunate Chevalier La Riviere had, before his death, informed the Turkish general that large and powerful succours were expected daily from Sicily. Secretly disquieted by this news, which he had at the time affected to disbelieve, Mustafa now urged immediate action. His opinion was that, in the first instance, they had better attack the castle of St. Elmo. It was a small and insignificant fort which at best would only delay them some five or six days; when this had fallen they could proceed to the more serious business of taking Il Borgo, the principal fortress on the island in which the grand master and most of the Knights were established. By the time St. Elmo had been taken they might reasonably expect that Dragut and his corsairs would have arrived, and, with these seasonable reinforcements, proceed to the really formidable portion of their task. In their decisions both admiral and general were wrong; to delay attack, once the troops were landed, was a counsel of pusillanimity hardly to be expected of Piali, but showing at the same time how he dreaded above all else departing one iota from the instructions which he had received. To attack the castle of St. Elmo first was a military mistake, because it could be—and was during the whole of the siege—reinforced from its larger sister Il Borgo.

The discourse of Mustafa prevailed in the council of war, and the siege of St. Elmo was decided upon and immediately begun.

CHAPTER 20

The Siege of Malta

There was an entire disregard of human life among the leaders of the Ottoman Turks at this time which is almost incredible; to attain their end in war they sacrificed thousands upon thousands of men with an absolutely callous indifference. In no chapter of the blood-stained history of their Empire was this trait more in evidence than it was at the siege of Malta. There was, however, a reason for this, which developed itself more and more as the ceaseless assaults on the positions of the Knights went on. From a military point of view, all the operations which took place were those of the siege of a fortress; as when at length St. Elmo fell the Turks turned their attention to the fortress of Il Borgo. The time-honoured method of the attack on a fortress, of approaching it by sap and mine, was here almost an impossibility, as the island of Malta is composed of solid rock through which it was practically impossible to drive trenches. It is true that the rock is of an exceptionally soft nature, easily cut through with proper tools; but you cannot cut through rock, no matter how soft it may be, when your operations are opposed at every step by a brave and vigilant enemy. Mustafa and the council of war had, as we have said, decided to begin operations by the siege of the fortress of St. Elmo. This place had been built from the designs of the Prior of Capua, an officer of the order, and was situated at the extreme end of the promontory of Mount Sceberass, which juts out between the Great Port and the harbour of Marsa Muzetto. The fort was in a commanding position and dominated the entrance to the two principal harbours in the island. It was admirably adapted for repulsing an attack from the sea; but, owing to the proximity of other points of land upon which artillery could be mounted, was easily capable of attack by such an enemy as that by which it was now assailed.

The principal preoccupation of the militant Prior of Capua had

JEAN PARISOT DE LA VALETTE, GRAND MASTER OF THE KNIGHTS OF MALTA, AT THE SIEGE OF THAT ISLAND BY THE TURKS IN 1565

been to make it formidable on the side facing the sea; perhaps the designer had never contemplated the possibility that the day might dawn when it would be attacked from the landward side! However this may have been, Mustafa decided that it could and should be carried on this, its weakest face, and made his preparations accordingly.

As far as it was possible to open trenches this was done, at the most prodigal expenditure of the lives of the pioneers. Where the rock proved absolutely impossible of manipulation redoubts were constructed of massive beams on which thick planks were bolted, the whole covered with wet earth which had to be collected with incredible toil from the country at the back. Disembarking their siege-guns, and utilising the cattle of the islanders for transporting them, the great cannon of the Turks were dragged up the slopes of the Mount and got into position; and by the 24th of May fire was opened on St. Elmo with ten guns which threw balls weighing eighty pounds. Besides these there were two culverins which threw balls of sixty pounds, and a huge basilisk, the projectile from which weighed no less than one hundred and sixty pounds. A terrible fire was opened against the walls of the fort, and so destructive did it immediately become that the Bailli of Negropont, the Knight in command, very soon became aware that his trust must be in the stout hearts and strong arms of his garrison; as the walls by which they were surrounded were hourly crumbling into nothingness.

Regarding the matter from this point of view, he sent at once to the grand master by the Chevalier La Cerda demanding succour; this officer, "rendered eloquent by fear," exaggerated the peril to which the fort was exposed and stated that it could not possibly hold out for more than another eight days.

"What losses have you had?" demanded the grand master.

"Sire," replied La Cerda, "the fort may be compared to a sick man in his extremity, in the last stage of weakness, unable to sustain himself except by perpetual cordials and remedies."

"Then I myself will be your physician," said the grand master with contempt, "and I will bring others with me. If that cannot cure you of fear it will, at all events, prevent the infidels from seizing upon the fort."

There was no real hope in the mind of La Valette that St. Elmo could be saved from the enemy. The place was too weak, and none knew this fact better than the man to whom all the defences of the island were as familiar as the hilt of his own good sword; but, though he secretly deplored the necessity, he felt that if Malta were to be preserved it could only be done by delaying until succour should come from outside; every day, nay, every hour, was of importance, and he was prepared to sacrifice St. Elmo and the lives of its entire garrison to attain his end. He did not, however—to continue the simile of La Cerda—prescribe for others a medicine which he himself was not prepared to take, and when he said that he would go to the fort of St. Elmo it was no mere figure of speech. The council of the Knights, however, would not hear of the grand master thus sacrificing himself; well did these noble gentlemen know that there was none among them like unto him, that his name and his influence were worth an army in themselves. The outcry was so loud that La Valette had to yield; which he did the more readily when he saw the splendid emulation among his brethren to cross over to the beleaguered and crumbling fortress which promised nothing but the grave to those who should pass within the circle of fire by which it was now surrounded. To the Chevaliers Gonzales de Medran and de la Motte was conceded the proud privilege for which all the Knights were clamouring; and, accompanied by the tears and the prayers of their brethren, they passed to that place where, if death were certain, honour at least was immortal. Truly the heart warms somewhat to the days of chivalry when one reads of what was done at the siege of Malta. The motto of *Noblesse oblige* was no dead letter in the sixteenth century. By this time the whole of Europe was awake to the peril of the order, and, galloping for dear life across Europe, came the Knights, anxious and willing to share in the danger. For most of these gentlemen Sicily was the goal at which they aimed; arrived there they flung themselves into any boat or shallop which they could hire, and, heedless of the risk of capture by the Turkish fleet, totally ignorant of what was passing in Malta save that the *infidel* was at her gates, they passed across the channel which separates the two islands and joined their fellows at Il Borgo.

Greatly heartened by the reinforcements brought to them by de Medran and de la Motte, the garrison of St. Elmo made a sortie, surprised the Turks in their entrenchments, and, under cover of the guns of the fort, succeeded in destroying nearly all the works which the enemy had so painfully built up. The Turks, however, when they had recovered from the surprise, were in such large numbers as to be able to rally and drive the Christians from the vantage points which they had gained; and to oblige them once again to retire into the fort. From this time onward there was never a day in which the garrison and the besiegers were not hand to hand in the trenches.

Just after the first reinforcements had been thrown into St. Elmo there arrived on the scene Ali, the Lieutenant of Dragut. This corsair came from Alexandria with six galleys, on board of which were nine hundred men, reinforcements for the Turkish army. A few days after this the famous Dragut himself appeared, with thirteen galleys and two *galleots*, on board of which were sixteen hundred men.

What must not have been the despairing feelings with which the defenders viewed the arrival of this augmentation to the swarming ranks of their foes! From afar they noted the vessels and knew, while Philip of Spain and Garzia de Toledo still procrastinated, that now was added to the number of their enemies the most famous captain who served the autocrat of the Eastern world. Very naturally the arrival of Dragut was hailed with acclamation by the Turks: every gun in that vast armada spoke in salute, every trumpet blared, every drum rolled to welcome the man honoured of the Padishah, notorious throughout the whole world of Europe for his implacable enmity to the Knights. The first preoccupation of the corsair was to inform himself as to the conduct of the operations. These, when disclosed to him, by no means met with his approval. This real leader immediately made it clear to Piali and Mustafa that which they should have done. In the first place they should have made themselves masters of the castle of Gozo, and then captured the Città Notabile. By doing this the supplies to the town and fortress of Il Borgo would have been cut off: besides—and more important than aught else—they would in this manner have closed the road to those succours expected by the Christians. Piali, who had desired from the first to undertake nothing without the advice of Dragut, now said that the siege of St. Elmo was not so far advanced after all, and, if the Basha of Tripoli should so direct, it could be raised at once. To this, however, Dragut would by no means consent.

"That would have been well enough," he said, "if the affair had not gone so far; but, after the opening of the trenches and several days of attack, it is not possible to raise the siege without sullying the honour of the Sultan and discouraging the valour of the soldiers."

It cannot be denied that, in acting as he did, the corsair displayed a self-restraint and a loyalty to the Sultan hardly to be expected in the circumstances. The jealousy which so often obtains among rival commanders was singularly in evidence in the forces of the Padishah: Dragut had good cause to be dissatisfied with the dispositions which had been made, and yet, for the reasons which we have quoted, he allowed them to proceed. Before the Basha had left Tripoli he had been engaged in communications with Muley Hamid, the then King of Tunis, who was feudatory of Spain. Anxious as was the corsair to aid in attacking his implacable enemies, the Knights, he could not afford to leave his own flank unguarded in Africa. He succeeded, however, in arriving at an understanding with the King of Tunis, and, further than this, he had assured himself, by means of his spies, that the succours which were to be sent from Sicily by the Spanish King could not possibly arrive for another two months. It was the negotiations which he was obliged to undertake with Muley Hamid which had caused his late arrival. As far as it is possible to judge, it was this circumstance, which (added to their own incomparable valour) turned the scale in favour of the Knights.

Among all those brave men at Malta, on both sides, in this flaming month of June 1565, there were none who excelled the Basha of Tripoli. "No one had ever seen a more intrepid general officer," says de Vertot. "He passed entire days in the trenches and at the batteries. Among his different talents none understood better than did he the direction and conduct of artillery, which was his special *métier*. By his orders on June 1st a second battery was constructed closer to the fort and parallel to the one already in existence, in order that an absolutely continuous fire might be maintained. He mounted four guns on the opposite side of Marsa Muzetto Harbour on a projecting point of land, from which a further enfilading fire smote the doomed fortress on the flank: this point has been known ever since as the Point Dragut."

A ravelin in advance of the fortress on the land side was scourged without ceasing by the *arquebus* fire of the Janissaries. One evening, as the return fire had slackened and all seemed quiet within this work, some Turkish engineers stole forth from the trenches to reconnoitre. Approaching the cavalier, all was still as death; the bold sappers pushed on as far as the ditch by which the work was surrounded, creeping on hands and knees. They let themselves down noiselessly into the ditch, and then, one standing on the shoulders of another, peeped in upon their Christian foes. Whether or no the sentry had been slain by a stray shot, or whether he too slept, can never be known; but the cavalier was unguarded; all within it slept the sleep of men utterly exhausted. The sappers crept back to their trenches, fetched scaling-ladders, swept like a flood over the rim of the cavalier, and put to death every man whom they found. Profiting by their advantage, the Turks dashed over the bridge connecting the cavalier with the fort; here, however, they were met by Sergeant-Major Guerare and a handful of soldiers aroused by him. These men were instantly succoured by the Chevaliers de Vercoyran and de Medran, who were immediately followed by the Bailli of

Negropont and several other Knights. An obstinate hand-to-hand combat now ensued; fresh Turks came up to the attack, but were mown down in swathes by an enfilading fire from two cannons which the defenders of the fort managed to bring to bear upon them. More pioneers arrived from the trenches, carrying planks and sacks filled with wool. These men tried to effect a permanent lodgement, but the fire was too hot on the Christian side, and men fell in hundreds. Nothing daunted, the Turks reared their scaling-ladders against the sides of the fortress itself, and attempted to scale the walls; but for this the ladders were too short, and the assailants were hurled back into the ditch. This attack, in which the Turkish arms were rewarded by the capture of the ravelin behind the cavalier, is said to have cost them the lives of three thousand men. It lasted from daybreak until midday.

On the side of the Christians twenty Knights and one hundred soldiers were slain; but worst of all, from their point of view, the ravelin remained in the hands of their enemies. The chevalier Abel de Bridiers de la Gardampe having received a ball through his body, some of his comrades ran to place him under cover. "Count me no longer among the living," said the Knight. "You will be better employed in defending the rest of our brethren." He then, unassisted, dragged himself to the foot of the altar in the chapel, where his dead body was discovered when all was over.

So far communication remained established between St. Elmo and their comrades in Il Borgo on the opposite side of the harbour; in consequence the wounded were removed and their places taken by one hundred fresh men under the Chevalier Vagnon. To the Bailli of Negropont and the Commandeur Broglio, La Valette sent a message to return to Il Borgo. These gallant and aged veterans, both of whom were wounded, whose faces were scorched by the sun and blackened with powder, whose bodies were well-nigh worn out with perpetual vigil and hand-to-hand fighting, refused stoutly to quit their post, which now was naught but a dreadful shambles filled with corpses mangled out of recognition and heads and limbs which had been torn and hacked from their bodies.

Dragut now proposed to erect batteries on the same side of the Great Port as that on which Il Borgo was situated; on the point now known as Ricasoli, but which was then and for centuries afterwards known as the Punta Delle Forche (or Point of the Gallows, because it was here that all pirates was executed; and their bodies, swinging in chains, were the first objects that met the eye on entering the Great Port). In this he was overruled ruled by Piali, who declared that he had not sufficient men to spare, and the Knights of Il Borgo would soon render the battery untenable even if they should succeed in erecting it, which the Turkish admiral now considered extremely doubtful. The siege of St. Elmo, which Mustafa had said would last at the outside for five or six days, had now been in progress for four weeks; and, although the fort was in a ruinous condition, nothing seemed capable of daunting those invincible warriors by which it was held.

The position in St. Elmo now was that the Turks still held on to the ravelin which they had captured; this they had built up to such a height that they could look over the parapet of the fortress and shoot down with *arquebus* fire any one whom they could see. Meanwhile the Turkish sappers delved night and day in their endeavour to undermine the parapet, which, if blown up, would give them free access to the interior of the fort; while another party, by use of the yards of galleys and huge planks of wood, busied themselves in constructing a bridge to connect the ravelin with the parapet. Lamirande, one of the most active of the defenders of the fort, viewed these preparations without undue alarm, as he was aware that, by the nature of the ground, it would be almost impossible to excavate sufficiently under the parapet to place an effective mine. As, however, the sapping was causing the parapet to incline outwards, and it was possible that it might almost at any moment fall over into the ditch, he caused a second parapet to be erected inside the first and artillery to be mounted thereon. Having done this he caused a false sortie to be made on the following night, and when the Turks rushed to the attack he, accompanied by a party of sappers, sallied out into the ditch and burned the bridge which had been made. The Turks, returning after their fruitless assault, found their bridge destroyed, but with untiring activity set to work and constructed it afresh. Dragging cannon to the very edge of the ravelin, they, on the very next evening, revenged themselves by also making a false attack: they swarmed into the ditch, and, placing their scaling-ladders against the walls, pretended that an escalade was to be attempted. The garrison, deceived, appeared on the parapet in large numbers, when a murderous fire at point-blank range was opened upon them from the ravelin. So great was the execution done on this occasion that the garrison lost more men than had hitherto been the case in the most determined attacks which they had sustained.

It now seemed as if indeed the end had come, that the garrison had done all that was in the power of mortal man and nothing was left for them but to retire while there was yet time. Accordingly choice was made of the chevalier Median to represent the desperate extremities to which they were reduced to La Valette. It was well known that for none among the Knights had the grand master more respect than he had for Medran, one of the bravest and most chivalrous of them all. He, at least, could never be suspected of cowardice, feebleness, at a desire to desert his post. This gallant Knight crossed the harbour on his dolorous errand and was received by his chief: to him he represented the state of affairs as it has here been set down, assuring him that at best the fort could but hold out for a few days longer.

A chapter of the Knights Grand Cross was immediately held and the most part of them were of opinion that the time had come to abandon a hopeless position. But this decision did not meet with the approval of the grand master. No one was more sensible than he of the peril to which their brethren were exposed; at the same time, he contended, that there were occasions on which it was necessary to sacrifice a certain number for the good of the whole order. He had certain information that, if St. Elmo were abandoned, the Viceroy of Sicily would hazard nothing for the relief of the island; that upon the arrival of succours depended the existence of their ancient and honourable confederacy: therefore, at no matter what cost, they were bound to hold out as long as possible. So dominant was the personality of the grand master that, in a short time, he had won over the votes of the chapter and Medran was ordered to return to St. Elmo and deliver to the garrison a message that the siege must take its course.

Medran accordingly returned and reported to his comrades the result of his embassy. Several of the older Knights received the command with due submission, but among those who were younger there were murmurings. These men deemed the answer to their appeal hard and cruel; they could see no object in the loss of their lives, which they well knew would all be sacrificed in the next assault. They accordingly, to the number of fifty-three, wrote a letter to the grand master, demanding permission to abandon St. Elmo and retire to Il Borgo. If their request were denied they announced their design to sally forth, sword in hand, and perish in the ranks of the enemy. The Commandeur de Cornet was the bearer of this letter, which was received by the grand master with sorrow and indignation. To reassure them, he sent three commissioners to inspect the place. This was done, and one of them, a Knight of Greek descent named Constantine Castriot, reported that the fort could still hold out a while longer. When he announced this at St. Elmo the recalcitrant Knights were so furious with him that the Baili of Negropont had to sound "the alarm" to prevent a disgraceful fracas. The commissioners returned to Il Borgo. After hearing their report La Valette wrote a letter to those by whom he had been memorialised to the following effect:

> Return to the convent, my brothers; you will there be in greater security; and on our part we shall feel a greater sense of security in the conservation of so important a place, on which depends the safety of the island and the honour of our order.

Never were men so taken aback as were the Knights in St. Elmo when they received this response; here it was intimated to them that that which they refused to do on account of the danger thereof was to be undertaken by others. This was no more than a fact, as La Valette was besieged with applications from, not only the Knights, but also the simple soldiers of the garrison, to be allowed to pass over to St. Elmo and die if necessary to the last man. It was, therefore, with prayers and tears that the Knights besought the grand master to allow them to remain. At first La Valette was adamant. He preferred, he said, the rawest militia which was prepared to obey his orders, to Knights who knew not their duty. In the end, however, he yielded, and in the fortress of St. Elmo, that crushed and ruined charnel-house, its defences gaping wide, its every corner exposed night and day to a sweeping murderous fire, there remained a host of men sadly torn and battered, but animated by such a spirit that nothing the Turks could devise made upon it the least impression. These great and gallant gentlemen had had their moment of weakness; they had been heartened to the right conception of their duty by the noble veteran who was their chief. To him had they turned at last, as his obedient children who had had their moment of rebellion in a trial as hard as was ever undergone by man. And now, as the inevitable end drew near, it was as if they would imitate the Roman gladiator with that terrible chorus of his: "*Ave Caesar morituri te salutant.*"

All day and every day did the garrison fight, snatching such repose as was possible when their pertinacious enemies, worn out by fatigue and the terrible heat, could no longer be led to the attack against those whom they now firmly believed to be in league with Shaitan himself; "For how else," demanded Janissary and Spahi alike, "could infidels like these make head against those chosen of the Prophet like ourselves."

At this time the garrison took into use a device attributed to the grand master himself. This consisted in hoops of wood which were first thoroughly soaked in alcohol and then boiled in oil; they were then tightly bound with cotton or wool, also soaked in inflammable liquids mixed with *saltpetre* and gunpowder. Once these fiendish contrivances were set alight nothing availed to put them out, and they were feared as was naught else by the Turks during the remainder of the time they were in Malta. They were particularly deadly against the Turks, and at times two or more soldiers mounting the breach would be caught in one of these fiery circles, and the unfortunate wretches would be burnt alive. Even the Janissaries refused to advance at times when these fireworks were being flung down upon their flowing garments.

On June 16th another attack was made on the fortress, and, incredible as it may seem, it was repulsed with such awful slaughter that at last the Turks would not face the swords of the garrison. Alter this the enemy succeeded in drawing so close a cordon round the place that no more succours could reach it, and the end was but a matter of time. The day before it came Dragut, who, with his usual intrepidity, was standing in the midst of a hot fire, was struck on the side of the head by a stone dislodged from a wall by a cannon-ball. At the moment when this happened he was holding a council of war in the trenches with Piali, a Sanjak, and the principal Turkish engineer. The same shot which wounded Dragut killed the Sanjak on the spot. Piali caused a cloak to be thrown over the body of the corsair in order that his state should not be observed by the soldiers, and as soon as possible had him removed to his tent, where he lay unconscious till the following day.

The council on which the corsair had been engaged when he received his mortal wound had for its object the complete isolation of St. Elmo from Il Borgo; his dispositions were completed and his orders given to the engineer just before he was struck.

The agony of St. Elmo was drawing to an end; completely hemmed in by the latest dispositions of Dragut, the fortress was at its last gasp; a brave Maltese swimmer managed to slip through the cordon, swim the harbour, and deliver to the grand master a letter from the Bailli of Negropont. The grand master made one last effort to throw succours and reinforcements into the place, but these were beaten off with terrible slaughter: nothing now remained but to await the inevitable tragedy.

On the night of June 22nd the defenders of St. Elmo, having now lost all hope of being supported, made ready for death. Into them La Valette had breathed his own heroic spirit, and none among them

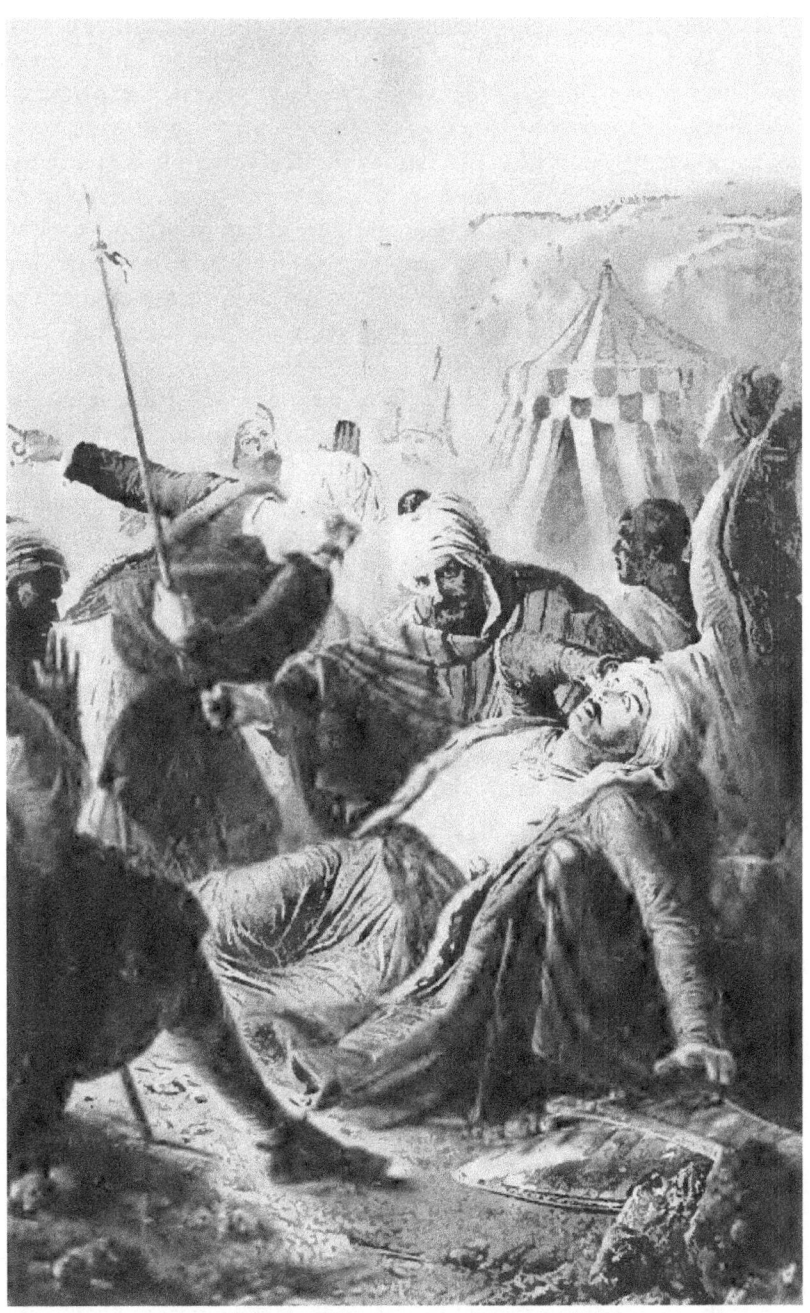
Death of Dragut at the siege of Malta

counselled or dreamed of surrender. The order to which they had given their allegiance now demanded of them the last sacrifice which it was in their power to make, and this was offered in the manner most fitting to its tenets. These exhausted, war-worn, battle-scarred warriors repaired to the chapel, where they confessed, and made ready by partaking together of the sacrament, "and, having thus surrendered their souls to God, each retired to his post to die on the bed of honour with arms in his hand." Those among the Knights who were too severely wounded or too ill to stand caused chairs to be carried to the breach in which they seated themselves and awaited the assault. For four hours did these indomitable men withstand the might of a host innumerable: at the conclusion of this period there remained alive but sixty of the garrison. Mustafa ceased the assault for a few moments only to replace the storming party by fresh troops, and then the end came. Almost the last to fall were the Chevalier Lamirande and the veteran Bailli of Negropont, and when the crescent banner was planted on the walls there remained alive not one of those defenders who had held the fort. Several of Dragut's officers ran to his tent and announced the taking of St. Elmo. The great captain was in his last extremity and unable to speak:

> He, however, manifested his joy by several signs, and, raising his eyes to heaven as if in thankfulness for its mercies, immediately expired: a captain of rare valour and even abundantly more humane than are ordinarily these corsairs.

The Basha Piali, on entering the fort and observing with what miserable resources it had so long been held exclaimed, as he looked across the harbour to Il Borgo:

"What will not the parent do to us, when so small a son has cost us the lives of our bravest soldiers?"

There is no record of what that cruel savage, Mustafa, said on this occasion; his deeds, however, spoke eloquently. He caused the bodies of the Knights to be decapitated and nailed to wooden crosses, while across their corpses were slashed a cross in derision of the religion of his foes. The bodies were then cast into the harbour, and were washed up at the foot of Il Borgo. Instantly the grand master ordered the decapitation of all the Turkish prisoners, and their heads were fired from cannon into the camp of Mustafa.

With the remainder of the siege, which was yet to last till September 18th, we have no concern in this book. It is only necessary to say that the men of Il Borgo were worthy to stand in the same category with the defenders of St. Elmo, which is equivalent to stating that in them also was discovered the last limit of heroism. The grand master survived the siege, his monument is the noble city of "Valetta" built on Mount Sceberras. The Turks abandoned the siege and returned to Constantinople on the arrival of some insignificant reinforcements from Sicily. So terrible had been the resistance of the Knights that no heart was left in their armada. Of Dragut there remains but little to be said: he was perhaps the best educated of the corsairs and less cruel than was usually their habit. Although not so renowned as his more celebrated master, Kheyr-ed-Din Barbarossa, this is, perhaps, because his career was cut short at the siege of Malta at a comparatively early age. Although he never attained the rank of *Admiralissimo* to the Grand Turk, that potentate, as we have seen, placed in him the greatest confidence, and relied largely on his judgment, especially when sea-affairs were in question. Like the Barbarossas before him, he rose from nothing to the height to which he eventually attained by sheer force of intellect and character. In the stormy times in which his lot was cast he never faltered in his onward way, never repined, never looked back, sustained as he was by a consciousness of his own capability to rule the wild spirits by whom he lived surrounded. So it is that, whatever other opinion we may hold of Dragut, we cannot deny that in this captain of the sea-wolves were blended rare qualities, which caused him to shine as a capable administrator, a fine seaman, but above all as a supreme leader of men. Dragut died with arms in his hands fighting those whom he considered to be his bitterest enemies. He did not live to see the repulse of Piali and Mustapha, and it is to be presumed that he died assured in his own mind that victory would rest with the Moslem host. For such a man as this no death could have been more welcome.

Chapter 21
Ali Basha

Now I have heard several mariners and captains of the sea, nay, even Knights of Malta, debate among themselves this question, as to which was the greater and better seaman, Dragut or Occhiali? And some held for one and some for the other; those who held for Occhiali declaring that he had held greater and more honourable charges than Dragut, because he commanded as General and Admiral for the Grand Turk and that *il fit belle action* at the battle of Lepanto.

Pierre de Bourdeille, the Seigneur de Brantôme, from whom we make the above quotation, was himself present at the siege of Malta and, besides this, as is well known, gossiped in his own inimitable way concerning men and women of his time, from corsairs to courtesans. When such contemporary authorities as those mentioned could not agree it is quite certain that we of the twentieth century cannot decide on the rival claims to distinction between the Bashaw of Tripoli and his follower Occhiali, as he was known to the Christians, or Ali Basha, as he was called by the Turks. Ali Basha has a title to fame in the fact that he is mentioned by Cervantes in his *Don Quijote de la Mancha* under the name of "Uchali" in chapter 39, *"Donde el cautivo cuenta su vida y sucesos."* The captive is supposed to have been no less a person than the famous Cervantes himself, and he briefly describes how Uchali became "Rey de Argel," or King of Algiers.

Ali was a Christian, having been born at a miserable little village in Calabria called Licastelli. Nothing whatever is known of his birth and parentage, and he does not appear even to have possessed a Christian name, although born in a Christian land. He followed from his earliest youth the calling of a mariner; "he was from infancy inured to salt water," says Joseph Morgan, in his *Compleat History of Algiers*, and he was, as a mere boy, captured by Ali Ahamed, Admiral of Algiers, and was chained to the starboard-bow oar in the galley of that officer. He was thus very early in life "inured" to suffering, and must have possessed a constitution of iron to withstand thus, in boyhood, the hardships of the life of a galley-slave, which as a rule broke down the endurance of strong men in a very few years. Morgan presents us with a description of him at this period which in these more squeamish days can certainly not be set down in its entirety: suffice it to say that he suffered all his days from what is known as "scald-head," and that personal filthiness was one of his principal characteristics.

For some years Ali remained at the heart-breaking toil of the rower's bench: cut off from home, which to him meant nothing, devoid of kinsfolk, alone—miserably alone in a world which, so far, had given him naught but the chain and the whip—it is not a matter for surprise that he became a Mussulman, thus freeing himself from slavery. From the time that he took this step his fortunes mended rapidly in that strange medley of savagery and bloodshed in which his lot was cast.

Alert, strong, capable, and vigorous, he became in early manhood chief boatswain in the galley in which his apprenticeship had been passed—a position which enabled him to accumulate a small store of ducats, with which he bought a share in a brigantine. Here he soon acquired sufficient wealth to become captain and owner of a galley, in which he soon gained the reputation of being one of the boldest corsairs on the Barbary coast. Having in some sort made a name for himself, his next step was to seek for a patron who could make use of his valour, address, and capability for command. His choice was soon made, as who in all the Mediterranean, in his early days, held such a name as Dragut? He accordingly entered the service of the Basha of Tripoli, and, under his command, became well known to the officers of the Grand Turk, particularly to the Admiral, Piali Basha, to whom he was able to render some important services.

There is no object to be gained in lingering over the earlier years of this notable corsair, as we should thus only be repeating what has been said about Dragut, whose lieutenant and trusted follower he became. He accompanied his master to the siege of Malta, and when Dragut was slain the Capitan-Basha, Piali, named him as successor to his chief as Viceroy of Tripoli. Ali sailed from Malta to Tripoli, taking with him the remains of Dragut, to be buried as that chieftain had directed. When he arrived on the Barbary coast he made himself master of the slaves and treasure which had been left behind by Dragut; shortly after this he was confirmed in his Vice-royalty of Tripoli by the

Grand Turk; thenceforward increasing, both his wealth and the terror in which his name was held, by continual raids upon the Christians, more particularly on the coasts of Sicily, Calabria, and Naples. It is curious to observe the sort of spite which all the *renegado*es seem to have harboured against the countries in which they were born.

In March 1568, owing to the fall of Mohammed Basha, the Viceroyalty of Algiers became vacant, and, through the good offices of his old friend Piali, Ali became Governor. He thus returned to occupy a position of literally sovereign power to the city which he had first entered as a galley-slave.

That he was no negligent Governor and that he took an entirely intelligent view of his functions, is proved by an occurrence which took place in this same year in Spain. The Moriscoes in the Kingdom of Granada revolted against their Spanish Governor, by whom they were sorely oppressed. They sent messages to Ali at Algiers, begging for succour against their persecutor. But the Basha would send no expedition; he permitted all and sundry to go as volunteers, but gave out publicly that "it more concerned him to defend well his own State than to interfere in the affairs of others." He even went farther than this, and when a number of Moriscoes, who were settled at Algiers, embarked a quantity of arms for transportation to the coast of Andalusia, he put an embargo on the vessels and would not allow them to sail, saying "he would never suffer the exportation of what was so necessary for the defence of his own dominions." At last, after much importunity, he consented "that all such as had two of a sort—as muskets, swords, or other weapons—might, if they thought fit, send over one of them, provided they did it gratis and purely for the cause' sake; but he would never allow any of them to strip themselves of their arms for lucre."

Ali, being now firmly established at Algiers, took up arms against the neighbouring State of Tunis. For long years now the King of Tunis had been protected by the Spaniards—a nation whom the sea-wolves always held in singular abhorrence as the most bigoted of the Christian Powers, and who held in thrall many of their co-religionists. Hamid, son of Hassan, who now ruled in Tunis, had reduced that unfortunate State to anarchy bordering on rebellion, and the whole country, torn by internal feud, was ready to rise against him. The Goletta was in the hands of the Spaniards; Carouan, an inland town, had set up a king of its own, while the maritime towns passed from the domination of the sea-wolves to that of the Christians, and from the Christians back to the sea-wolves, according to which party happened to be the stronger for the time being.

El Maestro Fray Diego de Haedo, "*Abad de Fromesta de la Orden del Patriarca San Benito*" and "*natural del Valle de Carranca*," whose *Topografia e Historia de Argel* (or Algiers) was printed in Valladolid in the year 1612, gives an account of Hamid at this time in which he describes that monarch as an—

> .... unpopular tyrant who sadly persecuted his vassals and the friends of his father; who could by no means suffer his tyrannies and those of his ministers, the scum of the earth ("*hombres baxos*"), to whom he had given the principal offices of the kingdom. Accordingly, since the time that Ali had become Basha of Algiers, letters had been written to him importuning him to come to Tunis that he might possess himself of that city and kingdom.

There were three principal conspirators—the Alcaid Bengabara, General of the Cavalry, the Alcaid Botaybo, and the Alcaid Alcadaar. Ali, however, was too shrewd a man to move until he had satisfied himself by reports from his own adherents; he, therefore, awaited the result of investigations made by spies from Algiers. At last, in the beginning of the year 1569, when the offers from the *alcaids* had been three times renewed and the Basha was assured that the people in Tunis were sincere in their offer to him of the sovereignty of the kingdom—which they begged him to conquer and hold in the name of the Ottoman Empire—the ex-galley-slave no longer hesitated. He left Algiers in the month of October, leaving that city in charge of one Mami Corso, a fellow *renegado*. Unlike Dragut, who would have gone by sea, he set out by land with some five thousand corsairs and *renegado*es. On the way he was reinforced by some six thousand cavalry of the wild tribes of the hinterland, then as ever ready to join in a fray with promise of booty: doubly ready in this case, as it was to harass so unpopular a tyrant as Hamid. Passing through Constantine and Bona, he continued to march towards Tunis, his following augmenting as he proceeded, and adding to his forces ten light field-guns. Arriving at Beja, a town which Haedo describes as being but two short days' march from Tunis, he came upon a fortress, recently erected by Hamid, mounting fourteen brass cannon. Here he halted, whereupon Hamid sallied out to give him battle at the head of some three thousand troops, horse and foot. The engagement had scarcely begun when the three *alcaids*, who had been in communication with Ali, deserted with all their following. Hamid fled to Tunis, expecting to find shelter there, but he was hotly pursued by the corsairs, who followed him up to Al-Burdon, where his summer palace was situated. Hamid, finding that his people were everywhere in revolt, fled to the Goletta, carrying with him a quantity of money, jewels, and portable valuables, and placed himself under the protection of the Spanish garrison—not, however, without the loss of the major portion of his baggage, plundered from him by certain Moors in the course of his flight.

Like Kheyr-ed-Din Barbarossa, Ali was now lord of Algiers and Tunis, and as he was, for a corsair, a man of wide views, he treated his new subjects with consideration. He made, however, one curious mistake not to have been expected from one so politic: he demanded tribute from the tribes of the hinterland. In those days, particularly in Northern Africa, men paid tribute to an overlord because he was stronger than they; because retribution followed swiftly and suddenly upon refusal. To order tribute to be paid without being ready to strike was merely to expose the man making the demand to derision. Particularly was this the case with the fierce land-pirates of the desert, whose habit it was to exact and not to pay tribute. To Ali the *sheiks* replied that "if he wanted tribute from them he must demand it lance in hand in the field, for there and nowhere else were they accustomed to pay: that their coin was steel lance-heads and not golden *aspers.*" After this, says Morgan, "the Basha thought it well to dissemble."

Ali, being in no position to wage war in the desert against these people, had to swallow the insult and to turn his attention to regulating the internal affairs of his newly acquired kingdom. This he succeeded in doing sufficiently by the month of June in the following year to enable him to leave Tunis in the hands of one Rabadan, a Sardinian *renegado*, and to start himself for Constantinople. His reason for doing this was the old one of attempting to consolidate his power in Northern Africa by appealing to the Sultan for help. As long as the Goletta remained in the hands of the Spaniards no corsair could feel himself secure in either Tunis or Algiers. The object of Ali was to beg from the Grand Turk men and ships to assist him to chase the Spaniards out of Africa.

The month of June 1570, in consequence, saw Ali once more at sea in his "Admiral galley," steering northwards to the Golden Horn. Carrying with them a favourable breeze from the south-east, the galleys spread their huge lateen sails, and the straining rowers had rest awhile. The squadron consisted of twenty-four galleys. Off Cape Passaro, in Sicily, a small vessel was captured which gave information that five galleys of the Knights of Malta were at anchor at Licata, a small harbour in the neighbourhood, and that they were on the point of sailing for Malta. The decision of Ali was taken on the instant: were he to go in and attack them with the overwhelming force at his command the crews might escape to the shore; even the Knights of Malta could hardly be expected to fight twenty-four galleys with five. He was anxious to capture the ships, but above all to capture those by whom they were manned: to have the satisfactory revenge of seeing the proud Knights stripped naked and chained to the benches of his own fleet.

The hot Mediterranean sun poured down out of a cloudless sky as the sea-wolves made their offing; out of sight of land they lay, but right in the course which the galleys of the Christians were bound to take. The great yards, with their lateen sails, were got down on deck, and, oar in hand, the Moslems awaited their prey. Presently the Maltese galleys were discovered coming leisurely along, under oars and sails, and then—when it was too late—the Knights discovered the snare into which they had fallen. There was but scant time for preparation or deliberation, and who shall blame four out of the five if they decided to try to escape? for it was escape or annihilation.

But there was one which did not fly, "*Una galera hizo cara a los Turcos*" (One single galley turned her bows towards the Turks), says that faithful chronicler Haedo. She was named the *Santa Ana*, but the name of her heroic commander has not come down to us. Even as Grenfell "at Flores in the Azores," stood upon the deck of the little *Revenge* on that memorable August day in 1591, when "he chose to die rather than to dishonour himself, his country, and her Majesty's ship," so also did this Knight of Malta bear down on the twenty-four that were his foes.

When Don John of Austria, being at the time young and inexperienced in warfare on the sea, wrote to the Marquis of Villafranca, General of the Galleys of Sicily, requesting advice on the subject of galley attacking galley, that officer replied to him, "Never fire your *arquebus* at the foe until you are so close at hand that his blood will leap into your face at the discharge."

If we bear in mind such an instruction as this it will help us to picture that close-packed sanguinary conflict upon which the Mediterranean sun looked down on this day. Eight to one, all that could find room to get alongside of the *Santa Ana*, fought with the Knight and his followers. The issue was, of course, never in doubt for a moment. "*Muertos y cansados*" (Dead and deadbeat), says Haedo, the *caballeros* and *soldados* of the Christian ship could at length hold out no longer. The sea-wolves were victorious, the proud banner of Saint John was lowered; but never in all its history had it been more nobly upheld, and the galley *Santa Ana,* commanded by that unknown member of the great Christian military hierarchy of the sixteenth century, may well stand in the roll of fame alongside of the *Revenge,* the *Vengeur,* and the *Victory.*

The *Capitana,* or "Admiral's galley," of the Knights, being hotly pursued, ran ashore with one of her consorts at Licata: the crews landed, but were pursued and overtaken. One galley escaped altogether, but four out of the five were taken. So notable a victory as this over the Knights caused so much rejoicing in the fleet of the sea-wolves that Ali determined to celebrate it by a triumphal return to Algiers instead of proceeding directly to Constantinople. Accordingly, the ships' heads were turned south once more, and upon July 20th, 1570, the fleet arrived in the African port, "*on sus galeras todas llenas de muchas banderas*"—with galleys gaily beflagged.

The procession entered the harbour in three divisions of eight galleys: and towing behind each division was one of the captured galleys of the Knights. In memory of his prowess Ali ordered that the shields and bucklers taken from the Maltese galleys, which bore upon them emblazoned the white cross of "the Religion," should be hung up in the great arched gate of the Marina. Also there was placed here the image of Saint John the Baptist, taken from the *Capitana* galley, "all of which remain," says Haedo, "until this day" (*i.e.* 1612), except the image of Saint John, which in the reign of Hassan Basha, a Venetian *renegado,* was taken down and burned at the instance of the Morabutos, "*los letrados de los Moros*" (the learned among the Moors). It is an instructive commentary on the fear and respect in which the Knights of Malta were held that such a man as Ali should have considered it a triumph worth the celebrating when he defeated five of their vessels with twenty-four of his own.

The next occurrence in the life of Ali was one of those to which the sea-wolves were subjected from time to time, and which do not seem to have caused them much trouble or anxiety. This was a mutiny of the Janissaries in Algiers, who very reasonably objected to being left without their pay. A mutiny of the Janissaries, however, was somewhat a serious matter, as they were accustomed to the enjoyment of many privileges, and were, as we have said elsewhere, a picked corps who had it in their power even to coerce the Sultan himself upon occasions.

Those of them who were in Algiers demanded "Who was this corsair who dared to keep the picked men of the army of the Grand Turk waiting for their pay, as if they were no better than his slaves?" Such a thing as a mutiny was, in the days of which we speak, a mat-

A Galley of the Knights of Malta

ter for which any prudent corsair had to be prepared. Ali was in no means discomposed, and, as the crisis had become acute on shore, he went to sea, where he was under no obligation to pay his men, who paid themselves at the expense of their enemies. He put to sea with twenty galleys, and, shortly after leaving Algiers, he met with a galley from the Levant, from which he received information that a powerful armada was preparing in Constantinople for an expedition against the Christians. He steered for Coron in the Morea, where he was almost immediately joined by the Ottoman fleet, the commander of which force was overjoyed to find so formidable a reinforcement under so renowned a captain as Ali.

Soliman the Magnificent had died in 1566, and had been succeeded by his son, Selim; this prince, bred in the Seraglio, was weak and licentious, given to that strong drink forbidden by the Prophet to an extent which caused him to be nicknamed by the Spaniards as "*el ebrio,*" or "*el bebedor.*"

This was a state of affairs which boded ill for the Turkish Empire, and Selim II. had been educated in a very different manner from that which had hitherto been the custom. Speaking of this, Gibbon says:

> Instead of the slothful luxury of the Seraglio, the heirs of royalty were educated in the council and the field. From early youth they were entrusted by their fathers with the command of provinces and of armies; and this manly institution, which was often productive of civil war, must have essentially contributed to the discipline and vigour of the monarchy.

Drunkard and weakling as he was, Selim had his ambitions. He wished to signalise his reign by some great conquest, such as had added lustre to the rule of his father; and in consequence he laid claim to the island of Cyprus, then belonging to Venice, The Venetians, having strengthened the fortifications of the island and fitted out their navy, sought alliances in Europe to curb the pretensions of the Porte. In this they found support, instant and generous, from the Pope Pius V. Of this great ecclesiastic Prescott says:

> He was one of those Pontiffs who seemed to have been called forth by the exigencies of the time to uphold the pillars of Catholicism as they were yet trembling under the assaults of Luther.

The Pope, Philip II. of Spain, and Venice formed what was known as the "Holy League," and, having formed it, immediately began to quarrel among themselves as to what its functions were to be. The

Venetians wished all its efforts to be directed to safeguarding Cyprus, while Philip and his viceroys were anxious to attack the sea-wolves on the coast of Africa in their strongholds. After much squabbling, an agreement was come to. The principal items of this were, that the Pope should pay one-sixth of the expenses, Venice two-sixths, and Spain three-sixths; that each party should appoint its own Commander-in-Chief, and that Don John of Austria should be in supreme command of the whole forces assembled. The contracting parties were to furnish 200 galleys, 100 transports, 50,000 foot, 4,500 horse, and the requisite artillery and stores.

While the Christians were negotiating and talking, the Turks were acting. It was in May that the Pope caused the treaty to be publicly read in full consistory; in April the Turkish fleet had got to sea and committed terrible ravages in the Adriatic, laying waste to Venetian territory.

While ships and men were gathering, and while the fleet which it was to be his fortune to defeat was pursuing its career in the Mediterranean, Don John of Austria left Madrid for the south on June 6th, 1571. When he arrived at Barcelona he made a pilgrimage to the Hermitage of Our Lady of Montserrat, where his father Charles V. had confessed and received the sacrament before he sailed on his voyage to the Barbary coast in his expedition against Barbarossa. From Barcelona he sailed with thirty galleys to Genoa, where he arrived on the 25th, and was lodged in the palace of Andrea Doria. In August he arrived by water at Naples.

By this time all Europe was aflame with excitement: warriors of noble birth were flocking to serve under the standard of the brother of the King of Spain, who was regarded as the very mirror of chivalry. The following description of Don John, at Naples, is from the pen of that great historian Prescott:

> Arrangements had been made in that city for his reception on a more magnificent scale than any he had witnessed on his journey. Granvelle, who had lately been raised to the post of Viceroy, came forth at the head of a long and brilliant procession to welcome his royal guest. The houses which lined the streets were hung with richly tinted tapestries and gaily festooned with flowers. The windows and verandas were graced with the beauty and fashion of the pleasure-loving capital, and many a dark eye sparkled as it gazed upon the fine form and features of the youthful hero, who at the age of twenty-four had come to Italy to assume the baton of command and lead the crusade

against the Moslems. His splendid dress of white velvet and cloth of gold set off his graceful person to advantage. A crimson scarf floated loosely over his breast, and his snow-white plumes drooping from his cap mingled with the yellow curls that fell in profusion over his shoulders. It was a picture which the Italian maiden might love to look on. It was certainly not the picture of the warrior sheathed in the iron panoply of war. But the young Prince, in his general aspect, might be relieved from the charge of effeminacy by his truly chivalrous bearing and the dauntless spirit which beamed from his clear blue eyes. In his own lineaments he seemed to combine all that was comely in the lineaments of his race.

At Naples Don John found a fleet at anchor under the command of Don Alvaro de Bazan, first marquis of Santa Cruz, of whom much was to be heard in the future in his capacity as Admiral of Castile. Here also he received from the hands of Cardinal Granvelle a consecrated banner sent to him by the Pope at a solemn ceremony in the church of the Franciscan Convent of Santa Chiara. On August 25th he left Naples and proceeded to Messina, where he landed under a triumphal arch of colossal dimensions, embossed with rich plates of silver and curiously sculptured with emblematical bas-reliefs. The royal galley in which the hero embarked was built at Barcelona: she was fitted with the greatest luxury, and was remarkable for her strength and speed; her stern was profusely decorated with emblems and devices drawn from history; no such warship had ever been seen in the world before.

Cayetano Rosell, in his *Historia del Combate Naval de Lepanto*, says that the number of vessels, great and small, in the Christian armada was over 300, of which 200 were galleys, the ordinary warships of the time. He goes on to say:

> In this spacious harbour (Messina) there were collected the squadrons of the League; the people who managed the oars and sails and the innumerable combatants making an immense number when added together. Since the days of Imperial Rome, never had been seen in these seas so imposing a spectacle, never had there been collected so many ships moving towards a single end dominated by a single will. Never was there a spectacle more gratifying in the eyes of justice, nor of greater incentive to men to fight for the cause of religion.

The Spanish fleet comprised 90 royal galleys, 24 *nefs*, and 50 *fregatas* and brigantines "*los mejores que en tiempo alguno se habrian visto*" (the finest that ever were seen at any time), as they were described by Don John. The Pope sent 12 galleys and 6 *fregatas*, under the command of Mark Antony Colonna. The Pope had also made a grant of the "*Crusada*" and "*Excusada*," and other ecclesiastical revenues which he drew from Spain, to the King of that country, to meet expenses.

Venice appointed Sebastian Veniero to the command of her fleet, which consisted of 106 galleys, 6 *galeasses* of enormous bulk and clumsy construction carrying each 40 guns, 2 *nefs*, and 20 *fregatas*. These vessels were, however, so miserably manned and equipped that Don John had to send on board Spaniards and Genoese to complete their complements. In a manuscript of the Bibliothéque du Roi (Number 10088) is an account of the battle of Lepanto by Commandeur de Romegas. He gives the number of the Turkish fleet at 333 ships, of which 230 were galleys, the rest *galeasses* and smaller craft. The total which he gives for the Christian fleet is 271. Ali Basha was in supreme command of the Turkish forces, "a man of an intrepid spirit, who had given many proofs of a humane and generous mature—qualities more rare among the Turks, perhaps among all nations, than mere physical courage." With Ali was the Basha of Algiers, that other Ali, the corsair, who since his arrival at Coron had done more than his share of the fighting, marauding, and devastating which were the preliminaries to the battle of Lepanto. In this historic conflict he was to show once again how, on the face of the waters, the sea-wolves were supreme; as it was he and his corsairs, out of the whole of the Moslem host, who acquitted themselves with the greatest credit on that day so fatal to the arms of the Ottoman Turk.

Chapter 22
Lepanto

Lepanto, the last battle of first-class importance in which the sea-wolves bore a leading part, is memorable in many ways. It is one of the most sanguinary which was ever fought, the element of personal hatred between the combatants, to which we have alluded more than once, being singularly in evidence on this occasion. As we have said, this campaign was brought about at the initiative of the Venetians, and an incident which occurred not long before the battle exacerbated the feelings with which the Turks were regarded by the Christians to the point of madness. The city of Famagusta, in Cyprus, had been captured by that Mustafa of whom we heard so much at the siege of Malta. The Venetian defenders made an honourable capitulation, but when the four principal Venetian captains were brought before Mustafa, that general caused three of them to be beheaded on the spot; the fourth, a noble and gallant gentleman who had been responsible for the magnificent defence of the city entrusted to his charge, he caused to be flayed alive in the market-square. He then had the skin stuffed with straw, and, with this ghastly trophy nailed to the prow of his galley, returned in triumph to Constantinople. Bragadino, the defender of Famagusta, did not die in vain; his terrible fate excited such a passion of anger in the whole of the armada of Don John that each individual of which it was composed felt that the sacrifice of his own life would be but a small thing if it only led to the destruction of such fiends as those against whom they were arrayed.

Lepanto was a magnificent triumph for the arms of Christendom, and taught a much-needed lesson to Europe that the Ottoman Turk was not invincible upon the sea; it was not, however, an interesting battle from the point of view of the student of war and its combinations. Of all the high officers in command on that memorable day there was only one who displayed real generalship and a proper ap-

IOANNES AVSTRIACVS CAR.V.F. PHI.R.CAT.NO APVD BELG. GVB. ET CAPIT. GENERAL.

DON JOHN OF AUSTRIA

preciation of the tactical necessities of the situation; that officer was Ali Basha, the leader of the sea-wolves. The account of the battle is somewhat obscured by the fact that on the side of the Moslems the name of the Ottoman Commander-in-Chief was also "Ali"; in order to avoid confusion in this narration, we shall allude to the Basha of Algiers by the name given to him by the Christians, "Occhiali."

It was on Sunday, October 7th, 1571, that the Christian fleet weighed anchor from Cephalonia and stood southwards along the Albanian coast, which is here fringed with rocky islets. The right wing was commanded by John Andrea Doria, the left wing by the Provéditeur Barbarigo, the centre, or "battle," as it was called, by Don John in person, who had on the one side of him Mark Antony Colonna, the General of the Galleys of the Pope, and on the other that fiery veteran Sebastian Veniero, the commander of the Venetians. Here also were stationed the Prince of Parma, nephew to Don John, Admiral of Savoy; Duke Urbino, Admiral of Genoa; the Admiral of Naples, and the Commandeur of Castile. The reserve, under the command of the Marquis of Santa Cruz, consisted of thirty-five galleys. Immediately in rear of the *Real*, or royal galley of Don John, was that of the Grand Commander Requesens. The number of seamen, soldiers, officers, and galley-slaves in the fleet amounted to over eighty thousand persons; twenty-nine thousand infantry had been embarked, of which number nineteen thousand were Spaniards. Opposed to the Christians on this day was a Turkish fleet which had on board no less than one hundred and twenty thousand men embarked in two hundred and fifty galleys, without counting an innumerable host of smaller vessels.

The authorities on whose accounts of the battle this description is based are Prescott, the famous historian; P. Daru, a member of the Académie Française, who wrote an exhaustive *Histoire de Venise* and Don Cayetano Rosell, member of the Spanish Academy, who is responsible for an exposition of the subject, known as *Historia del Combate Naval de Lepanto*. From a comparison of the works of these eminent men one fact emerges with great clearness, which is that the battle of Lepanto was an indiscriminate melee which was decided by some of the most desperate fighting ever recorded, but which depended hardly at all upon the tactical abilities of the men in chief command. It is true that we are told Don John issued written instructions to the commander of each ship, but we are left in the dark as to what these instructions were, while at the same time we discover that in his line of battle, which in the first instance appears to have been that of "single line ahead," the galleys of all nationalities were inextricably mixed

Sebastian Veniero. Inset, portraits of Don John and Pope Pius V. Heroic statue of Don John dominating Christian and Turkish fleets. The breath of the Almighty destroying the Turkish fleet at Lepanto.

up; making it thereby impossible for the Papal, Spanish, and Venetian commanders to deal, as they should have done, exclusively with their own men. On the other hand, Occhiali kept together the squadron of the sea-wolves; he out-generalled and had all but defeated John Andrea Doria, when the end came and he was obliged to retreat.

We are, however, anticipating. Don John passed down his own line in a light *"fregata"* giving a few words of exhortation and advice to each ship under his command. If the bastard brother of the King of Spain did not exhibit any large measure of ability as a leader on this occasion, he was perhaps none the less the right man in the right place, as he had about him so winning a way, he was so striking and gallant a figure, that the hearts of all under his command went out to him. The seamen and soldiers of the great armada greeted him with enthusiastic shouts of delight as he bade them remember in whose cause it was that they fought. The last of the Knights-errant must have made a brave show as he passed down that line four miles in length, the sun shining on his damascened armour, and his yellow curls streaming out from beneath his helmet.

Soon after sunrise the Turkish fleet was descried sailing towards the Christians, in such apparently overwhelming force that several of the Spanish commanders represented to Don John that it would be imprudent to risk a battle. To his honour be it recorded that he replied he had come out to fight the Turks and that the time for talk was now over. He then hoisted all his banners, and the executive signal for the combat to begin was given by displaying at his mainmast head the sacred banner blessed by the Pope. As this standard floated out upon the breeze there went up a great shout in unison from all that were under the command of Don John. The scene of the combat was that area of the Ionian Sea which is enclosed on the east by the coasts of Albania and Morea and on the west by the islands of Ithaca and Cephalonia, Just to the northward, at the entrance to the Gulf of Arta, sixteen hundred years before had been fought the battle of Actium between Antony and Octavius; the same spot had witnessed, in 1538, the memorable battle of Prevesa between Andrea Doria and Kheyr-ed-Din Barbarossa.

From the point of view of the seaman, who is naturally anxious to discover the dispositions of their fleets made by the rival Commanders-in-Chief, Lepanto is an almost hopeless puzzle. As far as can be gathered, however, it was that the two armadas approached one another in what is known as "line ahead," each ship being immediately astern of its next ahead in one long continuous line; and that, when they got within striking distance, these lines turned so that they formed "line abreast," when each ship, having turned at right angles, simultaneously the line advances abreast, the ships forming it being broadside to broadside.

When the Turks discovered the allies they were issuing from between the islets and the shore. Seeing John Andrea Doria moving to the right, they judged that he was executing a turning movement with the object of escaping to the northwards, from whence he had come; they were, at the time, unable to see the rest of the fleet, which was hidden by the land. With sound tactical judgment they accordingly advanced to attack the allies before they should have time to issue from the strait. They were, however, too far off to accomplish this, and, by the time they arrived within striking distance, the Christian fleet had cleared the strait and was ready for them, "drawn up for battle," says Monsieur Daru, which is somewhat vague in describing the disposition of a fleet. What is certain, however, is that in advance of the galleys of Don John were six great *galeasses*, which were armed with guns of immensely superior power to anything which could be mounted in galleys. As the Turks advanced to the attack these vessels opened fire, and did so much execution that Ali, the Turkish Commander-in-Chief, ordered his line to open out and thus avoid their fire. Whatever formation the fleet was in at the time—which was, as far as we can gather, "line abreast"—this opening-out process, to avoid the *galeasses*, threw it into hopeless confusion. The Turkish right wing, which was hugging the coast, and was the first to come into action, passed on in an endeavour to turn the left wing of the allies. While this manoeuvre was in progress Ali, the Capitan-Basha of the Turks, arrived in his vessel opposite to the royal galley of Don John. At the masthead of the galley of the Capitan-Bashaw floated the sacred standard of the Ottomans. This, the ancient banner of the Caliphs, was covered with texts from the Koran, and had upon it the name of Allah emblazoned no less than twenty-eight thousand nine hundred times in letters of gold. "It was," says Prescott, "the banner of the Sultan, having passed from father to son since the foundation of the dynasty, and was never seen in the field unless the Grand Seigneur or his lieutenant was there in person."

Ali, the Commander-in-Chief, a favourite of the Sultan, had been entrusted with this most precious of all the possessions of the Padishah, as an incentive to him and all under his command to fight their hardest to do honour to the Prophet, and to prevent this symbol of their religion from falling into the hands of the Christian. Ali, like

Don John, was young, and burning to distinguish himself; accordingly, as soon as the ships of the two leaders came opposite to each other neither regarded any enemy save his rival Commander-in-Chief. Ali drove his great galley straight on board of the vessel of Don John, and a most obstinate conflict ensued. Veniero and Colonna hastened to the assistance of their chief, who was sore beset.

The combat now became general, and, as has been said, was for the most part nothing but a melee, in which each ship sought out the nearest of her foes and closed with her. For some time the fight went hard with Don John; time and again the galley of the Moslem leader was boarded, but on each occasion the Spaniards were hurled back upon their own decks. Loredano and Malipier, two Venetian captains, fell upon seven Turkish galleys which were hastening to reinforce the attack on Don John, and sank one of them. They then fought with such fury and resolution with the six that remained that, although both captains were killed, it was conceded that they had saved their general, entirely altered the complexion of the battle in their neighbourhood, and facilitated the capture of the Turkish admiral. The determined conduct of the two Venetians allowed the Spanish division to close in on the Turkish flagship, which, after an heroic resistance, was captured, principally because there were practically none left alive to fight. The head of Ali was struck off by a Spanish soldier, the banner of the Moslems was replaced by the flag of the Cross, the head of Ali on a pike being exhibited in derision above it. The conquerors seem to have seen no incongruity in this performance. The lowering of the sacred standard of the Capitan-Basha had a disheartening effect upon the Turks; they knew by this that their Commander-in-Chief was dead and his ship captured, the result being that the resistance of the Ottomans began to weaken. Then thirty galleys took to flight from the neighbourhood of the Christian flagship; so hotly were they pursued that they ran on shore, the crews swimming or wading to the beach and making off inland.

On the right of the Christian line things had not been going so propitiously for them. Here Occhiali had managed, by his apparently persistent attempts to outflank John Andrea Doria, to decoy that commander away from his supports and from the main body of the Christians. This tactical manoeuvre of the corsair was successful; having drawn off some fifteen of the Christian galleys, he suddenly flung the whole of his greatly superior force into the gap and surrounded them. These galleys were Spanish, Venetian, and Maltese, and, although they offered a most vigorous resistance, they were mostly destroyed or captured. Doria, in spite of all his efforts, was on this day both out-generalled and outfought: the sea-wolves, under their grim leader, manoeuvring for position, obtaining it, and then falling like a thunderbolt on the foe. They were all brave men at Lepanto on this memorable October day; but few there were like the corsair king, in whom a heart of fire was kept in check by a brain of ice, who, during the whole combat, never gave away a chance, or failed to swoop like an eagle from his eyrie when the blunders of his enemy gave him the opportunity for which he watched. It was the old story of "the veritable man of the sea" pitted against gallant soldiers fighting on an unfamiliar element. And yet it was against the best seaman on the Christian side that Occhiali pitted himself on this stricken field; and none can deny that with him rested such honour as was gained by the Turks on this day, the day which broke up for ever the idea of the invincibility of the Ottomans on the water. It needs not to say, to those who have read the story of the siege of Malta, how the Knights comported themselves in the battle; and yet Occhiali captured the *Capitana*, or principal galley of the order, He was towing her out of action, a prize, when the Marquis of Santa Cruz bore down upon him with the reserve. By this time the battle was lost; the Moslems were in full retreat.

The corsair recognised that he could do no more: sullenly he cast off the tow, and, forming up some thirty of his galleys, still in a condition to navigate, stood boldly through the centre of where the battle had once raged, and escaped. The *Capitana* of Malta had been taken; and to the Sultan did Occhiali present the great standard of Saint John, as an earnest of his achievement.

Bernardino de Escalente, in his work *Diálogos del Arte Militar*, printed in Seville in 1583, says that the Captain Ojeda, of the galley *Guzmana*, recaptured the *Capitana* of Malta; and that, in recognition thereof, "the Religion" pensioned him for life. Ojeda, it is to be presumed, was under the orders of the Marquis of Santa Cruz during the battle.

There remains one incident connected with the battle of Lepanto which must be told. In the *Marquesa* galley, in the division of Doria, was lying in his bed sick of a fever a young man twenty-four years of age; a Spaniard of Alcala de Henares, "*de padres hidalgos y honrados,*" we are told, although these parents were poor. When this young man heard that a battle was imminent he rose from his bed and demanded of his captain, Francisco San Pedro, that he should be placed in the post of the greatest danger. The captain, and others, his friends, counselled him to remain in his bed. "*Señores,*" replied the young man, "what would be said of Miguel de Cervantes should he take this advice? On every occasion up to this day on which his enemies have offered battle to his Majesty I have served like a good soldier; and to-day I intend to do so in spite of this sickness and fever." He was given command of twelve soldiers in a shallop, and all day was to be seen where the combat raged most fiercely. He received two wounds in the chest and another which cost him the loss of his left hand. To those to whom he proudly displayed them in after-years he was accustomed to say, "wounds in the face or the chest are like stars which guide one through honour to the skies." Of him the chronicler says: "He continued the rest of his life with honourable memory of this wonderful occurrence, and, although he lost the use of his left hand, it added to the glory of his right." How glorious was that right hand is known to all readers of *El Ingenioso Hidalgo Don Quijote de la Mancha*.

The losses at the battle of Lepanto are something so prodigious that imagination boggles at them. It is said that the Christians lost five thousand men and the Turks no less than thirty thousand. Enormous as these numbers are, they represent probably a very conservative estimate of the loss. The Turks lost two hundred vessels, and when we recollect the number of men embarked on board of the sixteenth-century galleys we can see that the numbers are by no means exaggerated, especially as no quarter was given on either side. When the Captain Ojeda recaptured the battered wreck which had been the *Capitana* of Malta, we are told that on board of her were three hundred dead Turks; if this were the cost of the capture of one galley we need not be surprised at the total.

With the results to Europe of this amazing battle we have nothing to do in this book. That which it demonstrated, as far as the sea-wolves were concerned, was that they still remained the most competent seamen and sea-fighters in the Mediterranean, and that the legend of the invincibility of the Ottomans at sea rested on what had been accomplished during a long period of years by these insatiable pirates and magnificent warriors.

That which the fighting Pontiff, Pius V., said when he heard of the victory is in character with everything which history has told us of this remarkable occupant of the chair of Saint Peter. It was short but very much to the point, consisting of the one sentence, "*Fuit homo misus a Deo cui nomen erat Joannes*."

In a collection of epitaphs printed in Colonia in 1623 (and edited by one Franciscus Swertius) is one in Spanish by an anonymous author on Don John of Austria. In this, which takes the form of question and answer, it is asked of him "who with so much real glory lies so humbly 'neath this stone," what it is that Spain can do for him, what temple or what statue can she raise to his honour. To this the hero is made to reply that "My temple is found in my works, my statue has been my fame." This is not only a pretty conceit, but it is very substantially true when we think of the place in history which this man attained.

It remains to speak of the future career of Ali Basha after his experiences at Lepanto. He now returned to Constantinople, where he found that the bitter complaints of the Janissaries concerning their lack of pay had preceded him; this must have been annoying, as by this time so insignificant a circumstance had probably escaped his memory. His old friend and patron Piali Basha was still in power; the Basha used his influence, and the corsair laid at the feet of the Sultan the great Standard of Saint John captured by him from the Knights—which was the only trophy which came to Constantinople from that disastrous battle; and in consequence we are told that "instead of reprimands he was loaded with caresses and applauses."

There was in Ali the same dauntless quality of never knowing when he was beaten which had distinguished Kheyr-ed-Din Barbarossa. His exploits at Lepanto had secured him the high favour of the Sultan, which he used in a manner most grateful to that sovereign by approaching him with a request that he might be allowed to fit out another fleet to revenge himself on the Christians. The Sultan acceded to his request, and such diligence did he use that in June 1572, only eight months after the crushing defeat of the Turks, Ali took the sea with two hundred and fifty galleys besides smaller vessels. So powerful had he now become that Selim nominated him as his *Admiralissimo*, allowing him also to retain the Bashalic of Algiers. With his new fleet he sought out the allies once more, finding them at anchor in a port in the Morea. He lay outside the harbour defying them to come out, which they refused to do—"but they parted without bloody noses"—is Morgan's comment. Haedo attributes this inertia on the part of the allies to dissension among their leaders; but, however that may have been, Ali gained almost as much favour with the Sultan as if he had defeated them in a pitched battle. "But these are the judgments of God and things ordered by His divine providence and infinite wisdom," says Haedo. The connection is somewhat hard to establish.

In 1573 the Bashalic of Algiers passed into the hands of Arab Ahmed, and in this same year Don John of Austria recaptured Tunis from the Turks. Ali, with a fleet of two hundred and fifty galleys and forty smaller vessels, recaptured it again in a siege lasting forty days, and once more returned to Constantinople in triumph with thousands of Spanish captives. He was yet to live some years to harass the Christians, against whom he ever displayed a most inveterate rancour. In 1576 he set out from Constantinople with sixty galleys and ravaged the Calabrian coast, where he had been born. In 1578, the Janissaries of Algiers having assassinated Arab Ahmed the Basha, he was sent to chastise them, which he did with a heavy hand.

Ali was never married, and left no descendants; in the later years of his life he built himself a sumptuous palace some five miles from Constantinople, and no man in all the realm save the Sultan himself was so great a man as the Calabrian *renegado*, the unknown waif from Southern Italy who possessed neither name nor kindred. He was tall and robust in stature, but all his life suffered from "scald-head"; for a definition of which ailment we may refer the curious to the dictionary. He possessed, for a chieftain and a fighting man, the disadvantage of a voice so hoarse as to be inaudible at a few paces distant. In default of offspring he maintained at his charges five hundred corsairs, whom he called his children. He died in the year 1580, and with him what has been called the "Grand Period of the Moslem Corsairs" in this book may be said to have come to an end.

By the men whose deeds have been here chronicled the pirate States of Northern Africa were established; and, as we have seen, they maintained an unceasing warfare against all that was mightiest in Christendom, aided and abetted by the Sultans of Constantinople. In the sixteenth century the sea-wolves had this at least to recommend them, that they feared neither King nor Kaiser, albeit these great ones of the earth were bent on their destruction. Villains as they were, they were none the less men to be feared, men in whom dwelt wonderful capabilities of leadership. Such, however, was not the case with those by whom they were succeeded; and the great and civilised nations of the world tolerated for centuries in their midst a race of savage barbarians whose abominable insolence and fiendish cruelty were only equalled by their material weakness and military impotence. Algiers, Tunis, and Tripoli became recognised States, and the Great Powers degraded themselves by actually accrediting diplomatic agents to the "Courts" of these people.

"The Algerines are robbers, and I am their chief," was the remark made by the Dey of Algiers to the English Consul in 1641, and the man spoke the plain unvarnished truth. Yet at this time the Algerines had no more than sixty-five ships, and no organisation which could have held out for twenty-four hours against such attacks as had been successfully resisted on many occasions in the previous century.

On April 10th, 1682 (O.S.), "Articles of peace and commerce between the most serene and mighty Prince Charles II., by the Grace of God King of Great Britain, etc., and the most illustrious (*sic*) Lord, the Bashaw, Dey, and Aga, Governor of the famous city of Algiers in Barbary," were concluded by "Arthur Herbert, Esquire, Admiral of His Majesty's Fleet." It need hardly be said that such a treaty as this was not worth the paper on which it was written; that the barbarians by whom it was signed were as ignorant as they were unprincipled, and that the only argument which they understood at that, or any other time, was that of the right of the strongest.

When we of the present day read of the deeds of the corsairs we are filled with horror, we fail to understand how such things could have been tolerated, we seek for some explanation. When we hear of a "League of Christian Princes," and find that all its members could accomplish was to turn their arms the one against the other, we are even still more puzzled. What was it, then, that lay at the root of this problem? The answer would appear to be in the ethical standpoint of the sixteenth century. We are so accustomed in the present day to hear of the rights of man that we are apt to forget that, in the time of Barbarossa, of Dragut, of Charles V., and the Medicean Popes such a thing did not exist, and the only rights possessed by the common man were those vouchsafed to him by his sovereign lord. We have also to take another factor into consideration, which is that what we call "humanity" simply did not exist, the result being that the raids of the sea-wolves were not judged by the great ones of the earth from the standpoint of the amount of suffering which they inflicted, but in what manner these proceedings affected the wealth and power of the lord of the territory which had been despoiled. So differently was society constituted in those days that the very victims acquiesced more or less meekly in their fate, each one unconsciously voicing that most pathetic saying of the Russian peasant that "God is high and the Czar is far away."

The fact of the intolerable lot of the common man in these times helps us to understand one thing which otherwise would be an insoluble problem: which was, why did Christian soldiers so often become *renegado*es and fight for the corsairs under the banner of those who were the fiercest and most irreconcilable foes of themselves and their kindred? The life of the common soldier or sailor did not offer many advantages; it was generally a short and anything but a merry one, and the thing by which it was most profoundly affected was capture by the corsairs.

When this happened he became either a "gallerian," rowing out his heart on the benches of the Moslem galleys, or he festered in some noisome dungeon in Algiers, Oran, or Tlemcen. For him, however, there was always one avenue of escape open: he had but to acknowledge that Mahomet was the Prophet of God and the prison doors would fly open, or the shackles be knocked off the chain which bound him to the hell of the rower's bench. Many of the Christian captives had really nothing to bind them to the faith of their fathers—neither home nor lands, wealth nor kindred, and they were doubtless dazzled by the amazing success which accompanied the arms of the leaders of the pirates. Is it wonderful, then, that such men in such an age should grasp at the chance of freedom and throw in their lot with their captors?

It was treachery, it was apostasy, and no amount of sophistry can prove it to have been otherwise; but the man who would sit in judgment in the present day must try to figure to himself what the life of a galley-slave meant—a life so horrible and so terrible that it is impossible, in the interest of decency, to set down a tithe of what it really was.

We who in the present day sit in judgment upon the virtues and vices of a bygone age can, in the ordered security of our modern civilisation, see many things which were hidden from our forefathers, even as in another three hundred years our descendants will be able to point the finger of scorn at the mistakes which we are now committing. We have seen how it was that the pirate States arose; we have seen also how, in future generations, they were allowed to abide. We cannot, in common honesty, echo the words already quoted of the historian that "these are the judgments of God, and things ordered by His divine providence and infinite wisdom," neither can we acquit the heirs of the ages for that slackness which prevented them from doing their duty; we have, however, to ask ourselves this question, that, had it fallen to our own lot to deal with the problem of the extermination of the pirates, should we have done better?

One word in conclusion. That which they did has been set down here; the record, however, is not complete, as many of their acts of cruelty, lust, and oppression are not fitted for publication in the present day. It has been said, with truth, that no man is much better or much worse than in the age in which he lives; and to hold the scales evenly—if one were tempted to shock contemporary opinion by too literal a transcript of all that was done by the corsairs—it would also be necessary to cite the reprisals of their Christian antagonists. It has seemed better to leave such things unchronicled: to present, with as much fidelity as possible, the public lives and acts of these troublers of the peace of the sixteenth century. Looking back, as we do, over three hundred and fifty years, and judging as fairly as is possible, it would seem that there is little which can be said in their favour.

But we may at least concede that, no matter how infamous were the Barbarossas, Dragut, and Ali, they proved that in them dwelt one rare and supreme quality, which, in all the ages, has covered a multitude of sins. At a time when every one was a warrior and the whole world was an armed camp, men sought great captains in whose following to serve. Among the Moslems of Northern Africa, in ordered succession, there rose to the surface "veritable men of the sea," in the wake of whose galleys ravened the sea-wolves. When we consider how undisciplined and how stupidly violent these pirates were by nature, and how they were welded into a homogeneous whole by those of whom we speak, we are forced to the conclusion that seldom, in all the ages, have abler captains arisen to take fortune at the flood, to dominate the minds and the bodies of a vast host, to prove that they were, in deed and in truth, supreme as leaders of men.

ALSO FROM LEONAUR
AVAILABLE IN SOFTCOVER OR HARDCOVER WITH DUST JACKET

AFGHANISTAN: THE BELEAGUERED BRIGADE by G. R. Gleig—An Account of Sale's Brigade During the First Afghan War.

IN THE RANKS OF THE C. I. V by Erskine Childers—With the City Imperial Volunteer Battery (Honourable Artillery Company) in the Second Boer War.

THE BENGAL NATIVE ARMY by F. G. Cardew—An Invaluable Reference Resource.

THE 7TH (QUEEN'S OWN) HUSSARS: Volume 4—1688-1914 by C. R. B. Barrett—Uniforms, Equipment, Weapons, Traditions, the Services of Notable Officers and Men & the Appendices to All Volumes—Volume 4: 1688-1914.

THE SWORD OF THE CROWN by Eric W. Sheppard—A History of the British Army to 1914.

THE 7TH (QUEEN'S OWN) HUSSARS: Volume 3—1818-1914 by C. R. B. Barrett—On Campaign During the Canadian Rebellion, the Indian Mutiny, the Sudan, Matabeleland, Mashonaland and the Boer War Volume 3: 1818-1914.

THE KHARTOUM CAMPAIGN by Bennet Burleigh—A Special Correspondent's View of the Reconquest of the Sudan by British and Egyptian Forces under Kitchener—1898.

EL PUCHERO by Richard McSherry—The Letters of a Surgeon of Volunteers During Scott's Campaign of the American-Mexican War 1847-1848.

RIFLEMAN SAHIB by E. Maude—The Recollections of an Officer of the Bombay Rifles During the Southern Mahratta Campaign, Second Sikh War, Persian Campaign and Indian Mutiny.

THE KING'S HUSSAR by Edwin Mole—The Recollections of a 14th (King's) Hussar During the Victorian Era.

JOHN COMPANY'S CAVALRYMAN by William Johnson—The Experiences of a British Soldier in the Crimea, the Persian Campaign and the Indian Mutiny.

COLENSO & DURNFORD'S ZULU WAR by Frances E. Colenso & Edward Durnford—The first and possibly the most important history of the Zulu War.

U. S. DRAGOON by Samuel E. Chamberlain—Experiences in the Mexican War 1846-48 and on the South Western Frontier.

AVAILABLE ONLINE AT **www.leonaur.com**
AND FROM ALL GOOD BOOK STORES

ALSO FROM LEONAUR
AVAILABLE IN SOFTCOVER OR HARDCOVER WITH DUST JACKET

THE 2ND MAORI WAR: 1860-1861 *by Robert Carey*—The Second Maori War, or First Taranaki War, one more bloody instalment of the conflicts between European settlers and the indigenous Maori people.

A JOURNAL OF THE SECOND SIKH WAR *by Daniel A. Sandford*—The Experiences of an Ensign of the 2nd Bengal European Regiment During the Campaign in the Punjab, India, 1848-49.

THE LIGHT INFANTRY OFFICER *by John H. Cooke*—The Experiences of an Officer of the 43rd Light Infantry in America During the War of 1812.

BUSHVELDT CARBINEERS *by George Witton*—The War Against the Boers in South Africa and the 'Breaker' Morant Incident.

LAKE'S CAMPAIGNS IN INDIA *by Hugh Pearse*—The Second Anglo Maratha War, 1803-1807.

BRITAIN IN AFGHANISTAN 1: THE FIRST AFGHAN WAR 1839-42 *by Archibald Forbes*—From invasion to destruction-a British military disaster.

BRITAIN IN AFGHANISTAN 2: THE SECOND AFGHAN WAR 1878-80 *by Archibald Forbes*—This is the history of the Second Afghan War-another episode of British military history typified by savagery, massacre, siege and battles.

UP AMONG THE PANDIES *by Vivian Dering Majendie*—Experiences of a British Officer on Campaign During the Indian Mutiny, 1857-1858.

MUTINY: 1857 *by James Humphries*—Authentic Voices from the Indian Mutiny-First Hand Accounts of Battles, Sieges and Personal Hardships.

BLOW THE BUGLE, DRAW THE SWORD *by W. H. G. Kingston*—The Wars, Campaigns, Regiments and Soldiers of the British & Indian Armies During the Victorian Era, 1839-1898.

WAR BEYOND THE DRAGON PAGODA *by Major J. J. Snodgrass*—A Personal Narrative of the First Anglo-Burmese War 1824 - 1826.

THE HERO OF ALIWAL *by James Humphries*—The Campaigns of Sir Harry Smith in India, 1843-1846, During the Gwalior War & the First Sikh War.

ALL FOR A SHILLING A DAY *by Donald F. Featherstone*—The story of H.M. 16th, the Queen's Lancers During the first Sikh War 1845-1846.

AVAILABLE ONLINE AT **www.leonaur.com**
AND FROM ALL GOOD BOOK STORES

ALSO FROM LEONAUR
AVAILABLE IN SOFTCOVER OR HARDCOVER WITH DUST JACKET

THE FALL OF THE MOGHUL EMPIRE OF HINDUSTAN by H. G. Keene—By the beginning of the nineteenth century, as British and Indian armies under Lake and Wellesley dominated the scene, a little over half a century of conflict brought the Moghul Empire to its knees.

LADY SALE'S AFGHANISTAN by Florentia Sale—An Indomitable Victorian Lady's Account of the Retreat from Kabul During the First Afghan War.

THE CAMPAIGN OF MAGENTA AND SOLFERINO 1859 by Harold Carmichael Wylly—The Decisive Conflict for the Unification of Italy.

FRENCH'S CAVALRY CAMPAIGN by J. G. Maydon—A Special Correspondent's View of British Army Mounted Troops During the Boer War.

CAVALRY AT WATERLOO by Sir Evelyn Wood—British Mounted Troops During the Campaign of 1815.

THE SUBALTERN by George Robert Gleig—The Experiences of an Officer of the 85th Light Infantry During the Peninsular War.

NAPOLEON AT BAY, 1814 by F. Loraine Petre—The Campaigns to the Fall of the First Empire.

NAPOLEON AND THE CAMPAIGN OF 1806 by Colonel Vachée—The Napoleonic Method of Organisation and Command to the Battles of Jena & Auerstädt.

THE COMPLETE ADVENTURES IN THE CONNAUGHT RANGERS by William Grattan—The 88th Regiment during the Napoleonic Wars by a Serving Officer.

BUGLER AND OFFICER OF THE RIFLES by William Green & Harry Smith—With the 95th (Rifles) during the Peninsular & Waterloo Campaigns of the Napoleonic Wars.

NAPOLEONIC WAR STORIES by Sir Arthur Quiller-Couch—Tales of soldiers, spies, battles & sieges from the Peninsular & Waterloo campaigns.

CAPTAIN OF THE 95TH (RIFLES) by Jonathan Leach—An officer of Wellington's sharpshooters during the Peninsular, South of France and Waterloo campaigns of the Napoleonic wars.

RIFLEMAN COSTELLO by Edward Costello—The adventures of a soldier of the 95th (Rifles) in the Peninsular & Waterloo Campaigns of the Napoleonic wars.

AVAILABLE ONLINE AT www.leonaur.com
AND FROM ALL GOOD BOOK STORES

ALSO FROM LEONAUR
AVAILABLE IN SOFTCOVER OR HARDCOVER WITH DUST JACKET

AT THEM WITH THE BAYONET by *Donald F. Featherstone*—The first Anglo-Sikh War 1845-1846.

STEPHEN CRANE'S BATTLES by *Stephen Crane*—Nine Decisive Battles Recounted by the Author of 'The Red Badge of Courage'.

THE GURKHA WAR by *H. T. Prinsep*—The Anglo-Nepalese Conflict in North East India 1814-1816.

FIRE & BLOOD by *G. R. Gleig*—The burning of Washington & the battle of New Orleans, 1814, through the eyes of a young British soldier.

SOUND ADVANCE! by *Joseph Anderson*—Experiences of an officer of HM 50th regiment in Australia, Burma & the Gwalior war.

THE CAMPAIGN OF THE INDUS by *Thomas Holdsworth*—Experiences of a British Officer of the 2nd (Queen's Royal) Regiment in the Campaign to Place Shah Shuja on the Throne of Afghanistan 1838 - 1840.

WITH THE MADRAS EUROPEAN REGIMENT IN BURMA by *John Butler*—The Experiences of an Officer of the Honourable East India Company's Army During the First Anglo-Burmese War 1824 - 1826.

IN ZULULAND WITH THE BRITISH ARMY by *Charles L. Norris-Newman*—The Anglo-Zulu war of 1879 through the first-hand experiences of a special correspondent.

BESIEGED IN LUCKNOW by *Martin Richard Gubbins*—The first Anglo-Sikh War 1845-1846.

A TIGER ON HORSEBACK by *L. March Phillips*—The Experiences of a Trooper & Officer of Rimington's Guides - The Tigers - during the Anglo-Boer war 1899 - 1902.

SEPOYS, SIEGE & STORM by *Charles John Griffiths*—The Experiences of a young officer of H.M.'s 61st Regiment at Ferozepore, Delhi ridge and at the fall of Delhi during the Indian mutiny 1857.

CAMPAIGNING IN ZULULAND by *W. E. Montague*—Experiences on campaign during the Zulu war of 1879 with the 94th Regiment.

THE STORY OF THE GUIDES by *G.J. Younghusband*—The Exploits of the Soldiers of the famous Indian Army Regiment from the northwest frontier 1847 - 1900.

AVAILABLE ONLINE AT **www.leonaur.com**
AND FROM ALL GOOD BOOK STORES

ALSO FROM LEONAUR
AVAILABLE IN SOFTCOVER OR HARDCOVER WITH DUST JACKET

ZULU:1879 *by D.C.F. Moodie & the Leonaur Editors*—The Anglo-Zulu War of 1879 from contemporary sources: First Hand Accounts, Interviews, Dispatches, Official Documents & Newspaper Reports.

THE RED DRAGOON *by W.J. Adams*—With the 7th Dragoon Guards in the Cape of Good Hope against the Boers & the Kaffir tribes during the 'war of the axe' 1843-48'.

THE RECOLLECTIONS OF SKINNER OF SKINNER'S HORSE *by James Skinner*—James Skinner and his 'Yellow Boys' Irregular cavalry in the wars of India between the British, Mahratta, Rajput, Mogul, Sikh & Pindarree Forces.

A CAVALRY OFFICER DURING THE SEPOY REVOLT *by A. R. D. Mackenzie*—Experiences with the 3rd Bengal Light Cavalry, the Guides and Sikh Irregular Cavalry from the outbreak to Delhi and Lucknow.

A NORFOLK SOLDIER IN THE FIRST SIKH WAR *by J W Baldwin*—Experiences of a private of H.M. 9th Regiment of Foot in the battles for the Punjab, India 1845-6.

TOMMY ATKINS' WAR STORIES: 14 FIRST HAND ACCOUNTS—Fourteen first hand accounts from the ranks of the British Army during Queen Victoria's Empire.

THE WATERLOO LETTERS *by H. T. Siborne*—Accounts of the Battle by British Officers for its Foremost Historian.

NEY: GENERAL OF CAVALRY VOLUME 1—1769-1799 *by Antoine Bulos*—The Early Career of a Marshal of the First Empire.

NEY: MARSHAL OF FRANCE VOLUME 2—1799-1805 *by Antoine Bulos*—The Early Career of a Marshal of the First Empire.

AIDE-DE-CAMP TO NAPOLEON *by Philippe-Paul de Ségur*—For anyone interested in the Napoleonic Wars this book, written by one who was intimate with the strategies and machinations of the Emperor, will be essential reading.

TWILIGHT OF EMPIRE *by Sir Thomas Ussher & Sir George Cockburn*—Two accounts of Napoleon's Journeys in Exile to Elba and St. Helena: Narrative of Events by Sir Thomas Ussher & Napoleon's Last Voyage: Extract of a diary by Sir George Cockburn.

PRIVATE WHEELER *by William Wheeler*—The letters of a soldier of the 51st Light Infantry during the Peninsular War & at Waterloo.

AVAILABLE ONLINE AT **www.leonaur.com**
AND FROM ALL GOOD BOOK STORES

ALSO FROM LEONAUR
AVAILABLE IN SOFTCOVER OR HARDCOVER WITH DUST JACKET

OFFICERS & GENTLEMEN *by Peter Hawker & William Graham*—Two Accounts of British Officers During the Peninsula War: Officer of Light Dragoons by Peter Hawker & Campaign in Portugal and Spain by William Graham .

THE WALCHEREN EXPEDITION *by Anonymous*—The Experiences of a British Officer of the 81st Regt. During the Campaign in the Low Countries of 1809.

LADIES OF WATERLOO *by Charlotte A. Eaton, Magdalene de Lancey & Juana Smith*—The Experiences of Three Women During the Campaign of 1815: Waterloo Days by Charlotte A. Eaton, A Week at Waterloo by Magdalene de Lancey & Juana's Story by Juana Smith.

JOURNAL OF AN OFFICER IN THE KING'S GERMAN LEGION *by John Frederick Hering*—Recollections of Campaigning During the Napoleonic Wars.

JOURNAL OF AN ARMY SURGEON IN THE PENINSULAR WAR *by Charles Boutflower*—The Recollections of a British Army Medical Man on Campaign During the Napoleonic Wars.

ON CAMPAIGN WITH MOORE AND WELLINGTON *by Anthony Hamilton*—The Experiences of a Soldier of the 43rd Regiment During the Peninsular War.

THE ROAD TO AUSTERLITZ *by R. G. Burton*—Napoleon's Campaign of 1805.

SOLDIERS OF NAPOLEON *by A. J. Doisy De Villargennes & Arthur Chuquet*—The Experiences of the Men of the French First Empire: Under the Eagles by A. J. Doisy De Villargennes & Voices of 1812 by Arthur Chuquet .

INVASION OF FRANCE, 1814 *by F. W. O. Maycock*—The Final Battles of the Napoleonic First Empire.

LEIPZIG—A CONFLICT OF TITANS *by Frederic Shoberl*—A Personal Experience of the 'Battle of the Nations' During the Napoleonic Wars, October 14th-19th, 1813.

SLASHERS *by Charles Cadell*—The Campaigns of the 28th Regiment of Foot During the Napoleonic Wars by a Serving Officer.

BATTLE IMPERIAL *by Charles William Vane*—The Campaigns in Germany & France for the Defeat of Napoleon 1813-1814.

SWIFT & BOLD *by Gibbes Rigaud*—The 60th Rifles During the Peninsula War.

AVAILABLE ONLINE AT www.leonaur.com
AND FROM ALL GOOD BOOK STORES

ALSO FROM LEONAUR
AVAILABLE IN SOFTCOVER OR HARDCOVER WITH DUST JACKET

ADVENTURES OF A YOUNG RIFLEMAN by Johann Christian Maempel—The Experiences of a Saxon in the French & British Armies During the Napoleonic Wars.

THE HUSSAR by Norbert Landsheit & G. R. Gleig—A German Cavalryman in British Service Throughout the Napoleonic Wars.

RECOLLECTIONS OF THE PENINSULA by Moyle Sherer—An Officer of the 34th Regiment of Foot—'The Cumberland Gentlemen'—on Campaign Against Napoleon's French Army in Spain.

MARINE OF REVOLUTION & CONSULATE by Moreau de Jonnès—The Recollections of a French Soldier of the Revolutionary Wars 1791-1804.

GENTLEMEN IN RED by John Dobbs & Robert Knowles—Two Accounts of British Infantry Officers During the Peninsular War Recollections of an Old 52nd Man by John Dobbs An Officer of Fusiliers by Robert Knowles.

CORPORAL BROWN'S CAMPAIGNS IN THE LOW COUNTRIES by Robert Brown—Recollections of a Coldstream Guard in the Early Campaigns Against Revolutionary France 1793-1795.

THE 7TH (QUEENS OWN) HUSSARS: Volume 2—1793-1815 by C. R. B. Barrett—During the Campaigns in the Low Countries & the Peninsula and Waterloo Campaigns of the Napoleonic Wars. Volume 2: 1793-1815.

THE MARENGO CAMPAIGN 1800 by Herbert H. Sargent—The Victory that Completed the Austrian Defeat in Italy.

DONALDSON OF THE 94TH—SCOTS BRIGADE by Joseph Donaldson—The Recollections of a Soldier During the Peninsula & South of France Campaigns of the Napoleonic Wars.

A CONSCRIPT FOR EMPIRE by Philippe as told to Johann Christian Maempel—The Experiences of a Young German Conscript During the Napoleonic Wars.

JOURNAL OF THE CAMPAIGN OF 1815 by Alexander Cavalié Mercer—The Experiences of an Officer of the Royal Horse Artillery During the Waterloo Campaign.

NAPOLEON'S CAMPAIGNS IN POLAND 1806-7 by Robert Wilson—The campaign in Poland from the Russian side of the conflict.

AVAILABLE ONLINE AT **www.leonaur.com**
AND FROM ALL GOOD BOOK STORES

ALSO FROM LEONAUR
AVAILABLE IN SOFTCOVER OR HARDCOVER WITH DUST JACKET

OMPTEDA OF THE KING'S GERMAN LEGION by *Christian von Ompteda*—A Hanoverian Officer on Campaign Against Napoleon.

LIEUTENANT SIMMONS OF THE 95TH (RIFLES) by *George Simmons*—Recollections of the Peninsula, South of France & Waterloo Campaigns of the Napoleonic Wars.

A HORSEMAN FOR THE EMPEROR by *Jean Baptiste Gazzola*—A Cavalryman of Napoleon's Army on Campaign Throughout the Napoleonic Wars.

SERGEANT LAWRENCE by *William Lawrence*—With the 40th Regt. of Foot in South America, the Peninsular War & at Waterloo.

CAMPAIGNS WITH THE FIELD TRAIN by *Richard D. Henegan*—Experiences of a British Officer During the Peninsula and Waterloo Campaigns of the Napoleonic Wars.

CAVALRY SURGEON by *S. D. Broughton*—On Campaign Against Napoleon in the Peninsula & South of France During the Napoleonic Wars 1812-1814.

MEN OF THE RIFLES by *Thomas Knight, Henry Curling & Jonathan Leach*—The Reminiscences of Thomas Knight of the 95th (Rifles) by Thomas Knight, Henry Curling's Anecdotes by Henry Curling & The Field Services of the Rifle Brigade from its Formation to Waterloo by Jonathan Leach.

THE ULM CAMPAIGN 1805 by *F. N. Maude*—Napoleon and the Defeat of the Austrian Army During the 'War of the Third Coalition'.

SOLDIERING WITH THE 'DIVISION' by *Thomas Garrety*—The Military Experiences of an Infantryman of the 43rd Regiment During the Napoleonic Wars.

SERGEANT MORRIS OF THE 73RD FOOT by *Thomas Morris*—The Experiences of a British Infantryman During the Napoleonic Wars-Including Campaigns in Germany and at Waterloo.

A VOICE FROM WATERLOO by *Edward Cotton*—The Personal Experiences of a British Cavalryman Who Became a Battlefield Guide and Authority on the Campaign of 1815.

NAPOLEON AND HIS MARSHALS by *J. T. Headley*—The Men of the First Empire.

AVAILABLE ONLINE AT www.leonaur.com
AND FROM ALL GOOD BOOK STORES

ALSO FROM LEONAUR
AVAILABLE IN SOFTCOVER OR HARDCOVER WITH DUST JACKET

COLBORNE: A SINGULAR TALENT FOR WAR by *John Colborne*—The Napoleonic Wars Career of One of Wellington's Most Highly Valued Officers in Egypt, Holland, Italy, the Peninsula and at Waterloo.

NAPOLEON'S RUSSIAN CAMPAIGN by *Philippe Henri de Segur*—The Invasion, Battles and Retreat by an Aide-de-Camp on the Emperor's Staff.

WITH THE LIGHT DIVISION by *John H. Cooke*—The Experiences of an Officer of the 43rd Light Infantry in the Peninsula and South of France During the Napoleonic Wars.

WELLINGTON AND THE PYRENEES CAMPAIGN VOLUME I: FROM VITORIA TO THE BIDASSOA by *F. C. Beatson*—The final phase of the campaign in the Iberian Peninsula.

WELLINGTON AND THE INVASION OF FRANCE VOLUME II: THE BIDASSOA TO THE BATTLE OF THE NIVELLE by *F. C. Beatson*—The final phase of the campaign in the Iberian Peninsula.

WELLINGTON AND THE FALL OF FRANCE VOLUME III: THE GAVES AND THE BATTLE OF ORTHEZ by *F. C. Beatson*—The final phase of the campaign in the Iberian Peninsula.

NAPOLEON'S IMPERIAL GUARD: FROM MARENGO TO WATERLOO by *J. T. Headley*—The story of Napoleon's Imperial Guard and the men who commanded them.

BATTLES & SIEGES OF THE PENINSULAR WAR by *W. H. Fitchett*—Corunna, Busaco, Albuera, Ciudad Rodrigo, Badajos, Salamanca, San Sebastian & Others.

SERGEANT GUILLEMARD: THE MAN WHO SHOT NELSON? by *Robert Guillemard*—A Soldier of the Infantry of the French Army of Napoleon on Campaign Throughout Europe.

WITH THE GUARDS ACROSS THE PYRENEES by *Robert Batty*—The Experiences of a British Officer of Wellington's Army During the Battles for the Fall of Napoleonic France, 1813 .

A STAFF OFFICER IN THE PENINSULA by *E. W. Buckham*—An Officer of the British Staff Corps Cavalry During the Peninsula Campaign of the Napoleonic Wars.

THE LEIPZIG CAMPAIGN: 1813—NAPOLEON AND THE "BATTLE OF THE NATIONS" by *F. N. Maude*—Colonel Maude's analysis of Napoleon's campaign of 1813 around Leipzig.

AVAILABLE ONLINE AT **www.leonaur.com**
AND FROM ALL GOOD BOOK STORES

ALSO FROM LEONAUR
AVAILABLE IN SOFTCOVER OR HARDCOVER WITH DUST JACKET

BUGEAUD: A PACK WITH A BATON by *Thomas Robert Bugeaud*—The Early Campaigns of a Soldier of Napoleon's Army Who Would Become a Marshal of France.

WATERLOO RECOLLECTIONS by *Frederick Llewellyn*—Rare First Hand Accounts, Letters, Reports and Retellings from the Campaign of 1815.

SERGEANT NICOL by *Daniel Nicol*—The Experiences of a Gordon Highlander During the Napoleonic Wars in Egypt, the Peninsula and France.

THE JENA CAMPAIGN: 1806 by *F. N. Maude*—The Twin Battles of Jena & Auerstadt Between Napoleon's French and the Prussian Army.

PRIVATE O'NEIL by *Charles O'Neil*—The recollections of an Irish Rogue of H. M. 28th Regt.—The Slashers—during the Peninsula & Waterloo campaigns of the Napoleonic war.

ROYAL HIGHLANDER by *James Anton*—A soldier of H.M 42nd (Royal) Highlanders during the Peninsular, South of France & Waterloo Campaigns of the Napoleonic Wars.

CAPTAIN BLAZE by *Elzéar Blaze*—Life in Napoleons Army.

LEJEUNE VOLUME 1 by *Louis-François Lejeune*—The Napoleonic Wars through the Experiences of an Officer on Berthier's Staff.

LEJEUNE VOLUME 2 by *Louis-François Lejeune*—The Napoleonic Wars through the Experiences of an Officer on Berthier's Staff.

CAPTAIN COIGNET by *Jean-Roch Coignet*—A Soldier of Napoleon's Imperial Guard from the Italian Campaign to Russia and Waterloo.

FUSILIER COOPER by *John S. Cooper*—Experiences in the 7th (Royal) Fusiliers During the Peninsular Campaign of the Napoleonic Wars and the American Campaign to New Orleans.

FIGHTING NAPOLEON'S EMPIRE by *Joseph Anderson*—The Campaigns of a British Infantryman in Italy, Egypt, the Peninsular & the West Indies During the Napoleonic Wars.

CHASSEUR BARRES by *Jean-Baptiste Barres*—The experiences of a French Infantryman of the Imperial Guard at Austerlitz, Jena, Eylau, Friedland, in the Peninsular, Lutzen, Bautzen, Zinnwald and Hanau during the Napoleonic Wars.

AVAILABLE ONLINE AT **www.leonaur.com**
AND FROM ALL GOOD BOOK STORES

ALSO FROM LEONAUR
AVAILABLE IN SOFTCOVER OR HARDCOVER WITH DUST JACKET

CAPTAIN COIGNET *by Jean-Roch Coignet*—A Soldier of Napoleon's Imperial Guard from the Italian Campaign to Russia and Waterloo.

HUSSAR ROCCA *by Albert Jean Michel de Rocca*—A French cavalry officer's experiences of the Napoleonic Wars and his views on the Peninsular Campaigns against the Spanish, British And Guerilla Armies.

MARINES TO 95TH (RIFLES) *by Thomas Fernyhough*—The military experiences of Robert Fernyhough during the Napoleonic Wars.

LIGHT BOB *by Robert Blakeney*—The experiences of a young officer in H.M 28th & 36th regiments of the British Infantry during the Peninsular Campaign of the Napoleonic Wars 1804 - 1814.

WITH WELLINGTON'S LIGHT CAVALRY *by William Tomkinson*—The Experiences of an officer of the 16th Light Dragoons in the Peninsular and Waterloo campaigns of the Napoleonic Wars.

SERGEANT BOURGOGNE *by Adrien Bourgogne*—With Napoleon's Imperial Guard in the Russian Campaign and on the Retreat from Moscow 1812 - 13.

SURTEES OF THE 95TH (RIFLES) *by William Surtees*—A Soldier of the 95th (Rifles) in the Peninsular campaign of the Napoleonic Wars.

SWORDS OF HONOUR *by Henry Newbolt & Stanley L. Wood*—The Careers of Six Outstanding Officers from the Napoleonic Wars, the Wars for India and the American Civil War.

ENSIGN BELL IN THE PENINSULAR WAR *by George Bell*—The Experiences of a young British Soldier of the 34th Regiment 'The Cumberland Gentlemen' in the Napoleonic wars.

HUSSAR IN WINTER *by Alexander Gordon*—A British Cavalry Officer during the retreat to Corunna in the Peninsular campaign of the Napoleonic Wars.

THE COMPLEAT RIFLEMAN HARRIS *by Benjamin Harris as told to and transcribed by Captain Henry Curling, 52nd Regt. of Foot*—The adventures of a soldier of the 95th (Rifles) during the Peninsular Campaign of the Napoleonic Wars.

THE ADVENTURES OF A LIGHT DRAGOON *by George Farmer & G.R. Gleig*—A cavalryman during the Peninsular & Waterloo Campaigns, in captivity & at the siege of Bhurtpore, India.

AVAILABLE ONLINE AT **www.leonaur.com**
AND FROM ALL GOOD BOOK STORES

ALSO FROM LEONAUR
AVAILABLE IN SOFTCOVER OR HARDCOVER WITH DUST JACKET

THE LIFE OF THE REAL BRIGADIER GERARD VOLUME 1—THE YOUNG HUSSAR 1782-1807 *by Jean-Baptiste De Marbot*—A French Cavalryman Of the Napoleonic Wars at Marengo, Austerlitz, Jena, Eylau & Friedland.

THE LIFE OF THE REAL BRIGADIER GERARD VOLUME 2—IMPERIAL AIDE-DE-CAMP 1807-1811 *by Jean-Baptiste De Marbot*—A French Cavalryman of the Napoleonic Wars at Saragossa, Landshut, Eckmuhl, Ratisbon, Aspern-Essling, Wagram, Busaco & Torres Vedras.

THE LIFE OF THE REAL BRIGADIER GERARD VOLUME 3—COLONEL OF CHASSEURS 1811-1815 *by Jean-Baptiste De Marbot*—A French Cavalryman in the retreat from Moscow, Lutzen, Bautzen, Katzbach, Leipzig, Hanau & Waterloo.

THE INDIAN WAR OF 1864 *by Eugene Ware*—The Experiences of a Young Officer of the 7th Iowa Cavalry on the Western Frontier During the Civil War.

THE MARCH OF DESTINY *by Charles E. Young & V. Devinny*—Dangers of the Trail in 1865 by Charles E. Young & The Story of a Pioneer by V. Devinny, two Accounts of Early Emigrants to Colorado.

CROSSING THE PLAINS *by William Audley Maxwell*—A First Hand Narrative of the Early Pioneer Trail to California in 1857.

CHIEF OF SCOUTS *by William F. Drannan*—A Pilot to Emigrant and Government Trains, Across the Plains of the Western Frontier.

THIRTY-ONE YEARS ON THE PLAINS AND IN THE MOUNTAINS *by William F. Drannan*—William Drannan was born to be a pioneer, hunter, trapper and wagon train guide during the momentous days of the Great American West.

THE INDIAN WARS VOLUNTEER *by William Thompson*—Recollections of the Conflict Against the Snakes, Shoshone, Bannocks, Modocs and Other Native Tribes of the American North West.

THE 4TH TENNESSEE CAVALRY *by George B. Guild*—The Services of Smith's Regiment of Confederate Cavalry by One of its Officers.

COLONEL WORTHINGTON'S SHILOH *by T. Worthington*—The Tennessee Campaign, 1862, by an Officer of the Ohio Volunteers.

FOUR YEARS IN THE SADDLE *by W. L. Curry*—The History of the First Regiment Ohio Volunteer Cavalry in the American Civil War.

AVAILABLE ONLINE AT **www.leonaur.com**
AND FROM ALL GOOD BOOK STORES

ALSO FROM LEONAUR
AVAILABLE IN SOFTCOVER OR HARDCOVER WITH DUST JACKET

LIFE IN THE ARMY OF NORTHERN VIRGINIA *by Carlton McCarthy*—The Observations of a Confederate Artilleryman of Cutshaw's Battalion During the American Civil War 1861-1865.

HISTORY OF THE CAVALRY OF THE ARMY OF THE POTOMAC *by Charles D. Rhodes*—Including Pope's Army of Virginia and the Cavalry Operations in West Virginia During the American Civil War.

CAMP-FIRE AND COTTON-FIELD *by Thomas W. Knox*—A New York Herald Correspondent's View of the American Civil War.

SERGEANT STILLWELL *by Leander Stillwell*—The Experiences of a Union Army Soldier of the 61st Illinois Infantry During the American Civil War.

STONEWALL'S CANNONEER *by Edward A. Moore*—Experiences with the Rockbridge Artillery, Confederate Army of Northern Virginia, During the American Civil War.

THE SIXTH CORPS *by George Stevens*—The Army of the Potomac, Union Army, During the American Civil War.

THE RAILROAD RAIDERS *by William Pittenger*—An Ohio Volunteers Recollections of the Andrews Raid to Disrupt the Confederate Railroad in Georgia During the American Civil War.

CITIZEN SOLDIER *by John Beatty*—An Account of the American Civil War by a Union Infantry Officer of Ohio Volunteers Who Became a Brigadier General.

COX: PERSONAL RECOLLECTIONS OF THE CIVIL WAR--VOLUME 1 *by Jacob Dolson Cox*—West Virginia, Kanawha Valley, Gauley Bridge, Cotton Mountain, South Mountain, Antietam, the Morgan Raid & the East Tennessee Campaign.

COX: PERSONAL RECOLLECTIONS OF THE CIVIL WAR--VOLUME 2 *by Jacob Dolson Cox*—Siege of Knoxville, East Tennessee, Atlanta Campaign, the Nashville Campaign & the North Carolina Campaign.

KERSHAW'S BRIGADE VOLUME 1 *by D. Augustus Dickert*—Manassas, Seven Pines, Sharpsburg (Antietam), Fredricksburg, Chancellorsville, Gettysburg, Chickamauga, Chattanooga, Fort Sanders & Bean Station.

KERSHAW'S BRIGADE VOLUME 2 *by D. Augustus Dickert*—At the wilderness, Cold Harbour, Petersburg, The Shenandoah Valley and Cedar Creek..

AVAILABLE ONLINE AT **www.leonaur.com**
AND FROM ALL GOOD BOOK STORES

ALSO FROM LEONAUR
AVAILABLE IN SOFTCOVER OR HARDCOVER WITH DUST JACKET

THE RELUCTANT REBEL by *William G. Stevenson*—A young Kentuckian's experiences in the Confederate Infantry & Cavalry during the American Civil War..

BOOTS AND SADDLES by *Elizabeth B. Custer*—The experiences of General Custer's Wife on the Western Plains.

FANNIE BEERS' CIVIL WAR by *Fannie A. Beers*—A Confederate Lady's Experiences of Nursing During the Campaigns & Battles of the American Civil War.

LADY SALE'S AFGHANISTAN by *Florentia Sale*—An Indomitable Victorian Lady's Account of the Retreat from Kabul During the First Afghan War.

THE TWO WARS OF MRS DUBERLY by *Frances Isabella Duberly*—An Intrepid Victorian Lady's Experience of the Crimea and Indian Mutiny.

THE REBELLIOUS DUCHESS by *Paul F. S. Dermoncourt*—The Adventures of the Duchess of Berri and Her Attempt to Overthrow French Monarchy.

LADIES OF WATERLOO by *Charlotte A. Eaton, Magdalene de Lancey & Juana Smith*—The Experiences of Three Women During the Campaign of 1815: Waterloo Days by Charlotte A. Eaton, A Week at Waterloo by Magdalene de Lancey & Juana's Story by Juana Smith.

TWO YEARS BEFORE THE MAST by *Richard Henry Dana. Jr.*—The account of one young man's experiences serving on board a sailing brig—the Penelope—bound for California, between the years 1834-36.

A SAILOR OF KING GEORGE by *Frederick Hoffman*—From Midshipman to Captain—Recollections of War at Sea in the Napoleonic Age 1793-1815.

LORDS OF THE SEA by *A. T. Mahan*—Great Captains of the Royal Navy During the Age of Sail.

COGGESHALL'S VOYAGES: VOLUME 1 by *George Coggeshall*—The Recollections of an American Schooner Captain.

COGGESHALL'S VOYAGES: VOLUME 2 by *George Coggeshall*—The Recollections of an American Schooner Captain.

TWILIGHT OF EMPIRE by *Sir Thomas Ussher & Sir George Cockburn*—Two accounts of Napoleon's Journeys in Exile to Elba and St. Helena: Narrative of Events by Sir Thomas Ussher & Napoleon's Last Voyage: Extract of a diary by Sir George Cockburn.

AVAILABLE ONLINE AT **www.leonaur.com**
AND FROM ALL GOOD BOOK STORES

ALSO FROM LEONAUR
AVAILABLE IN SOFTCOVER OR HARDCOVER WITH DUST JACKET

ESCAPE FROM THE FRENCH by *Edward Boys*—A Young Royal Navy Midshipman's Adventures During the Napoleonic War.

THE VOYAGE OF H.M.S. PANDORA by *Edward Edwards R. N. & George Hamilton, edited by Basil Thomson*—In Pursuit of the Mutineers of the Bounty in the South Seas—1790-1791.

MEDUSA by *J. B. Henry Savigny and Alexander Correard and Charlotte-Adélaïde Dard*—Narrative of a Voyage to Senegal in 1816 & The Sufferings of the Picard Family After the Shipwreck of the Medusa.

THE SEA WAR OF 1812 VOLUME 1 by *A. T. Mahan*—A History of the Maritime Conflict.

THE SEA WAR OF 1812 VOLUME 2 by *A. T. Mahan*—A History of the Maritime Conflict.

WETHERELL OF H. M. S. HUSSAR by *John Wetherell*—The Recollections of an Ordinary Seaman of the Royal Navy During the Napoleonic Wars.

THE NAVAL BRIGADE IN NATAL by *C. R. N. Burne*—With the Guns of H. M. S. Terrible & H. M. S. Tartar during the Boer War 1899-1900.

THE VOYAGE OF H. M. S. BOUNTY by *William Bligh*—The True Story of an 18th Century Voyage of Exploration and Mutiny.

SHIPWRECK! by *William Gilly*—The Royal Navy's Disasters at Sea 1793-1849.

KING'S CUTTERS AND SMUGGLERS: 1700-1855 by *E. Keble Chatterton*—A unique period of maritime history-from the beginning of the eighteenth to the middle of the nineteenth century when British seamen risked all to smuggle valuable goods from wool to tea and spirits from and to the Continent.

CONFEDERATE BLOCKADE RUNNER by *John Wilkinson*—The Personal Recollections of an Officer of the Confederate Navy.

NAVAL BATTLES OF THE NAPOLEONIC WARS by *W. H. Fitchett*—Cape St. Vincent, the Nile, Cadiz, Copenhagen, Trafalgar & Others.

PRISONERS OF THE RED DESERT by *R. S. Gwatkin-Williams*—The Adventures of the Crew of the Tara During the First World War.

U-BOAT WAR 1914-1918 by *James B. Connolly/Karl von Schenk*—Two Contrasting Accounts from Both Sides of the Conflict at Sea D uring the Great War.

AVAILABLE ONLINE AT **www.leonaur.com**
AND FROM ALL GOOD BOOK STORES

ALSO FROM LEONAUR
AVAILABLE IN SOFTCOVER OR HARDCOVER WITH DUST JACKET

IRON TIMES WITH THE GUARDS *by An O. E. (G. P. A. Fildes)*—The Experiences of an Officer of the Coldstream Guards on the Western Front During the First World War.

THE GREAT WAR IN THE MIDDLE EAST: 1 *by W. T. Massey*—The Desert Campaigns & How Jerusalem Was Won---two classic accounts in one volume.

THE GREAT WAR IN THE MIDDLE EAST: 2 *by W. T. Massey*—Allenby's Final Triumph.

SMITH-DORRIEN *by Horace Smith-Dorrien*—Isandlwhana to the Great War.

1914 *by Sir John French*—The Early Campaigns of the Great War by the British Commander.

GRENADIER *by E. R. M. Fryer*—The Recollections of an Officer of the Grenadier Guards throughout the Great War on the Western Front.

BATTLE, CAPTURE & ESCAPE *by George Pearson*—The Experiences of a Canadian Light Infantryman During the Great War.

DIGGERS AT WAR *by R. Hugh Knyvett & G. P. Cuttriss*—"Over There" With the Australians by R. Hugh Knyvett and Over the Top With the Third Australian Division by G. P. Cuttriss. Accounts of Australians During the Great War in the Middle East, at Gallipoli and on the Western Front.

HEAVY FIGHTING BEFORE US *by George Brenton Laurie*—The Letters of an Officer of the Royal Irish Rifles on the Western Front During the Great War.

THE CAMELIERS *by Oliver Hogue*—A Classic Account of the Australians of the Imperial Camel Corps During the First World War in the Middle East.

RED DUST *by Donald Black*—A Classic Account of Australian Light Horsemen in Palestine During the First World War.

THE LEAN, BROWN MEN *by Angus Buchanan*—Experiences in East Africa During the Great War with the 25th Royal Fusiliers—the Legion of Frontiersmen.

THE NIGERIAN REGIMENT IN EAST AFRICA *by W. D. Downes*—On Campaign During the Great War 1916-1918.

THE 'DIE-HARDS' IN SIBERIA *by John Ward*—With the Middlesex Regiment Against the Bolsheviks 1918-19.

AVAILABLE ONLINE AT **www.leonaur.com**
AND FROM ALL GOOD BOOK STORES

ALSO FROM LEONAUR
AVAILABLE IN SOFTCOVER OR HARDCOVER WITH DUST JACKET

FARAWAY CAMPAIGN *by F. James*—Experiences of an Indian Army Cavalry Officer in Persia & Russia During the Great War.

REVOLT IN THE DESERT *by T. E. Lawrence*—An account of the experiences of one remarkable British officer's war from his own perspective.

MACHINE-GUN SQUADRON *by A. M. G.*—The 20th Machine Gunners from British Yeomanry Regiments in the Middle East Campaign of the First World War.

A GUNNER'S CRUSADE *by Antony Bluett*—The Campaign in the Desert, Palestine & Syria as Experienced by the Honourable Artillery Company During the Great War .

DESPATCH RIDER *by W. H. L. Watson*—The Experiences of a British Army Motorcycle Despatch Rider During the Opening Battles of the Great War in Europe.

TIGERS ALONG THE TIGRIS *by E. J. Thompson*—The Leicestershire Regiment in Mesopotamia During the First World War.

HEARTS & DRAGONS *by Charles R. M. F. Crutwell*—The 4th Royal Berkshire Regiment in France and Italy During the Great War, 1914-1918.

INFANTRY BRIGADE: 1914 *by John Ward*—The Diary of a Commander of the 15th Infantry Brigade, 5th Division, British Army, During the Retreat from Mons.

DOING OUR 'BIT' *by Ian Hay*—Two Classic Accounts of the Men of Kitchener's 'New Army' During the Great War including *The First 100,000 & All In It*.

AN EYE IN THE STORM *by Arthur Ruhl*—An American War Correspondent's Experiences of the First World War from the Western Front to Gallipoli-and Beyond.

STAND & FALL *by Joe Cassells*—With the Middlesex Regiment Against the Bolsheviks 1918-19.

RIFLEMAN MACGILL'S WAR *by Patrick MacGill*—A Soldier of the London Irish During the Great War in Europe including *The Amateur Army, The Red Horizon & The Great Push*.

WITH THE GUNS *by C. A. Rose & Hugh Dalton*—Two First Hand Accounts of British Gunners at War in Europe During World War 1- Three Years in France with the Guns and With the British Guns in Italy.

THE BUSH WAR DOCTOR *by Robert V. Dolbey*—The Experiences of a British Army Doctor During the East African Campaign of the First World War.

AVAILABLE ONLINE AT **www.leonaur.com**
AND FROM ALL GOOD BOOK STORES

www.ingramcontent.com/pod-product-compliance
Lightning Source LLC
Chambersburg PA
CBHW031622160426
43196CB00006B/238